W9-DII-198

Also by Danny Schechter

Falun Gong's Challenge to China:
Spiritual Practice or "Evil Cult"?
(Akashic Books)

The More You Watch, The Less You Know:
News Wars, [sub]Merged Hopes, Media Adventures
(Seven Stories)

Mediaocracy: Hail to the Thief
How the Media "Stole" the U.S. Presidential Elections 2000
Editor, with Roland Schatz
(Innovatio Verlag and Electronpress.com for MEDIAchannel.org)

NEWS DISSECTOR
passions, pieces, and polemics • 1960–2000

danny schechter

LIBRARY
FRANKLIN PIERCE COLLEGE
RINDGE, NH 03461

Akashic Books
New York

All rights reserved. No part of this book may be reproduced in any
manner whatsoever without the permission in writing from the publisher.

Published by Akashic Books
©2001 Danny Schechter
An earlier version of *News Dissector* was published digitally
by Electron Press (www.electronpress.com).

Cover photo: Danny Schechter interviews financier George Soros for
Globalvision's *Globalization and Human Rights* documentary.
Cover photo ©1998 R. Romano
Other photos by various friends over various years, with thanks.
Book design by Sohrab Habibion

ISBN: 1-888451-20-3
Library of Congress Catalog Card Number: 00-112239
All rights reserved
First printing
Printed in Canada

Akashic Books
PO Box 1456
New York, NY 10009
Akashic7@aol.com
www.akashicbooks.com

Nothing can now be believed which is seen in a newspaper.
Truth itself becomes suspicious by being put into that polluted vehicle.
—Thomas Jefferson, farmer and writer, 1789

A would-be satirist, a hired buffoon,
A monthly scribbler of low lampoon,
Condemned to drudge, the meanest of the mean,
And furbish falsehoods for a magazine.
—Lord Byron, author and poet, 1809

I do not propose to write an ode to dejection, but to brag
as lustily as a chanticleer in the morning, standing on his roost,
if only to wake his neighbors up.
—Henry David Thoreau (1817-1862), writer

Our duty is to keep the universe thoroughly posted concerning murders
and street fights, and balls, and theaters, and pack-trains, and churches,
and lectures, and school houses, and city military affairs, and highway
robberies, and Bible societies, and a thousand other things which it is the
province of local reporters to keep track of and to magnify into undue
importance for the instruction of the readers of this great daily newspaper.
—Mark Twain (1835-1910), reporter, *Territorial Enterprise*,
Virginia City, Nevada Territory

You can't wait for inspiration; you have to go after it with a club.
—Jack London (1876-1916), writer

[The Internet] . . . is an amazing communications tool that's bringing
the whole world together. I mean, you sit down to sign on to America
Online in your hometown, and it's just staggering to think they're
hearing the exact same busy signal that you're hearing.
—Dennis Miller, comic, 2001

TABLE OF CONTENTS

PART 4: ENGAGING AFRICA

PART 5: MEDIA MAKER

PART 6: MEDIA CRITIC

DEDICATION

No one in modern journalism does it all by their lonesome. My own work over the years—in print, radio, cable, television, film, and now, online—has always been collaborative to some degree. Much as I have fought them, there have been editors and executive producers to improve my work, colleagues to critique it, and sometimes critics to . . . what is it that we critics do?

So here's to all of my co-workers over all these years who have put up with me, stood by me, and helped me do my thing. I may have been the "News Dissector"—but without them, I'd have been one hand clapping. They were there, in the background and the foreground, prodding me to sharpen it up, cut it down, and restrain tendencies towards self-promotion, self-indulgence, and delusional self-importance.

Keep your sense of humor, they counseled, and I have.

Thank you all for what you did then, and to my colleagues on the Media Channel (www.mediachannel.org) in this new century, thank you for what you are doing now.

News Dissector is dedicated to the media dreams we are still determined to realize; also to my brother Bill, my brother Rory, and our many tribes of Globalvisioneers; and, as always, to Sarah Debs Schechter, who has joined the movie world now, going "Hollywood"—at least in the geographical sense.

ACKNOWLEDGMENTS

It is a thrill after all these years, and after chasing so many assignments and reporting so many stories including these many adventures, that two publishers wanted to reprint versions of this book and the selections from the body of work over four decades that it includes. One, Phillip Harris at Electron Press (www.electronpress.com), compiled a longer e-book version for Electronpress.com. Now, a child of another generation, Johnny Temple, an unusual musician-publisher who put out an earlier book of mine, *Falun Gong's Challenge to China*, has released this edition with a different and perhaps more modern, even hipper attitude. Working with a talented editor, Joel Schalit, he sliced and diced the material another way entirely, making it less chronological and more thematic. Some of the material I liked best was left on the "edit-room floor" but, that, alas, comes with the territory. The truth is no one would necessarily want to plod through an *Encyclopedia Schechtercana*.

One of the great joys of working in the media is interacting with people you respect. I was honored to have Ahmed Kathrada contribute a fore-word to the book, and I appreciate Anant Singh's help in arranging it. Kathy, as Kathrada is known to friends, has been one of the great stal-warts of the liberation struggle in South Africa, and a man on whom Nelson Mandela relied during his long years of isolation and confinement.

FOREWORD
A Salute from South Africa by Ahmed Kathrada

For nearly three decades, the apartheid system tried to make us non-persons. We couldn't be mentioned by name in the press. Our pictures couldn't be shown. We couldn't be quoted. By the force of law and threats, a compliant media went along. Only a very few journalists or media organizations had the courage to challenge censorship laws and the dictates of the propagandists of the old order.

When we emerged from prison, we were shocked to learn that for many years some sectors of the international media had been taking cues from Apartheid South Africa. Cold War attitudes framed the news. Our democratic movement was often labeled as "Moscow-backed," when we actually enjoyed support from people all over the world. The African National Congress had to work extremely hard to get its positions before the world public. At one point, in the late '80s, as human rights abuses were increasing against the people of South Africa, the TV coverage overseas in some countries actually decreased.

While we were being told to shut up within South Africa, we were being shut out by some media institutions in the West, who for a time believed that sanctions couldn't work, and that the struggle against apartheid couldn't win. Happily, their skepticism did not prevail.

As developments on the ground changed, coverage changed along with it, but it was still all too often focused on violence, and not on the real political situation. The world public that mobilized to help free Nelson Mandela, with whom I shared a cell block in the notorious Robben Island prison, was often not aware of the collective nature of our movement, and other ANC leaders like Oliver Tambo. The people's structures in the townships that led the struggle so bravely under the ANC's leadership were often deemed unworthy of media support.

We heard about a group of journalists in New York working with media workers inside South Africa who were, despite the odds and obstacles, determined to get the real and full story out. Led by Danny Schechter, they fought censorship here, and self-censorship there, with the weekly *South Africa Now* TV series, which won many awards for telling the story that the networks wouldn't. That broadcast was also seen throughout Africa and other parts of the world; people could now hear the voices of our struggle, with reports filed from the inside out, from the bottom up. *South Africa Now* was important not only for *what* it reported, but for *how* it reported—working with the people closest to the actual reality. I am sure that efforts like this played a key role in educating and mobilizing the victorious anti-apartheid movement worldwide.

Afterwards, Nelson Mandela invited Danny and his colleagues from their production company, Globalvision, to document his trip to America in 1990, and, later, the historic 1994 election here at home. Working with South Africa's leading film producer, Anant Singh, Danny directed inspirational documentary films including *Countdown to Freedom: Ten Days that Changed South Africa*, *Prisoners of Hope: Reunion on Robben Island*, and *A Hero for All: Nelson Mandela's Farewell*. These films will help future generations understand why we struggled like we did—and how the people of the world responded.

Many journalists bravely challenged apartheid and helped the world understand what was wrong and why it had to be righted. We appreciate all of their efforts. But after reading this collection of Danny Schechter's writings over all these years, including an account of his first visit to our country in 1967 (when he attended the funeral of the great former president-general of the ANC, Chief Albert Luthuli), I recognize and salute his long-standing committment to human rights journalism, and his continuing involvement in telling stories that must get out and be heard.

South Africa Now has become *South Africa Then*. Continued coverage is called for in this period when the struggle for liberation, which seemed so black and white, has become more complex as we battle for development, and, in the face of AIDS challenges, for survival. We need world support as much now as we did then.

I am pleased that Danny Schechter is still with us in the trenches as an independent observer and a journalist of conscience. He is truly a News Dissector.

***

Ahmed Kathrada was sentenced to life imprisonment in 1964 by South Africa's apartheid regime. He served twenty-six years in the notorious Robben Island prison alongside Nelson Mandela before being released on October 15, 1989. His experiences are described in Letters From Robben Island: A Selection of Ahmed Kathrada's Prison Correspondence, 1964-1989 *(Michigan State University 1999). Kathrada was elected to the South African parliament in 1994.*

INTRODUCTION
Bringing Back the News Dissector

In 1999, I brought the "News Dissector" back to life, this time as the title of a weekly column for a global media Internet portal, mediachannel.org. We created the site to challenge a media industry that I've managed to survive in while fighting the good fight to improve coverage on the inside for so many years. One of the people in that industry—formerly a network executive, now the CEO of a promising new media venture—commented to me during a panel dicussion I was moderating that he remembered me as the WBCN/Boston News Dissector from his college days. "Danny," he told me, "you were into branding before all of us. You branded yourself." So now the brand is back, this time on the Internet, and as the title of this collection of essays and reports going back to the 1960s. In some ways it feels like a dissection of a dissector.

Through *News Dissector's* pages, you will be able to join me on some of the many media adventures that took me around the world over the past forty years. It's sometimes hard for me to acknowledge that I've traveled to over fifty countries, stood in the presence of presidents, been shot at in two wars, and, yes, walked on the wild side. I've been in the company of UN Secretary Generals, interviewed rock musicians, debated media moguls and many media-defined newsmakers. But I have also walked on back roads and alleys with the poor and the less well-known. I have spent time with people who have always lived and died outside the media's glare. People whose dignity and courage have often moved me to a deeper understanding of the world I am part of, and sometimes moved me to action.

You'll meet me first as a precocious teenager just discovering the world of journalism, but unable to escape the issues of the day. I became aware of the fight for civil rights by covering one of the first New York press conferences by students who were staging sit-ins against racial segregation way back in the spring of 1960. Their stories shocked me and touched me. Spurred on by their challenge, I got involved.

That brought me face to face with a persistent dilemma facing journalists: When is it right to "cross the line" between "objective" reporting and more values-driven journalism? The activists I was covering were my own age, and yet they were clearly making history. I decided to join them and *then* try to chronicle their struggle from the inside. That engagement with the "Movement" (as we called it, and we always thought of it with a capital M) was to put me on a trajectory that I haven't left to this day, although there have been some unexpected twists and detours and even an occasional U-turn on that bumpy road to a better America and a more just world. It's a path on which you get engaged even when you don't always think you should. It is a road that respects and demands participatory journalism.

Like many of those who came before and after me, my views were shaped by the crises and moral challenges facing the years in which I came of age. In the early 1960s, I was a civil rights activist and a community organizer, working on voter registration drives in the deep South and helping to organize rent strikes "up north." I was immersed in "Negro" culture and the civil rights struggle and was blessed to be able to march alongside the Reverend Doctor Martin Luther King Jr. and interact personally with Malcolm X.

As I grew older, my life took a turn from activism to politics, when as part of an eight-month fellowship program that included now–Vice President Dick Cheney, I became an assistant to the mayor of Detroit and saw how political insiders operate. From there it was off to the London School of Economics, to earn a master's degree in political sociology and learn about other cultures, in part by plunging into the "dawning of that Age of Aquarius" and revolution in the streets. Mick Jagger, who went to the LSE before me, was not the only "street fighting man."

I returned to the States in the pivotal year of 1968 and moved to Boston, where I began a two-pronged immersion in issues and media. I worked full-time researching and writing about Africa, only to fall unexpectedly into an on-air job in rock and roll radio and broadcast news. It was then that the "News Dissector" was first born. After a decade as a radio newscaster, it was on to a career in television as a reporter and producer, and ultimately into the establishment world of networks and media conglomerates. I was an outsider who became an insider only to turn myself into an outsider again.

That transition comes through in these pages as I continue to seek to define a role for myself in the media business and in life; a role that marries money with meaning and permits me to pursue my many passions. It hasn't always been easy, but I have no regrets. To borrow a phrase from my late mom, the poet Ruth Lisa Schechter, I feel that I can now tell it like it is because I was there when it was.

Once I began watching the world with new eyes, America's various intelligence agencies began watching me. The CIA and the FBI were on my case and tracking my not-all-that-subversive activities. Later, thanks to the Freedom of Information Act, I was fortunate to get a glimpse of how they work and some of the pathetic reports their spooks came up with. Fortunately, I did not meet the fate of some of my colleagues in other countries who found themselves in an early grave because of unsolicited attention from state security services and undercover agents.

My current plunge into working on the web has brought me, in my late fifties, into a new medium that both seems to belong to a younger generation, the current twentysomethings, but has also been quite open to my own involvement in the online world. The Internet is, as James Brown used to sing, "a brand new bag." It's an interactive medium with a global reach for those who have access to it; a still emerging medium with a technology that seems to change every day. All the rules are not yet in place; all of the controls associated with broadcasting and print media have thus far not been imposed.

For years, critics railed that the means of media production were concentrated in the few hands that could afford expensive printing plants and TV studios. But once new technologies became widely available—low-cost cameras, audio and video editing equipment, along with computer-based publishing systems—there was a tectonic shift in publishing and broadcasting opportunities. Suddenly the tools of radio and television production became more affordable, and anyone could become a publisher or producer. This ushered in a technology-driven democratization of the means of production after electronic-product manufacturers discovered that consumers welcome equipment that allows ordinary people to *make* media as well as consume it.

The presence of these new technologies did not in itself revolutionize—nor will it—the class structures responsible for the "digital divide": a world divided between information haves and have-nots. It seemed as one means of communication became accessible, another one became more remote. The ability to reach large audiences stayed locked up under the control of a smaller and smaller number of larger and larger media companies. In the search for synergies to boost their bottom lines, a wave of media mergers accelerated industry consolidation at the top.

One consequence for independent producers into whose ranks I "descended" (one newspaper called me a "hero of downward mobility") was that as production became easier, distribution became harder. Yes, we could post insurgent and provocative content of all kinds. But building an audience requires marketing muscle and publicity. That costs a lot of money. Large conglomerates have it, smaller entities don't. Our own film and video production company, Globalvision, which I co-own with Rory O'Connor, could now produce important programming at a relatively low cost, but getting it seen in an unfiltered environment became problematic.

If we were just willing to make slimy films about serial killers for channels that insisted on owning and controlling all valuable rights, we could easily find work. If we wanted to do stories about human rights and corporate injustice under our own banner, and also own and control the product, the obstacles could be overwhelming. Competing as a small company in an age of media giants makes you feel like an ant in a field of elephants. You have to tread carefully, lest you be crushed. Nevertheless, I'm not the least bit daunted. These are challenges I've faced before.

I entered professional journalism at a time when independent and alternative media was in ascendance and was beginning to reach large audiences. I was part of what we called the "underground press," a spunky countercultural challenge to the mainstream. I joined the FM radio revolution and became a fixture on Boston's WBCN, once one of the country's most innovative music stations. As the "news guy," I found the freedom to pioneer a different style of newscasting: audio-rich, collage-driven, critically inflected, and determined to tell the truth as I saw it. Fortunately, it became very popular and propelled me to some degree of notoriety. As I later joked, I had become a legend in my own mind.

'BCN was a commercial station, and soon my colleagues and I were face-to-face with an acquisition by a far straighter and more conventional company. Fortunately, we had organized ourselves into a union. After nineteen of us were arbitrarily fired, we fought back by striking and mobilizing solidarity in our vast audience. We won the strike. However, with the passage of time, we changed along with the station. Listeners could hear the difference, as the station lost its identity (and soul) as an outlet that stood apart from the morass of mediocrity on the dial. In these pages, you can read about what happened when self-styled "King of All Media" Howard Stern was moved into the morning slot.

I joined the media to spotlight serious problems in the world, and soon realized that the media was not only one of those problems, but a problem that was barely recognized as such. Activists for social change wanted to get on the media, not transform it. They saw media exposure as a means to other ends, not always aware that media companies had their own agendas closely wedded to the status quo. The media decided what news was, and how to present it. And for the most part, they froze critics and activists out, along with many of the issues they cared about.

When I think about the issues that I devoted so much of my time to—South Africa, racism, human rights, economic fairness—I realize that getting what I considered to be the real story was often easier than getting that story out. Media gatekeepers intervened to block ideas and perspectives deemed "too controversial," while conventional formats restricted who could tell what. That may be built into the logic of a commercial media system, although as I discovered, mainstream public broadcasting can be even worse.

It's always potentially embarrassing to dust off yellowed articles from a filing cabinet and think they may be of contemporary interest. I would like to believe that the articles in *News Dissector* meet that test. Looking back at where I have been and what I have done, I can see some breakthroughs I never imagined when I originally wrote some of these essays and reports. I know it is unfashionable to be optimistic, but we actually won many of the fights we took on. The civil rights movement achieved more than it expected, but less than it deserved. Racial inequality is still with us and still needs to be transformed. But segregation, in a formal sense, belongs largely to the past.

The anti-apartheid struggle in South Africa prevailed at great cost but without the type of civil war and mass bloodletting that most of the "experts" expected. Years after the freeing of Nelson Mandela, a new plague, AIDS, is killing more people than died in the freedom struggle. And that issue has engaged my current interest and involvement. But South Africa is a far different place than the "Beloved Country" (to quote Alan Paton) that I first visited in 1967, and describe in these pages.

The war on Vietnam that so many of us opposed finally ended too, and in the last months of the Clinton administration, an American president visited Hanoi, signaling that normal relations between our two countries may still be possible. At the same time, it would be disingenuous to employ the solution Vermont's former senator, George Aitken, once proposed for the US role in Vietnam: "Declare victory and come home." Over many years of banging my own head up against many unmoving walls, I recognized how conservative our country is and how powerful and resilient the powers of the status quo can be. The simple black and whites of my youth turned into complex grays along with some of my hair. I now see many more nuances and contradictions in middle age, as I am sure we all do. It's far easier to know what you are *against* than precisely what you are *for*. My basic values haven't changed, but my appreciation of how difficult it is to transform the world has. Yet I still identify more with the values of our "we" generation than the conformism of the "me" generations that followed.

I've come to see that the problem is not just "them," but also "us." The progressive side of the spectrum may have an accurate analysis, but its organizing and media strategies have often been naïve and ineffective—when there is any strategy at all. What's left in the left is all too often reactive and protest-centered, railing at what's wrong rather than building a constituency for what's right. It is impossible to live in a dynamic and materialist society like ours without it affecting one's worldview or often corroding one's idealism or sense of what's possible. The progressive movements with which I've identified have failed to build strong organizations, and are often as self-marginalizing as they are constrained by larger powers. Sometimes this leads one into a low-grade despair, or a Sancho Panza–like tilting at windmills. As a young activist, I was certain that our '60s generation would be triumphant. But after eight years of living under a president younger than myself, and someone who marched alongside us earlier in his life, I'm not so sure.

We have to accept our share of the responsibility for this condition. The failure of the movements of the '60s to deal with deep contradictions led to many implosions and the dramatic growth of identity politics. The women's movement was in part a reaction to male domination and insensitivity within the student and activist communities. I had my own painful experiences in recognizing the many unconscious ways that I and other "male heavies" contributed to a rage that led to the painful breakups of organizations and relationships. Ditto for the disaffections of many people of color. Close friends and colleagues like the late journalist Andrew Kopkind and his partner John Scagliotti sensitized me to the legitimate aspirations of gay people. Sadly, the upwardly mobile or counter-cultural trajectories that many of us followed distanced us from the needs and organizations of working people. To be sure, the unwelcoming atmosphere in much of the labor movement contributed to that rupture. And beyond all of this—a litany which can easily turn into self-flagellation—must be the recognition that the powers-that-be demonstrated in countless ways that, in the words of Al Haig, they were "in charge," and would resist (and sometimes try to destroy) the emergence of serious opposition movements, no matter how democratic or non-violent. Power only yields to counter-power, and anti-democratic media systems need to be challenged by more democratic ones.

Co-optation and neo-conservative rationalizations in the name of being "effective" have a way of worming their way into the minds of many potentially progressive leaders who cannot resist the seductions of power. This is also true in the media, where people who choose to become journalists betray their callings in the name of pragmatism—often masking careerism. None of these insights have slowed me down or stopped my own immersion in activist-supporting media work. I am old-fashioned enough to believe that active citizenship trumps passive consumerism every time. But it has chastened me somewhat. I try to avoid the perennially fashionable skepticism of some of my jaded, know-it-all colleagues. (The media magazine *Brill's Content* employs "skepticism is a virtue" as its motto.) However, I admit that I am more sensitive now to what seem at times to be impossible barriers to achieving a more just world. I also know that skills and savvy are needed more than good intentions.

At the beginning of a new century, it feels like I've moved on to yet another struggle that seems just as unwinnable as the battles I first chose to fight when I was younger. Can our media system be transformed? How do you change that beast? I'm still struggling to find out. I started writing at the time of the "New Frontier," when a youthful president, John F. Kennedy, appeared to represent the hopes for change that many younger people yearned for. This book is coming out as the Dubya presidency begins under a cloud of illegitimacy, in a country where politics is mortgaged to special interests, and corporate journalism is too often a handmaiden.

The problems I have been concerned with over these years seem to be permanent features of our culture and country. They remain part of the landscape, so the struggles with which I have always identified will remain with us as well. All are unfinished. Wars for development have replaced wars of liberation. Spies and surveillance have become more covert, yet they remain just as insidious. But activism and honest journalism remain. It is gratifying to see a new global justice movement taking shape and so many sharp voices and new outlets. It is exciting to sense that the web may still become the global news and information outlet that so many of us desire.

The articles and essays in this book were written over a span of forty years. They reflect some of the print journalism and reporting I filed "on the side," usually when I was doing other things like going to school, organizing for civil rights actions, protesting against the Vietnam War, newscasting, filmmaking, or producing for television. They were written to supplement other forms of expression, since I've always found myself trying to do at least nine things at once. Many of my stories for broadcast were produced with teams in a collaborative process; most of these articles were scribbled and typed alone, late at night, on planes, trains, and in hotel rooms.

I always knew I could never live on my writings alone, but I could never really live without them either. The life of a freelancer was never for me. Yet, I've always made mental notes and observations, or obsessively clipped publications for later use. I write because the other mediums I work in have never enabled me to explore the most fascinating details of the stories I have been drawn to. Print can allow you to sustain real arguments, offer perspectives, or even, from time to time, express emotion. I write because other mediums seem more transitory, while the written word, on paper, in print, had permanence. Or so I've always thought. I always believed they could last forever. Of course they didn't. Even libraries chuck books for which there is little demand.

As it turns out, many of the publications in which the pieces in this book first appeared are long gone, along, I would note, with many of the "big magazines" I grew up with, like *Life, Look,* and the *Saturday Evening Post.* They are buried in the media cemetery alongside *Ramparts, Dialogue,* and the smaller alternative magazines that carried my byline. Happily, I am still here, and as we used to say in my teenage years, "keeping on keeping on."

Stay tuned.

I am.

Onward!

Your News Dissector,
Danny Schechter, editor@mediachannel.org
June 2001

PRESS ACCREDITATION—STUDENT PRESS ASSOCIATION

2117 S Street NW
Washington, D.C. 20006

July 3, 1967

To Whom it May Concern:

Mr. Daniel Schechter is an official correspondent of the United States Student Press Association. Would you please extend to him all the courtesies as a bona fide member of the student press?

The U.S. Student Press Association is an independent organization owned and operated by three hundred member college papers, which pay dues to finance the organization.

Yours sincerely,
Robert A. Gross
General Secretary

part one **MOVEMENT DAYS**

passions, pieces, and polemics • 1960–2000

STUDENT FORUM
1960

The New York Post *ran a student forum for debate. As the editor of my high school paper, the* Clinton News, *I was invited to have a say. I was seventeen, and I was wrong. It was my first exposure in the mainstream press. The issue: Should eighteen-year-olds be allowed to vote?*

Age eighteen is the magic number for many teenagers. They feel this brings complete maturity and an official entrance into the adult world. Accordingly, they clamor for the privilege of voting.

However, maturity, especially in the political sense, comes only with education and experience. The majority of today's youth are uninformed and apathetic about the workings of government and demonstrate little interest in important issues.

This is not to say that all teenagers aren't informed; a good many could certainly vote intelligently. Unfortunately, their number is not sufficient to warrant a lowering of the voting age.

Another danger of permitting the vote at eighteen is the gullibility of the teenage mind. This ability to be influenced easily has been shown by the fervent support given to Hitler and Mussolini by German and Italian youths during their rise to power. It is also significant that both lowered the voting age as soon as they came into power.

Of the seventeen nations in the world with voting ages under twenty-one, eight are Communist states and seven are in Latin America, an area not noted for political stability.

The age of legal maturity in the U.S. is twenty-one. Lowering the age for voting would eventually lead to lowering the age for jury duty, right to make contracts, etc., and might upset the country's social and economic order in an undesirable way.

Many cry that "if you are old enough to fight, you are old enough to vote," yet few realize the enormous differences between physical and mental maturity. The ability to fight has nothing to do with the abilities of thought and evaluation. In fact, armed forces discipline leaves little room for free thought.

This article originally appeared in the New York Post, *May 13, 1960.*

WHAT IS A REVOLUTIONARY?
1968

This morning I am in a cinema packed with London's film buffs, watching "Lenin in Poland." The film embodies socialist realism, employing flashbacks and images to recount Lenin's stay in Polonia in 1914, his imprisonment, his fear of the coming war in Europe. There he was, Vladimir Ilyich, the frenetic revolutionist embracing his comrades, hungering for news of the international struggle—a man pictured as human, warmly concerned about children, but also a calculating Marxist, displaying disciplined outrage and faith in the ultimate victory of the proletariat. For him, the revolution was inevitable.

This was the Lenin, the grandfatherly "hero of the Socialist Revolution." Communism's main man! "Overthrow the capitalists," he had written, and it shall be done. "It may not happen in my generation," he told some Swiss workers before the Russian revolution erupted. So he did have doubts. He never stopped thinking, writing, advocating, agitating. "He is the most male of all these reformers," Wilson writes, "because he never weeps; his attitude begins with impatience." The most male? What does that mean? Lenin was the idea man, the man with the plan. He gave Gorky the "impression of the physical pressure of the irresistible truth." And yet look at his legacy. I wouldn't want to live under Leninist rule.

Is that what it will take in America? Must one be like Lenin—driven by a fantastic egotism and macho commitment to the revolution at all costs, by all means? Or more likely, will aping Lenin drive us to the fringes of sectarian political irrelevance, into ineffective sects fighting over obscure doctrinal issues about theory and practice?

If Lenin were alive there is no doubt that he would dismiss our movements—SNCC, SDS etc.—as an infantile disorder. After all, we have little elaborated ideology, and virtually no real organization. We have forsaken the proletariat—or they us—to work with mobile shifting lumpen elements or kids like ourselves. How can they substitute for the masses, he would ask. That most "male" of men would see our insurgency as a form of political juvenile delinquency.

I don't buy it. Look at the utopia he built.

From a letter, London 1968.

HOFFA AND HAZARD
1963

I grew up in a labor movement home. I went to Cornell's School of Industrial and Labor Relations. In 1963, I met Teamsters Union leader Jimmy Hoffa, then America's most feared labor leader. I wanted to understand why the labor movement was in the shape it was.

Jimmy Hoffa's private plane landed in Ithaca less than a week after Berman Gibson, the leader of the striking miners in Hazard, Kentucky, returned to hunger and floods in the coalfields. More than two thousand Cornell students listened to the Teamster boss boast about the conditions and $3.03 hourly minimum his truckers enjoy; less than four hundred heard Gibson's report about men making less than $3 a day in the mines. The gulf that stands between those hourly and daily minimums represents the distance that the labor movement has come in this country. A look at these two men and what they represent suggests, at once, both the source of organized labor's undoing, and its possible regeneration.

"Unions and their members," Hoffa told a group of students, "have changed much since the days of Gompers." The emphasis he placed on "bread and butter" gains continues unchanged. Unions have become, as George Bernard Shaw put it, "the capitalism of the proletariat," playing an important and acknowledged role in the free enterprise system. It is James Riddle Hoffa, more than most labor leaders, who embodies the spirit of Samuel Gompers. Having accepted the National Association of Manufacturers' definition of the American dream, Hoffa has risen to a position of power respected by his peers in the labor "business." Militant in the pursuit of self-interest, Hoffa is not interested in the moral content of his programs or approach; yet it is Hoffa's philosophy of unionism, not his over-publicized and exaggerated underworld associations, that pose the greatest threat to the type of movement that American workers might create.

The rise of Jimmy Hoffa is a testimonial to the notion that no matter how humble one's beginnings, opportunity to climb or claw to the top still exists in America. Born in poverty, one of a family of four children whose father died young, Hoffa was early cast into the role of a breadwinner. At eighteen, in the midst of the depression, he went to work as a warehouseman. "I got interested in unions," he says, "because we were being kicked around." Self-interest and antagonism towards his employer's practices motivated him to organize an independent union which was later incorporated into the Teamster brotherhood. Things were rough in those days. "The employers," he recalls, "hired thugs who were out to get us, and brother, your life was in your hands every day. There was only one way to survive—fight back. And we used to slug it out on the strikes. They found out we didn't scare. The police would beat your brains in for even talking union. If you went out on strike, you got your head broken." Violence was not unusual during the massive organizing campaigns of the thirties. Jimmy Hoffa learned early that strategy without muscle could never be successful.

As he would be the first to tell you, Jimmy Hoffa is tough. It is this impression that above all he seeks to convey. Armed with an impressive array of facts and figures as well as a competent speaking ability, Hoffa makes no pretenses to intellectualism. Uneasy with social philosophy, he is anxious to be identified solely with the union's rank and file. Ambitious and shrewd, Hoffa is quick to catalogue the pragmatic achievements his brand of unionism has chalked up. Success goes to the strong and tough; power, not a crusading spirit, begets benefits. Hoffa's militancy and zeal are reserved for extending and consolidating his union's influence, strengthening its contracts, and enlarging its membership. Undaunted by its biting critics in and around the house of labor, the 1.7 million member International Brotherhood of Teamsters, Chauffeurs, Warehousemen, and Helpers is the largest union in the country and is growing while others lose members or fight to stand still.

While Jimmy Hoffa tightens control over his union, Berman Gibson stands abandoned by the union he grew up in. "I was too strong a union man for the United Mine Workers," explains the leader of the protracted wildcat revolt against the mine operators and the union in the southeastern corner of Kentucky. Operating in an area where most of the large mines have shut down, the UMW appears to be trying to pull out of this depressed mountain region. The marginal operators, likewise, are anxious to aid the unions' departure by relying on scab labor and "injunction-happy" judges. Without a sufficient number of operators paying the negotiated forty-cents-a-ton royalty to support the miners' welfare program, the UMW has announced that it is closing four of its hospitals in the area come July. Union members in and around Hazard have been blacklisted from employment while the sheriff's office coordinates a harassment campaign against those on strike.

And so, Berman Gibson brought his case to the school kids, and

Cornell's sorority sisters responded by sending their winter clothes to mountain folk who go without.

The American Way

Berman Gibson embraces the original spirit of protest which built and may even save the American labor movement. "I believe in the American way," he announced to those who came and gaped in disbelief at the story he told, "but I believe there is enough here for all of us if it is done right." Speaking simply in a rapid-fire dialect, the stocky miner told of having taken an oath when he first joined up with the union back in the thirties: "I swore then and I'll swear now never to harm a brother or leave him in distress. All we askin' for is justice—men just shouldn't have to live this way."

The full implications of Gibson's demands challenge Attorney General Bobby Kennedy and his government far more fundamentally than do Hoffa's brash machinations. Gibson has pointed to the real enemies within: widespread deprivation, a stagnant economy unable to provide for those most in need, local systems of justice oblivious to constitutional rights, and a labor movement hamstrung by an approach to social and economic problems grounded in traditional and outmoded assumptions and practices. Even a victory for the strikers will not solve the basic problem of men being rendered "obsolete" by a combination of automation and shrinking markets. Real protection for Gibson's men lies with a labor movement that will rehabilitate its social engine and lead with a vision on political, economic, and social fronts.

Beyond Collective Bargaining

It is the role labor has chosen to play today that is responsible for the position it is in. Content to focus on winning immediate and tangible economic gains at the collective bargaining table, unions are unprepared and unequipped to tackle the basic problems of the changing nature and composition of the work force: a high unemployment rate, and automation. Sociologist Daniel Bell is quite right in insisting that to do so, labor must go beyond collective bargaining.

The present system of a narrow, ultimately ineffectual concentration on economic goals cannot fully confront those problems. As one union official recently told a reporter from *LOOK*: "Union leaders sit behind expensive desks with carpets under their feet and most of them don't know what they want, except to preserve the status quo inside their union and get themselves accepted by the community at large . . . they make a labor movement that's got nothing to say about politics to the politicians. And nothing to say to the Negroes in the South or to the unorganized farm laborers in California. Nothing really to say about automation and unemployment. No purpose—nothing to communicate." Is it this that the labor movement has come to, a short twenty-five years after seriously unfurling its banners on the American scene?

To expect the labor movement to act upon the demands being made of it by its most loyal but disillusioned well-wishers is to ask the near impossible. Realistically, the tenacity of the bread-and-butter tradition of AFL craft unionism cannot be wished away. The AFL-CIO, wed in federation since 1955, is now, according to observers, having serious marital difficulties: "AFL-CIO unity still stops at the hyphen." The house of labor is beset by deep personal and jurisdictional rivalries. Union enrollment is not climbing, an independent Teamsters union frequently raids its affiliated locals while protracted strikes in sensitive industries increase public and congressional anxiety about the need to regulate "big labor." And aging leadership, often insistent on maintaining traditional methods, in many cases no longer reflects the composition of a changing membership. These oligarchic tendencies within the unions have created bitter conflicts, particularly among the under-represented Negro workers who still face discriminatory practices in a diminishing number of unions. All the problems involve an inertia born of structural difficulties and limited horizons, a lassitude which many fear has permanently circumscribed labor's potential role as an agent of social change.

Unions Need a Creative Ferment

There are few signs of aggressive social action on the part of unions. Some unions, it is true, have embraced the civil rights movement. Others have embarked upon organizing campaigns among those workers who need unionization most. The Hospital Workers Union in New York City provides an encouraging example. Yet the large majority of unions stand on the sidelines, contributing little toward real social dialogue. It is ironic, as one critic has noted, that one of the few people standing up to the "new gauleiters of thought control and the manipulation of news is one who has no pretensions to intellectualism, radical or otherwise, James R. Hoffa." To rekindle the social zeal of a cynical and often materially satisfied rank and file is not an easy job. To allow the task to fall to an opportunistic Jimmy Hoffa is to abrogate the larger responsibility.

Yet the labor movement today needs both Jimmy Hoffa and Berman

Gibson. The spirit and courage displayed by Hoffa in combating a government vendetta against him could well be used to focus on other areas of government ineptitude and inaction on pressing social problems. The AFL-CIO might also borrow a leaf from Hoffa's organizing manual and employ the same type of financial and personnel resources in organizing the unorganized. The Teamsters' insistence on organizing interracial locals (especially in the South), providing important community services, and building comprehensive medical and pension plans stand as examples for the whole labor movement to emulate.

But the labor movement must also leave Hoffa's brand of unionism behind. It has to evolve a new philosophy for itself. Its social interests and conscience need to be broadened. Organized labor then could become a powerful political force for a more democratic and equitable society. Somehow a creative ferment is needed to shake loose the self-defeating structures and horizons limiting labor's role. The inspiration, imagination, and idealism which once guided labor unions needs rekindling. An upheaval of this sort will change not only the state of the unions but the state of the Union.

This article originally appeared in Dialogue Magazine, *Spring 1963.*

DISCOVERING HARLEM
1961/2000

*In 1961, as the civil rights movement erupted nationwide, I wanted a deeper
understanding of what was going on. I joined a group of Cornell students
under the rubric of the appropriately named "Project Understanding"—a
project of the Cornell United Religious Work (CURW)—to travel to the
South and North to see for ourselves. This appeared in one of the project's
reports.*

> "Parnell came down the road, he said t'a cheering mon:
> 'Ireland shall get her freedom and you still break
> stone.'"
> —W.B. Yeats

Note: The following impressions were gained mostly during an automobile tour of Harlem, led by Dan Schechter, a native New Yorker, and Sam Carradine, also a New Yorker and a Cornellian on leave to serve as administrative assistant on the staff of the Domestic Peace Corps pilot project in Central Harlem.

> "New York is proud of Harlem . . . today."
> —Mayor Robert Wagner, Harlem Youth Day ceremony

So we seven came to learn from Lenox Avenue, which, more than most streets in America, has a lesson to offer. There are men who do nothing more than stroll down this broad promenade, stopping for a "three-for-one" in the endless stream of bars that line the avenue. They are there when the avenue wakes up, and make sure she never goes to sleep. They, more than the others, taught Harlem to the black from Jackson, the white from Evanston, the New Jersey gentleman farmer, and the coeds from Scarsdale and points suburban. We have climbed back above Cayuga's Waters now, but the lesson of the valley stands freshly imprinted in our hearts and minds. If it isn't now, it never will be.

Life on the streets 125 blocks north of the power center of the free world moves sluggishly from day to day. *Daily News* is dropped off and gobbled up at 9:30 each night, and Harlem learns about who will win the fight or who won at Aqueduct. Kids check out the track meet results, and somewhere a matron moans about all the senseless killin' goin' on in the world. The bars on Eighth Avenue are broken up only by churches, and if they both didn't exist, Jimmy Baldwin assured me, there would be blood in the streets. But they do, and Harlem Hospital has yet to leave a Saturday night behind which has not seen its shootings and cuttings. The blood flows. That part of Harlem not killing the other part is high somewhere on Jesus, TV, Thunderbird, boo, or somethin' else.

We got their first real view of the valley up there in front of the High School of Music and Art where those bohemian foxes catch their classes. The housing projects were visible near the river, and the lines of tenements (seventy percent built before 1900) were broken only by the crisscross pattern of avenue and street. There was a gray mist hanging over the valley that afternoon but the Harlem River and the smelly East could be seen over the rooftops. The Park, I told them, was known more for its sexual crimes than its steps, but that only brought a chuckle. City College, that asphalt campus so unlike our own, was behind us now and the outline of the skyline stared back at us.

It was getting dark in the Volkswagen as we neared Seventh Avenue. The street began to turn on its lights to advertise for Sunday. "That's Sugar Hill," Sam told us, with as much disinterest as a guide who points to the tomb of someone he never knew. It was there that they once lived, to the envy of those who lived below. Today, it stands as a testimony to the glory of Black Manhattan. The cars stopped and we were in Riverton, Harlem's first privately built project. It looked clean and stark and a long way now from the front lawn of Cornell's Beta Sig house which Sam had also gotten to know. "I'm showing them around our Harlem," Sam chuckled as he introduced us to Doug, whose glassy eyes revealed his preoccupation. "This isn't a slum," I could sense our people thinking, "we want to see a slum." And then, I thought again of Jimmy Baldwin who had written: "Harlem watched Riverton go up . . . in the most violent bitterness of spirit and hated it long before the builders arrived. They began hating it about the moment people began moving out of their condemned houses to make room for this additional proof of how thoroughly the white world despised them." Harsh words, I thought. Jimmy is living downtown now. Riverton was clean that Sunday.

Slowly, Harlem came into focus. There were the churches and the schools, and the Schomburg Collection of Negro History—official New York's monument to the glory of Negritude. The Christians built their "Y," and the City was adding more operating rooms to Harlem Hospital. We visited the Honorable Elijah Muhammad's minister at the Temple No. 7 restaurant, who taught us that which was taught to him. We met Malcolm X who spoke about soul, and there were few among us who didn't dig the bean pie.

Where else in New York can you buy bean pie?

***

Author's Note, 2000: Malcolm was later to become a personal influence in my life, a larger than life figure with whom I was fortunate to cross paths. As an editor of the Cornell student magazine *Dialogue*, I invited him to campus for a debate with civil rights leader James Farmer of CORE, an organization I then supported. Up until that point, no national leader had agreed to appear with Malcolm, perhaps out of a concern about "legitimizing" him—this was long before the publication of his autobiography. Clearly, there was also the fear of being humiliated by the minister's intellectual prowess and charisma.

First, I persuaded Farmer to participate. Then, I wrote to Malcolm, hoping he would at least receive the letter and respond. Frankly, I didn't know what to expect. A few days later, he answered with a letter, written in his home in East Elmhurst, Queens—a house that would years later be firebombed. He had typed the letter himself, beginning with a yes:

> I accept your invitation to take part in the debate at
> Cornell University on March 7. Mr. James Farmer is the
> first of the nationally known so-called Negro "leaders"
> who has accepted the ever-present opportunity to dis-
> cuss "Integration and Separation" in a head-on debate
> with a black person who is against integration. It
> should prove most interesting.

The minister also raised some specifics, since the only room we had available was the rather small Moot Courtroom at the law school:

> Are you certain your auditorium has sufficient seating
> capacity? If so, it will be the smallest college crowd ever
> to attend a debate in which a Muslim was involved.

I had asked him to send along supplementary material to help publicize the event. He responded to this request curtly:

> I have no background material on myself. I'm the minister of the Muslim community here in New York City (Muhammad's Mosque No. 7), and National Representative of the Honorable Elijah Muhammad (Spiritual Head of the Muslims in the Western Hemisphere). We are against "forced integration," and we advocate complete separation of the races. We are not anti-white, but we are PRO-BLACK.
>
> Any other way we can be helpful to you beforehand, don't hesitate to let us know.
>
> Sincerely,
> Malcolm X

As a CORE partisan then, I feared Malcolm as a hate monger, and admired Farmer, who had moved from pacifism into unionism and then into civil rights activism. (Sadly, he would later be co-opted by Nixonism, taking a job in the Republican administration.) Though eloquent, Farmer was no match for the sharp-tongued Muslim minister, then working his way onto the national stage. Malcolm arrived five hours before I expected him, in the company of Captain Joseph of Elijah Muhammad's Fruit of Islam security force. As host, I spent the day with Malcolm, showing him around, arguing, challenging, being challenged—clearly outmatched on every assumption and liberal conviction. He blew me away with the consistency of his argument and the power of his belief in the separatist imperative—though I didn't totally agree with him, and later in life he revised his own thinking as well.

The atmosphere at the debate that night was charged. The Moot Courtroom was packed. Nearly every black student on campus was there. I welcomed the crowd.

Farmer went first. He recited the evils of segregation and praised the struggle against it. "Our program is clear," he concluded. "We are going to achieve our goals for integration by non-violent direct action on an interracial level. We ask you, Mr. X, what is your program?" The room erupted in cheers, then reverted to a stony silence.

It was Malcolm's turn. There he was, the man they once called "Big

Red": tall, impeccably attired. He began with a mantra: "In the name of Allah, the Beneficent, the Merciful, to whom all praise is due, to whom we forever thank for giving America's twenty million so-called Negroes the most honorable Elijah Muhammad as our leader and our teacher and our guide."

From there he made the case for separation. "We who are Muslims, followers of the honorable Elijah Muhammad, don't think that an integrated cup of coffee is sufficient payment for 310 years of slave labor." The rhetoric was intense; neither man gave an inch. No one who was there would ever forget it.

After the debate—the transcript of which is now reprinted in at least one history of the civil rights movement—Malcolm came to a reception to meet the students and duel some more with our questions. I was at his side when, for the third time, some young preppie asked him if he was just spewing violence. Having heard his response earlier, I leapt into the fray, saying, "Let me handle this one, Minister." He smiled when I lurched into his mantra: "The Honorable Elijah Muhammad teaches us that we are just undoing the violence that your people . . ." Malcolm watched me fooling around—mocking him perhaps, but with respect—and broke into a broad smile.

"Okay, Danny," he said to me, "you have your X." For the rest of the night, and on the several occasions afterwards when we met (including once in Harlem when he spoke alongside Mississippi's legendary share-cropper and political leader Fannie Lou Hamer—the night he gave his famous "Bullets or Ballots" warning), he remembered to call me "Danny X," always with a chuckle and a knowing wink. Malcolm had quite a few white friends, including a number of journalists. In private, he was a man with a great sense of humor and warmth.

Who could have predicted his expulsion from the Muslims, his turn away from racist politics to a more revolutionary stance, his trip to Mecca, his continuing quarrel with the Nation of Islam, and his awful fate? I was with a group of civil rights buddies when we heard that he had been shot down in Harlem. Assassinated. We were shocked. I cried. Years later I spent some time with his wife Betty before she, too, died tragically. At her funeral, many people were speechless.

I learned from Malcolm about human rights, Africa, and Islam. I also learned that people can and do change. And sometimes pay the price for doing so.

BLACK NATIONALISM
The Ghetto Seeks Identity
1962

> *"This innocent country set you down in a ghetto in which it intended that you should perish . . . You were born where you were born and faced the future that you faced because you were black and for no other reason."*
>
> —James Baldwin, "A Letter to My Nephew"

Harlem, like black ghettoes throughout the country, is reasserting its blackness. The men and women who walk the Lenox Avenues of America can no longer be viewed in terms of traditional and simplistic characterizations. While the rest of America wasn't looking, large numbers of her non-whites have forsaken her. A new mood has emerged among the children of the North's porters, cooks, and cleaning women. Born out of a historical isolation bred of rejection, discrimination, and exclusion, large numbers of Negroes are not only accepting the realities of separation, but demanding them.

Many Negroes today are wondering along with author James Baldwin if it is worth it to integrate into a burning house. The man who stands in Harlem's streets and the boy who has risen to CCNY on the "mountain" that overlooks the "valley," are today both asking this question and concluding, to the consternation of official America, the black bourgeoisie, and the archetypal white liberal, NO. These two brothers of the flesh are rejecting the hypocrisy of an official rhetoric which preaches equality while the unofficial reality of their city and their society remains as Jim-Crowed as any jail in Jackson, Mississippi. They are coming together, in ever-increasing numbers, to a feeling of black nationalism— the American Negritude. This term is used to embrace a multitude of feelings, many of them contradictory, but all having in common a search for identity on the individual and group level. It is a search stemming from impatience, and it reflects an awareness of the rapidity of changes taking place in black Africa. As a southern student put it: "At the rate things are going there, all of Africa will be free before we can get a lousy cup of coffee." His northern brother has his lousy cup of coffee, but has recognized that it has done little but quench his thirst.

Most prominent among adherents of black nationalism are the followers of the Honorable Elijah Muhammad, leader of the Black Muslims. Yet the mood of nationalism, no doubt spurred by the Muslims' message and taken up with their flamboyance, transcends the movement itself. "Black nationalism," notes Dr. C. Eric Lincoln, author of *The Black Muslims in America*, "is more than courage and rebellion; it is a way of life rejecting white symbols and culture and emphasizing pride in being black." Once the urban-dwelling Negro asked if he was as good as the white man; today he is wondering aloud if the white man is as good as him.

Young Negro intellectuals are becoming increasingly critical about the basic structure, strength, and weaknesses of American society. Baldwin quotes one as saying, "I might consider being integrated into something else—an American society more real and more honest—but this?"

This article originally appeared in a report by Project Understanding-Cornell 62.

DEEP IN THE HEART OF HARLEM
Rats, Roaches, and "Agents of Social Change"
1964

. . . Thousands of Harlem tenants continue to withhold their rent from slumlords, and the strikes are slowly spreading through other parts of old New York. A look at the strike movement suggests some of the problems, techniques, and prospects of sustaining organization as an outgrowth of single-issue agitation.

The New York rent rebellions began with the actions of an unemployed shipping clerk in a Harlem slum. (Tenant Granville Cherry later became director of the Harlem Action Group, an affiliate of the Northern Student Movement of which I was full-time staffer.) The uprisings were spread throughout Harlem by Jesse Gray, a community activist and politician with student help. The strikes present a fundamental challenge to the institutionalized patterns of landlord-biased indifference by municipal agencies, courts, and political clubs. The strikes, which require difficult and time-consuming organizing techniques, have also challenged most middle class–oriented civil rights groups (NAACP, CORE etc.) who have been spurred into more contact with ghetto residents. In many ways, the success of the strikes in involving thousands of people in participatory tenants council units shows that the task of reaching and mobilizing the urban masses can be successful where community leadership guides action towards relevant issues of importance to the community.

However, the rent strikes have built-in limitations as a tactic aimed at forcing improved building code enforcement and better housing. As Feldman and Meyers wrote in *NSM News,*

> In this situation, like so many other dilemmas that Negroes face today, even a little improvement in conditions requires major economic and political changes. Discrimination and deterioration are running rampant. Neither a rent strike nor any patchwork solution can deal in the long run with the problems of overcrowding and urban blight. Although rent strikes can help improve conditions to a certain extent, they cannot keep up with the decline. But the dynamism of the movement built around the rent strike can generate considerable pressure for solutions.

Rent strikes can be an exciting technique for community organization in the northern urban ghettoes. For the first time, they have involved deprived slum dwellers in a movement for substantive change. They have also expanded the political consciousness of the ghetto community and channeled frustrations into a socially effective response. By involving the "welfare poor" in a movement for change, rent strikes have given thousands new dignity, self-respect, and a sense of empowerment. In some cases the strikes have won improvements from landlords and rent reductions too. But they have yet to spur meaningful housing legislation. Nonetheless, as an organizing technique the rent strikes help nurture indigenous leadership and build organizations that can get involved in other activities (school boycotts, selective patronage, etc.).

Based on my own experience in Harlem and the work of the Northern Student Movement (NSM), the strikes illustrate that students, white and black, who work at developing organizing skills, and understand the sustained and long process of building a movement, can play an effective role in the squalid corner of deprivation and despair in the American community.

Excerpts from a paper originally prepared for an organizing strategy meeting that brought together civil rights workers and Students for a Democratic Society organizers in Ann Arbor, Michigan, in the fall of 1964. It was part of a transition from campus activism to community organizing that would continue for twenty years.

COMMUNITY ORGANIZER
1965/1999

By 1964 the civil rights movement was evolving, moving from protest into politics. The March on Washington ended one era, and the Harlem riots would soon signal the start of another. We discussed and debated the next steps. In Mississippi, the summer project had brought hundreds of student volunteers to run Freedom Schools and register voters. Goodman, Chaney, and Schwerner (whom I knew from Cornell) were murdered. The press was focusing on the dramas in the South. In the North we saw ourselves as community organizers. But what were we organizing, and how could we do it better?

It was questions like these that prompted three of us in the Northern Student Movement to go back to school and sign up with a federally funded program at Syracuse University: the Community Action Training Center. A social work professor, Warren Haggstrom, had won a large grant from the War on Poverty to demonstrate that mobilizing the poor in their own interests was an effective strategy for fighting poverty. His approach was modeled on the work of Saul Alinsky, a legendary Chicago-based organizer who had used trade union tactics and confrontational strategies to build powerful and politically potent community organizations like the Woodlawn Organization in Chicago. Alinsky had agreed to advise the Center and its corps of students who saw a way to get academic legitimacy, a stipend, and a graduate degree in organizing. Heading up the field organizing program was an Alinsky apostle and booster, Fred Ross, whose claim to fame was that he had recruited Cesar Chavez into the farm workers' movement.

If the civil rights movement was reactive and somewhat anarchistic, the Alinsky model was highly structured and very disciplined. It was built on a theoretical base, something that much of the movement lacked. It was serious and exciting. Only eight participants were chosen for an intensive one-year training program built around three seminars, including one focused on theoretical and critical organizing issues, along with hours of field work in poor neighborhoods and housing projects. For some of us living in the hothouse of unstable activist organizations, it seemed like a godsend. Ambitious. A break from the uncertainties of movement work. And we were paid to learn. What could we lose?

For the first few months, it was stimulating. We had to challenge all of our own assumptions about political work. We came to see that organization is crucial, and that it had to be set up so that the people themselves could be in control. It was democratic, bottom-up, and methodical. It was hard work—but it did work. Soon, organizations were sprouting up in the neighborhoods in which we worked. New leaders emerged. Poor people started shaking the dust off their lives, speaking out on their concerns, even marching on City Hall.

For me, this work had grown out of some studying and research papers I had been doing at Cornell. As the civil rights movement swept through the rural South, I began looking at the urban North, believing that in the end, that's where the real problem was. In 1965, one of the students hired to evaluate the program interviewed me. She transcribed our conversation, which I found thirty-four years later. Here's what I said—and sounded like—back then:

> . . . During the year between '62 and '63, I began to
> study more about the problems, you know, about
> Northern ghettoes and how they came to be, and why
> they were allowed to exist, and who was benefiting
> from their existence. And soon I began to see that this
> problem wasn't just something that happened, that it
> had been built right in; racism is very much a part of
> Americanism, you know, and exploitation is built into
> the very structure of the society . . . if it ever was going
> to be changed, the people who were part of the prob-
> lem had to be part of the solution, they had to be able
> to speak for themselves and determine their own des-
> tiny, because one thing that you learn about a ghetto is
> that it doesn't control itself.

Within a few months, certain contradictions within the program surfaced. While we were organizing the poor on government grants, our government was bombing the poor of Southeast Asia. That war overtook the War on Poverty. Soon, one of the issues that the people we were organizing started talking about was the draft, as their sons started getting sucked up in large numbers by the war. This was not an issue we were encouraged to work on. Protests against the war—or alliances between the organizations we were building and other poor peoples' groups world-wide—were discouraged. The war was not an issue that the Alinskyites wanted to take on. It didn't seem winnable. And besides, it was being led by Democrats and liberals. Alinsky, the author of *Reveille for Radicals*, had become more of a reformer and pragmatist. He disliked the rhetoric and ideology of the movement and the New Left. He hated militants because he thought they scared off ordinary people.

The social workers in the group really weren't as political as we civil rights movement grads. They were looking for jobs; we pressed for action. As the conditions of poverty that we worked with every day radicalized us, the people who ran the program seemed to become more moderate and cautious. They were worried about their funding, and the pressure that they were beginning to feel from the University, which was under attack from the city government for sponsoring our little den of troublemakers. Soon, conflicts and debates within the program intensified as the contradiction of fighting the government with government funding became more obvious. And soon the three of us from the Northern Student Movement who had come to Syracuse together were branded troublemakers. And fired.

One of the largest demonstrations mounted by the people organized by the Community Action Training Center took place outside the training center to protest our firing. As the war in Vietnam sapped funding from the War on Poverty, the Center would soon close its doors.

Author's Note: Although community organizer Saul Alinsky was an inspiration to me, his methodology was limited, as I pointed out in a two-part dissection, "Reveille for Reformers," which appeared in the now-defunct journal, *Studies on the Left*, in 1966.

INFILTRATING CITY HALL
Assistant to the Mayor
1966/1998

It was 1966. I was an assistant to the mayor of Detroit, a "highly paid" apparatchik under a Ford Foundation fellowship for doctoral students in government. I was a doctoral candidate in the sense that the only academic program I could get into easily after being fired by the War on Poverty was a Ph.D. program at Syracuse University. I was avoiding the draft and they were prospecting for tuition money. I won the fellowship, in part because, when asked to name my party affiliation, I was the only applicant to list the insurgent Freedom Democratic Party of Mississippi. The head of the program liked that, and I was in.

Now I was helping to write speeches for Jerome P. Cavanagh, a young Kennedyesque public official known for his boyish looks and charismatic style. For the first time I was wearing a tie and jacket every day. I was working alongside ex–*New York Times* reporter Tony Ripley during the day, and by night keeping detailed notes on everything I saw. Nominally, I was "a participant observer"—although I had taken an oath of confidentiality as the price of access. But now, thirty-two years later, with the mayor long in the grave, I guess the statute of limitations has run out on that pledge.

Truth be told, I felt like Herbert Philbrick, of 1950s TV-show fame, who lived three lives—one as a member of the Communist Party, one as a Soviet spy, and the third as a counterspy for the FBI. I saw myself as a mole for the Movement, an agent of the *other America* who had somehow infiltrated the halls of power. These were the last days of Lyndon Johnson's Great Society, and Cavanagh was considered by some to be the most liberal big-city mayor in America. He was determined to insure that Detroit would not be another Watts. "Despite its long history of rancorous race relations," *Time* magazine noted in 1965, "Detroit in recent years has been one of the few big northern cities to escape large-scale Negro rioting. The distinction was not won by accident—unless that accident is Jerome Cavanagh."

When other cities tried to turn away marches by Dr. King, Cavanagh invited him in and marched with him. King previewed his "I Have A Dream" Speech during Detroit's "Great March to Freedom." Cavanagh sounded like my kind of guy. I was interested in finding out what a city government could do for the people, and if the system could be made to work.

He only had a small team around him. His office worked on the entourage system. If you were in the entourage, you were in. If you weren't, you weren't, no matter what your title was. Ripley was the staff liberal and sophisticate; Dick Strickhartz, the controller, the centrist numbers man, a law professor and key adviser; and Jim Trainor, the conservative Irish press secretary, an older, old-style, cigar-smoking newspaper editor close to the cops.

As for me, I was a freebie. Cavanagh was pleased to get an extra hand on deck for no charge. When I interviewed with him I was taken aback when he dropped phrases like "the real nitty-gritty." He saw me coming. As did the *Detroit News*, which reported on my arrival, "For Free: SCHOLAR PUT ON MAYOR'S OFFICE STAFF" describing a twenty-three-year-old "scholar" as the new mayoral aide. "Other mayoral aides and secretaries refer to Schechter as the 'intern.'"

So, years before Monica burst on the scene, there I was, without her "talents" or special access—"the intern" on a $500 monthly stipend from the National Center for Education in Politics. Later on, I was blown away by how many people, lobbyist and advocate types, approached me as if I had real power; they all wanted something, mostly the mayor's ear. Soon I had a set of keys to the City-County Building for weekend work. When my used Ford got hit by one of the Motor City's vehicle-crazed maniacs, the mayor gave me use of an old detective's car from the motor pool, complete with an official X designation on the license plate, and the right to tank up in the municipal garage.

What Cavanagh and company didn't know was that privately I was living a third life. I was living with a black woman at the time, who had no use for politicians of any kind, or interest in my scholarly pursuits. Her name was Mardell. She was beautiful, brassy, and bold—an R&B singer, a wannabe part of the Motown world. And could she *siiiing*! I never brought it up at the office. I didn't think they would understand.

I had hooked up with her in Syracuse where a night of endearment turned into six months of shacking up. When we rolled into town, pulling a trailer loaded down with my books and records, we literally couldn't find an apartment to rent. It was straight-out, in-your-face racism, which at that time cut across all ethnic lines.

We were a strange-looking couple of contrasting pigments, cultures, classes, and regions. She was poor, from the Deep South; I was working class, from the Bronx. Two incompatible accents if you ever heard them. She was foxy; I was funky. We ended up nesting in a tiny hole, in the back of a small transient building, at 186 East Grand Boulevard, a not-quite-safe ghetto neighborhood. I came to experience the underside of liberal Detroit when two cops threw me up against my car one night after I parked in the alley behind the house. They didn't notice the mayor's office decal on my windshield and just did their usual thing. One pulled a weapon, pointed it at me, and asked what the fuck I was doing in that part of town. No, I didn't say "I live here motherfucker." I yes-sirred them to death, and nearly pissed in my pants.

So while I worked with the governing elite downtown in the suites, I was never far away from the rage in the streets. In 1967, an incident like the one I experienced escalated into the worst riot in American history, virtually destroying large sections of town and whatever hopes the mayor had of creating a stable oasis of urban enlightenment. (Years later, after the riots, I went back and found the building I had lived in trashed beyond recognition.) Parts of Detroit have never recovered.

In those days the city was in the first or second stage of white flight. The suburbs were becoming a white noose around a deteriorating black inner city. The auto companies, along with a few banks and the economic aristocracy, kept the local economy humming. This was before they began to export jobs and build factories globally. I actually sat in on meetings between the mayor and the presidents of the Big Three automakers, and watched how the business community assured that the city government met its needs. Detroit was largely a blue-collar town, where many blacks held good jobs, drawing down lots of overtime. The ghettoes there, unlike Harlem, were tree-lined, but all the same problems were present. Black workers owned homes and late-model cars. A black middle class, the third largest in the country behind Atlanta and Washington DC, conspicuously displayed its wealth. Berry Gordy's Motown sound of young America had become a booming business. A former autoworker, he was soon running a hit factory.

And the labor unions were powerful, especially the Detroit-based United Auto Workers. The UAW distrusted the mayor because he was not a Democratic Party stalwart. In those days, the union virtually ran the Party. Cavanagh had become mayor through a non-partisan election. He was a lawyer by training, young and cocky. He didn't owe them his job and they couldn't control him to their satisfaction. By the spring of '66, Cavanagh wanted to move up, out of Detroit and onto the national stage.

He became the president of the National League of Cities and the Conference of American Mayors. He made the cover of *Newsweek* as the voice of Urban America, with a youthful, clean image that appealed as well to many Republicans. He had his eye on an open Senate seat. The polls showed he could beat the GOP in the general elections. But, first, he had to win the primary by whipping the UAW's longtime booster, and virtual client, former four-term governor of Michigan and top Africa aide in the Kennedy Administration, G. Mennen ("Soapy") Williams, known for his green bow ties and penchant for shaking the hand of every voter in the state. Williams was the establishment; Cavanagh, the insurgent. To translate it into today's terms, Cavanagh was a Clintonite before his time; Williams an old-fashioned cold war liberal, a Hubert Humphrey Democrat and LBJ acolyte.

So there I was "working for the Man," as my friends put it, and at the same time, getting a real inside lesson on the guts of big-time politics. How do you fight a deeply entrenched, liberal-sounding machine? The real Clinton would do what he has done, move to the right, align with middle-class values, while blowing smoke about putting people first. Cavanagh, aware of how the cities were then losing the guns-versus-butter-budget fight because of the billions shoveled into the Vietnam War, decided to go after Williams from the left, challenging his support for the war and calling for a cease-fire. He was the first elected official to take such a radical stance as early as 1966, and I was thrilled to work on his end-the-war policy paper and help with the campaign. His position was popular even if his campaign lacked adequate funds and enough troops.

I became an advance man, shooting off to smaller cities and towns throughout Michigan, organizing the mayor's appearances. I'd call potential supporters, invite them to meet the mayor, and find venues for his talks. I felt like a hotshot political operative. I worked closely with a group of seasoned political consultants who functioned as hired guns for the campaign, advising on the nuts and bolts of building an organization. I took notes at all the strategy sessions.

Meeting, Hotel Pick Fort Shelby. April 13, 1966. Briefing on building the research operation. I will keep the consultants' names to myself. Otherwise, here is a taste of some verbatim snatches.

> C1: We want to talk frankly and candidly, and expect
> that much of what we say will stay in this room . . . I
> am a newspaperman and my partner is a lawyer . . .
> Our experience comes from working with Kefauver, the
> Johnson campaign, Bobby Kennedy, and Lindsay . . .

> First, you have to get all the available information
> about your opponent, ALL the available stuff . . .
> C2: You need a Xerox machine. It is expensive but
> probably worth it . . .
> C1: The first part of research is NEGATIVE research.
> This looks into everything Williams said and did. It must
> be exhaustive, thoroughly documented, authentic,
> accurate . . . (When you use this stuff, it is useful not to
> say anything directly but let others say it for you . . .)
> C2: Political literature is very important, but is usually
> not read because it is uninteresting. Action photos are
> very important. It should be attractive.

Those quotes are from my notes. I was fascinated by this detailed planning, by just how scientific and organized campaign strategizing had
become. What a contrast from our anarchistic New Left collective style of
debate and consensus building. These guys were like football coaches,
diagramming and running plays. This was not a bottom-up people's
movement, but a top-down marketing campaign, with the candidate as
the product. We weren't working with people, but on them.

The mayor is talking now:

> One of the criticisms is that we are a slick group of guys
> trying to PR our way though the campaign. But we *do*
> have to get Soapy talking . . .
> C1: We have to zing him and make him overreact.
> Make him talk. The best thing we can do is say some-
> thing critical about Africa and make him patiently
> explain the subtleties of African policy . . . No one cares.
> Mayor: [laughs] Even the Negroes don't care about that.

Later there's talk about giving the mayor a higher profile on civil rights:

> Cl: Send a secret check for $100 to Richmond Flowers
> in Alabama [a civil rights advocate] . . .'me and the
> wife were discussing this and thought it would be a
> good thing,' and then leak it . . . deny it at first, and
> then admit it, play it down as a personal thing.
> Mayor's aide: Has he ever done anything like that?

> Another aide [Sarcastically]: All the time, but we never
> knew about it . . . [Laughter]

I have no evidence that the mayor tried a stunt like that, but this snatch of conversation gives you a feel of how calculated and contrived politics in America had become. Cavanagh lost the primary, and then, just as we predicted, Williams was beaten in the general election. A Republican became Michigan's second senator and stayed for what seemed like forever.

I didn't. The politics of power and maneuver had become a game I didn't want to play anymore, although I wasn't half bad at it. My stint in the big show of mainstream politics was ending.

When the campaign was over, the mayor moved me as his "eyes and ears" into the local version of the War on Poverty, an oversized bureaucracy and pacification program, a place for patronage slushed with federal funds. I wrote long memos to the director pointing out that the program, Total Action Against Poverty, was not so total; in fact, not very effective at all. (From one my memos: "It is as if we are all straight men in a comic con-game because the money is in poverty this year.")

It wouldn't be for long. We didn't know then but the real war, the one in Vietnam, had another nine years to run, while the poor were being poured into its service. Lyndon Johnson had no use for cease-fires in Asia, ours or anyone's, and funds for the inner cities began to dry up. Within a year, parts of Detroit would look like Vietnam, and there would be soldiers in the streets. The war would come home. I discovered that Detroit was burning when I arrived for the first time in, of all places, South Africa.

My internship was over. In August, I bid adieu to Stroh's beer, Cobo Hall, the Tigers, and my sweet girlfriend Mardell, who was having trouble finding a job or breaking into the big time. We loved each other but it was not to be.

Society was polarizing. Students were beginning to speak up and act out. The confrontational '60s were about to explode. Soon I would be leaving town and the country—off to the London School of Economics and the "old world," which opened up new worlds for me. The future did not shine on the city or the mayor. Within a few years, his career went up in flames too. Like Bill Clinton years later, he would get caught in a sex scandal and then a messy divorce. His political career was over. And soon he was too. Dead of a heart attack at an early age. A good man.

He could have been a contender.

DRAFT BOARD
1966/1999

I remember the night I went to meet my draft board. River Avenue, the Bronx, second floor, just around the corner from Yankee Stadium. I don't think the Bombers were in town the night I almost joined some other bombers. I would remember if there had been roaring in the bleachers. I was there to cop a plea, extend a 2-S student deferment. It wasn't fear of the fighting that motivated me, but opposition to the war. I was anxious to avoid the dreaded 1-A classification which back in '66 meant only one thing: Vietnam. The draft board had me down as eligible, but getting that reversed, I thought, would be a sure thing. The London School of Economics had admitted me for the fall. It was August, and so all I was asking for was a month's extension. Just one month! I wasn't taking chances. I had flooded the Board with letters, testifying to my seriousness as a student, my good services as a Ford Foundation fellow in the offices of Detroit's Mayor Cavanagh, my serious interest in urban affairs, surely a subject linked to preserving national security. At first, I was pretty cocky, impressed with myself, and my strategy.

Until I talked to Paul.

Paul Yergans had been a high school buddy, one of my closest running buddies. The son of mixed parents with a progressive background, he introduced me to black nationalist thinking years before it came into vogue. Paul had chuckled at my euphoria, my certainty. He was planning to go to Canada, ultimately did, and is still there.

"Their job is to draft you, man, don't you realize that? That's their job. You're a number and they have a quota. Look at the state of the cities. Do you think they give a shit about urban affairs? No, you're going down."

His logic jolted me. He could be right. Flashes of Fort Dix and basic training convinced me to seek outside help, and I did.

His name was Julius C.C. Edelstein, and he was at the time a professor of urban studies at the City University. Before that he had been the man who ran New York City for Mayor Robert Wagner. "Mr. Fixer," one newspaper called him. I had met Edelstein in Detroit, and perhaps our kinship as New Yorkers in the Motor City served as a bond. He had taken a liking to me, and offered support. Edelstein had written a letter to the draft board on my behalf, but I realized that these letters were just stuffing in a file. What if no one read them? Maybe they couldn't even read, because if they could, how could they stay on the draft board? No, a more personal approach was needed. So, presumptuously, and in a panic, I called on him to take another step, to actually come with me that night, to serve as an advocate. In person. I guess I needed someone to hold my hand and speak up for me. It was a lot to ask, but I was in a sweat after Paul's gritty dose of street realism. Edelstein agreed to come, no doubt as a favor for the mayor of Detroit. In a gesture of by then deeply engrained intra–New York politics, he even called the Bronx borough president to tell him he would be making a visit. Not only did he come, but we went in style, in his limo.

Draft boards are made up of volunteer-appointees, civil servants who made some extra per diem cash for going to meetings and sending young men to war. They owed their jobs to politicians like Edelstein and the machine he had served so faithfully. So when he showed up in the Bronx that night, live and in person, some eyebrows went up around the table. People of his stature didn't visit everyday. The Board heard his short testimonial and then asked me some perfunctory questions. Then, on the spot, my 2-S was granted.

I shouted. Mr. Edelstein smiled knowingly.

So would have Paul, because he always knew it was who you know that counts.

RAISING THE QUESTION: WHO DECIDES?
1967

> ". . . Cram them full of facts non-combustible data,
> chock them so damned full of 'facts' they feel stuffed . . .
> 'brilliant' with information. Then they'll feel they're
> thinking, they'll get a sense of motion without moving
> . . . We depend on you. I don't think you realize how
> important you are, to our happy world as it stands
> now."
> —Ray Bradbury, Fahrenheit 451

On Friday, March 17, 1967, three thousand students marched through the city of London and the West End, demonstrating national support for the "rebels of the London School of Economics." For Britain's universities, sharply divided by tradition and the "tracking" system, it was a rare moment of unity: students from Leeds, Manchester, Regent St., Polytechnic, and Cambridge (among others) carried banners together and wore a new symbol of quiet protest: yellow daffodils. The *London Times* called the demonstrations "unprecedented in British university history." The march was inspired by the round-the-clock sit-ins at the LSE that began on Monday, March 13. For ten days, between 200 and 800 students occupied LSE's main entrance hall, unfurling a banner that read "Beware the Pedagogic Gerontocracy"—beware the rule of the old men.

The old men—administrators, professors, journalists, and MPs—have advanced many theories in the past few weeks to explain the student unrest at the LSE, and its apparent national resonance. Some were quick to point out the "Berkeley-influenced American agitators" who objected to "any kind of authority." Others more intelligently viewed the crisis in the context of Britain's larger problems of higher education. The students themselves saw it both as a general social problem and as a result of specific events at the LSE.

It has taken acts of peculiar genius over the last five months by Sir Sydney Caine, outgoing Director of LSE, and his allies to bring the unquestioned authority of the School administration into a state of siege. Their actions have had a common theme: contempt for the students' position in the university, or at best, disbelief that worthwhile changes could be implemented outside ponderous bureaucratic channels. Thus, last fall, when students wanted to ask Director-designate Walter Adams some well-founded questions about his administration of University College, Rhodesia, the LSE authorities stuck to the letter of their regulations. The students had no "constitutional capacity" to raise doubts about the new director, and their questions were dismissed as a "vicious character attack."

In the second term, the administration intensified its opposition to student initiative. The president of the Graduate Students' Association, Marshall Bloom (an American), helped organize a meeting held January 31 to discuss opposition to the new director. Sir Sidney reacted to the discussion as if it were a conspiracy to overthrow a School appointment; he banned the meeting an hour before it was scheduled to take place. Four hundred students gathered outside the "banned room"; in the tension and confusion which followed, one of the School's elderly porters suffered a heart attack and died.

No one was singled out for blame in the porter's death, but the administration apparently decided that someone had to be punished for the disorder which preceded it. Six student officers, including David Adelstein (President of the Students' Union) and Marshall Bloom, were summoned before a disciplinary board to face charges of convening the meeting in defiance of the director's order. The four lesser officers were acquitted, but on Monday, March 13, Adelstein and Bloom were found guilty and suspended for the remainder of the academic year.

The verdicts suddenly defined the situation sharply: at LSE, power was monopolized by a small group of men and delegated to the director, who was unaccountable in practice to anyone. Six weeks of legal defense at the disciplinary hearings, quiet negotiations by moderate students and professors, and carefully restrained public protest had made no impression. Not eagerness, but monumental frustration led the former president of the Conservative Society to speak for almost all the students by proposing a sit-in and boycott "until the suspensions are rescinded."

The issues of the sit-in went far beyond the original opposition to Dr. Adams. The students were protesting the infringement of their right to speak, their subservient position within the School, and the lack of communications with School authorities. In the third day of demonstrations, with 104 students now suspended, the Director ventured to address a packed Union meeting; he was asked, "as a human being, as a man," to make some gesture of goodwill to help end the disruption of the School. He stood in front of his students, white-faced and tight-lipped, and shook his head.

To have visited the LSE during the long nights of its occupation was to be impressed by the earnestness of the students, their sense of drama, their strange humor, and their spontaneous democracy, which drove both elitist student politicians and administrators to the wall. A Harry Kidd, the embattled School secretary, told newsmen; "Democracy is almost a disease in the School." But the students had a different experience of the School's illness: concentrated power, which selected some issues for immediate action and relegated others to interminable debate. Thus, while the director refused to consider student proposals on the grounds that nothing could be decided without reference to several committees, his assistants suspended one hundred students en masse, without a hearing or an appeal, and then cynically used the suspensions as bargaining counters against the demonstrators.

The sit-ins were more than a demand for student participation; they were a crude exercise of student power. With the demonstrators in de facto control of the School, an administrator, initiating a new "routine," rang up to see if a scheduled Oxfam lecture would be permitted to go on. Of course it was. But students sitting in the main hall murmured that this was not what they really wanted: to command by force and coercion. If anything, they saw their actions as designed to end the climate of coercion and intimidation in the School. More positively, the desire for power—feared in all quarters of traditional respectability—meant to most students simply the right to a say, the affirmation of certain basic values, and the need for restraints on arbitrary actions by the director or anyone under his authority. In short, a more democratic and free university.

This is precisely what the authorities feared. Democracy of the type hinted at by the student protesters could be a very dangerous thing for men who had appropriated power for themselves; thus, some LSE professors branded the student plea for participation as a demand for "student control." Students at the LSE were raising the question of who decides—and who should decide—and that question, powerful in its implications for the School's future, quite rightly disturbed. Predictably, the question was skirted with wild charges of outside agitators, of "Berkeley-trained provos" skillfully manipulating the minds of some of Britain's finest students. These charges, and similarly inept and frightened responses, only exacerbated the conflict.

Many in Britain were surprised at this response by a school with a liberal and dissenting tradition. But the LSE's unique position in British higher education—an intimate research institute in the social sciences, dominated by the needs of faculty and graduates—has been undermined by the general problems of Britain's educational revolution. The Robbins Report of 1963 recommended that the LSE help ease the increased pressure for university places by expanding its undergraduate program. Short of space and funds, LSE became overcrowded and suffered under one of the worst staff-student ratios in Britain. As the *New Statesman* pointed out on March 17, the metaphor of the factory had become all too apt at LSE; in unconscious confirmation, a sociology professor told students (in an attempt to quiet their protest), "I am paid to be an intellectual. Whatever issues are under debate, the machine must go on." The *Observer* of March 19 related LSE's problems to Britain's general situation:

> The universities as a whole are in the middle of an industrial revolution . . . Higher education, from being a cottage industry, is becoming a large-scale mass-production process. Students are in danger of coming to regard themselves as a new kind of intellectual proletariat, with a new sense of grievance.

That "new sense of grievance" became a qualitative demand at the LSE. At bottom, it was a demand for an end to the absurdity of institutions which lived for themselves more than for the people within them. An administration which hobbled the Students' Union, refused to discuss seriously curriculum or rules reform, and which enforced its will through Olympian disciplinary committees (all comparing poorly with more progressive universities even in Britain), seemed to reflect an incorrect balance of power and priorities. As their education appeared more manifestly unsatisfactory, the students responded with a stronger plea for respect and for a community dedicated to a more genuine practice of freedom and relevant inquiry. Their response is less to felt exploitation—the traditional subject matter of both old-left and parliamentary politics—but to a pervasive frustration which some students describe as "dehumanization."

The student proposals to remedy this situation at the LSE are by no means impractical. New universities in Britain incorporate students on disciplinary boards, curriculum review committees, and some within the Academic Senates. In America, students are slowly winning bills of rights from university administrations. At San Francisco State College, a Free University operates within the college itself, subsidized entirely by student government funds. In Sweden, student unions have far greater parity with administrations than in Britain. There are other models for reform as well. None, we are sure, satisfies every objection or grievance. But nothing could stop experimentation and innovation at the LSE if administrative will and boldness existed.

Administrative will, unfortunately, has been used to date at the LSE only to enforce points of discipline. For six weeks in February and March, the administration exhausted the School with disciplinary hearings which most students and many faculty members thought fundamentally unnecessary and unjust. On the day the verdicts were announced, the administration barricaded itself in its building, lowering steel fire doors and establishing a checkpoint at the main entrance. In symbolic contrast, the students' occupation of LSE for ten days was dedicated to the idea of an "open university." In a recent letter from London, a friend described the round-the-clock seminars on educational theory and structure; lectures by sympathetic academics; and the general ferment of trying to discover what "freeing education" means, and how to implement such a revolution. "Time has lost its power at LSE"—such an achievement must inspire hope in a world where students usually feel only the pressures of time and power, and rarely the fruits of their control.

This article, written with Rand Rosenblatt, originally appeared in The New Republic, *December 16, 1967.*

LONDON GUERILLA FORCE (THEATRE) OPPOSES THE WAR
1967

LONDON (LNS)—It is 11:15 a.m. in the midst of the lunch hour on London's busy Fleet Street, the narrow thoroughfare which intersects the center of Britain's newspaper district. At the top of the street a small group of twenty gathers, quietly lines up in two rows, dons grotesque red, white, and blue Uncle Sam hats, and unveils several American flags and banners. On signal, to the count of a military cadence, they hup-two-three-four down the street. They leap upon a small monument framed on a traffic island, dramatically raise their flags, and announce that they have set up an Induction Center to draft Englishmen into the war in Vietnam.

Traffic slowly grinds to a halt, and onlookers gather as Yanks begin humming the familiar refrain of the Marine Corps hymn. Each actor plays a different role. A doctor, dressed in the long white garb of his profession, brandishes a sign identifying him as the "Medical unit—are you physically fit to fight?" A similarly dressed woman proclaims herself the "Psychological section—do you harbor subversive doubts?"

Suddenly, four of the soldiers, toy guns in hand, dart into the crowd and cajole suitably dressed and bowler-hatted "Englishmen" (plants) into the induction center and off to Vietnam.

To allay confusion in the crowd, still others wearing only the "camera" symbol of the American tourist distributed flyers which officially "drafted" the onlookers. The cards also called attention to the disloyal meeting being held that evening during which several resisters will turn themselves in.

Later that afternoon, a sparkling chauffeur-driven Jaguar turns into Downing Street, home of the British prime minister, and pulls to a stop outside No. 10. Both the police and tourists, who customarily line the sidewalk in hopes of getting a peek at the famous visitors, are puzzled. One new arrival looks like General Patton, and struts like a U.S. military commander, while the other is a beautifully dressed, broadly smiling curvaceous girl wrapped in a "Miss America" banner.

Something for the Prime Minister

They have something to deliver to the prime minister. "'And it 'ere,'" the copper says. Right! And out of the trunk comes an eight-by-eight-foot draft card informing Mr. Harold Wilson that he has been classified 1-A "until his policy changes," by order of the president. The accompanying letter advises the prime minister that since British diplomatic support is tantamount to military aid, he is being symbolically drafted into the U.S. Army. The copper is perplexed.

Suddenly a strange-looking man dressed in guerilla military outfit and wearing goggles and a gas mask tears up the street, waving his arms frantically. Several policemen rush to the front of the house. He tears off the gas mask, falls on his knees, and begins to plead (in a proper British accent): "Please Harold, I want to go. I want to kill Commies. Please lead us." The police have had enough. They tear the draft card, but the girl gets the letter through to the house itself. Meanwhile, the press photographers have been having a field day.

These were two brief exercises in "guerilla theatre." They were tried for the first time in the streets of London by members of the "Stop It Committee: Americans in Britain for U.S. Withdrawal from Vietnam." The actions were designed to coincide with the widespread return of draft cards organized in America. Four "Stop It" members announced at a public meeting that night why they also have rid themselves of their cards.

Not everything went smoothly during the afternoon. Experienced actors have an easier time improvising dialogue than hesitant activists. Clearly, role-playing or rehearsals are needed. A group should not "do its thing" in anticipation of being disrupted by the police and, if that doesn't happen, allow its action to peter out. A finale is as important as an entrance.

But clearly, actions such as these can be organized with little fanfare, with a small disciplined group, and attract both publicity and political attention. The "Stop It" committee is developing an expanding repertory of such actions, which can continue to keep the war in the British consciousness and expand the tactical imagination of local peace groups.

This article, distributed by Liberation News Service, *appeared in the* North Carolina Anvil, *December 16, 1967, and in other underground newspapers.*

CHICAGO EIGHT ATTACK
1969

In 1969, I reported on the Chicago Conspiracy trial. Here is one group report, written in the incendiary movement-speak of the time for Boston's underground newspaper, The Old Mole, *to which I contributed regularly:*

It must be seen to be believed! And we have just seen it. The trial of the Chicago Conspiracy is taking place within a courtroom that is of, by, and for Judge Julius J. Hoffman. Removed from the people, high on the twenty-third floor of the glass and steel federal building in downtown Chicago, our movement, our culture, and our life are on trial.

The luminescent waffle ceiling, the mahogany-paneled walls, and the thickly carpeted floor made us feel like we were in the cold sterility of the president's office at GE or MIT.

It is no easy chore to enter the courtroom; the ritual included first convincing the marshals that we were cousins of the defendants, and then undergoing a thorough frisking by stony-faced matrons. Once inside, we encountered a remarkable hodgepodge of characters:

- Spectators include Chicago socialites, trial "groupies" and a scattering of movement brothers, sisters, and other relatives.
- The press ranges from gray-suited network broadcasters to shaggy LNS reporters. Sketchers try in vain to capture some sense of the personalities and drama of the court scene.
- Tough, humorless marshals, trying to preserve discipline in the courtroom, permit no signs of life from the spectators. During the days before Bobby Seale was erased from the case, up to twenty-five marshals would worm their way out of the woodwork in seconds, crowding the aisles and walls of the court.
- The prosecution, Schultz and Co., are perfect organization men, bland yet sinister; they seem to match the décor of the room
- The jury, ten women and two men, is allowed into the courtroom only to hear so-called "evidence," missing most of what is politically important in the case.

This assortment of Cicero housewives, black (wigged) women, fashionably dressed suburbanites, nondescript men, and one young woman who doesn't quite fit, has been kept from families and the outside world since being impaneled. They are baffled, innocent victims of a court system that uses them as pawns.

• Judge Julius J. Hoffman, like America itself, is Magoo and Hitler rolled into one. On first sight it seems impossible that this man could rule anything. Seemingly senile and absurd, he is a wolf in clown's garb, determined to be center stage and in control at all times.

• Finally, the Conspiracy: the seven remaining defendants (minus Bobby Seale) represent different parts of the mosaic that is the American left: spokesmen for different strategies, yet all threatening the power of the ruling class.

For two months the Conspirators have been forced to listen to the parade of pigs, informers, and government henchmen. Outraged and frustrated, they must witness American justice doing its crippled thing. Bobby, expressing his anger at the denial of his constitutional rights, was shackled and taped, and eventually sentenced to four long years.

And it is now time for our side to be presented. The aim of the defense is to recreate Chicago, 1968, right in the courtroom of Judge Julius J. Hoffman. The trial will demonstrate, as Tom Hayden promises in *The Guardian*, "that our lifestyle and politics are incomprehensible except as a threat—to those who are persecuting us—that the terms of the social conflict are irreconcilable. We are not a pressure group which went beyond the permissible limits of dissent in liberal society, and we are not interested in having this trial redefine those limits. We came to Chicago as participants in the creation of a new society in the streets and parks, a society which constitutes its growth with its own natural laws, structures, language, and symbols. We will argue that Chicago revealed the necessity for a new American revolution against the dinosaurs controlling an obsolete and unrepresentative system." The defense will try to bring the real conspiracy to trial: the plan is to put Daley and Co., possibly even LBJ, on the stand. The outer limits of the court system will be tested; we must try to demystify the courts in America.

This is what the defense hopes to do. But without illusion. For as becomes menacingly apparent from our brief sojourn in the courtroom, they have us on their turf: they have the power and set the rules for this round.

Like the war in Vietnam, the Conspiracy trial is no accident. It fits neatly into the unfolding scheme of stepped-up repression. It is evidence that the ruling class is willing to escalate its tactics against us beyond our still liberal imaginations. Each American town has its own political scapegoats these days. More people are being busted and on heavier charges: the recent New York "bombers," welfare mothers around the corner, Black Panthers and Chicanos, and the "conspirators" of every variety.

No political defendants will be freed by some liberal faith in the ultimate justice of the American system. Just as Richard Nixon is not about to end imperialism in Vietnam, he is not about to alter the course of massive repression in this country unless people pressure him enough to do so. *Life* and many others may have faith, but the Chicago Conspiracy, for good reason, doesn't expect to win, even on appeal. For at the very least, they and their lawyers will probably serve time, like Bobby, for "contempt," for expressing anger at the obscenity of America as it has unfolded in that courtroom.

That conspiracy thing will continue to hang over all of us. They will keep dragging us into their courtrooms, and we must be prepared to face more repression. We must continue to defend our brothers and sisters, when necessary on The Man's turf. But we must also bring that defense into the streets—our turf—where we are mounting the assault against the American Monster.

FREE THE CONSPIRACY!

FREE ALL OF U.S.!

With Carol McEldowney and Randy Rappaport.

Note: On February 18, 1970, the jury returned verdicts of guilty against five of the remaining seven defendants, acquitting the other two. On November 21, 1972, the guilty verdicts were overturned by the Seventh Circuit Court of Appeals.

ON THE BEACH
The Movement for a Nude Society
1975

I wasn't able to escape covering political activism—even while on vacation on Cape Cod.

It is a beautiful beach, and socialists might take comfort in the fact that it has already been nationalized. It's part of a scenic National Seashore, one of those breathtaking vistas responsible for stimulating the seasonal tourist invasion of the region. A sand dune swoops several hundred feet above its deep sandy surface. It's been attracting national attention this summer—because all of the people on it are naked.

Truro's "free beach," as it has come to be called, is now at the center of a local controversy. Hundreds of folks have been flocking there, some out of curiosity, others out of a simple desire to swim in the increasingly popular *au naturel* style. Many bring their cars along, clogging the small country roads and creating a parking problem for a number of property owners, mostly summer people, who resent the intrusion and the inconvenience. In late August, nearly 200 middle and upper class *enrages* met at a local school under the auspices of a neighborhood association. They voted to call on the federal government, which administers the beach, to force the nudists to put their bathing suits back on or get out of town.

So far all of this sounds as one would expect, but it isn't that simple. The whole story involves the town of Truro, which voted at last year's annual meeting (remember New England democracy?) to regulate nudity. Advocates say there has been no crime to speak of. The beach's users are a fairly mellow and diverse collection of singles and families, gays and straights.

For some, nudism is an ideology and a way of life. Sunbathing cults still exist in America, although on the free beach, nudity is not particularly ideological. But it will undoubtedly become so when, and if, the authorities decide to repress it. Even then, there are not liable to be any barricades erected in the sand, although one could easily envision some form of resistance developing. So far, the question of the right to swim nude has been fought out in the courts. In at least two decisions, one in New York, the other in California, state courts have affirmed that nude swimming is not illegal so long as it doesn't jeopardize the rights of others.

In Truro, the town government itself is not committed to stamping out the nudists, although it would like to find some formula to placate the property owners. The prevailing official attitude is a low-key one. Nudity, as one official commented, is "no big thing and no new thing." "Skinny-dipping" has been going on in these parts for years.

As John Bell, an older Cape Codder, noted in the weekly *Provincetown Advocate*: "Years ago, before the National Seashore became a crowded reality [this was written in 1973], nude bathing at the ocean was the rule rather than the exception. If you took a bathing suit with you, it was just in case strangers happened to come by." A new book on Marilyn Monroe even reveals that her illicit sometime-beau, the late President Kennedy, used to hang out in the raw at his compound on the Cape at Hyannis. Even the *Register*, a stodgy local newspaper, thinks that the growing "nude problem" is no problem at all. Quite the contrary, as they explained in a recent editorial: "It always seemed to us that clothing, which is generally a nuisance, was worn for warmth, health, and adornment. Perfectly good reasons. Only they don't apply at the beach. The free beach, it seems to us, is saying that sometimes we abandon too much of our freedom without cause."

So, if just about everyone is for the beach, who is agin' it? Good question. And the answer, not surprisingly, is the liberals. Time and again, the people who rose to support the resolution adopted by a 200-1 vote by the property owners made it perfectly clear that they are not against nudity per se. Only one of their number, Adrian Murphy, who was one of Adlai Stevenson's speechwriters, has been waxing self-righteous on the issue.

Last year, he circulated his own petition from a posh address on New York's Upper East Side, calling on the citizenry not to be "naïve" about the hordes and their fringes. The alarming growth of the nude beach, he wrote, threatens the town "not only with sexual crimes against adults and children but also, inevitably, with other crimes against persons and property."

Homosexuals seem the real target of a good deal of this civic uptightness. The summer residents—many of whom are psychiatrists incidentally—apparently want to shield their children (and themselves) from the gays who have been visible on the beach for years. Nearby Provincetown is a nationally-known center for gay vacationers, and not a few of Truro's straight citizens would prefer to keep them segregated in P-town (which bans nudity).

And so hysteria turned a parking problem into an "intolerable" calamity, and the National Seashore was in the middle. Its reluctance to provide parking or other facilities at the beach had followed a pragmatic policy of not officially recognizing, and thereby legitimizing, the practice. As Lawrence Hadley, the Seashore's superintendent, rather delicately put it in a letter last spring to a local resident who had urged the provision of facilities: "I would be reluctant to formally recognize this activity by this means as it is not strictly in keeping with the purposes for which the seashore was established."

This official reluctance is undoubtedly not representative of anyone's personal feelings. The chief park ranger, Norton W. Bean, is an occasional "user" of the nude beach, as are many of the rangers under his command. He was apparently a bit shaken by the amount of verbal abuse directed towards the Seashore administration at the Neighborhood Association meeting. The next day, his rangers were busy putting "private property— no trespassing" signs back up on the thin strip of privately owned land that interfaces the Seashore's property with the town's road. Privately, they were urging free beach users to use an alternate route. "We have to keep it cool for a while," one of them told me. "They could, you know, just bring in the Park police from Washington, you know, the Nazis, and sweep the place. We would like to avoid that."

But even if the Nazis don't impose their final solution—a not entirely improbable outcome given the government's propensity towards repressive overkill to such threats to law and order—a resolution of the whole problem may be a while off. The simplest alternative would be to open other beaches for nude swimming and thus take the strain off Truro. The property owners did suggest such a recourse. But it's unlikely, at least as long as the nudists remain a minority. Building more parking lots requires money. It could also take quite a while.

Meanwhile, the problem is unsolved and Truro's beach commissioner and leading businessmen are not in any particular hurry to solve it. They are both profiting from the confusion. Both grocery store owner Joseph Schoonejongen and realtor Alfred Souza, who doubles as chairman of the Beach Commission, have opened commercial parking lots in the cross-roads that is the town's center. They're charging two bucks apiece for cars, and Souza says he doesn't see any conflict of interest.

On the seclusion of the beach, most of the subjects of this controversy are unaware of its dimensions. They're copping the rays, riding the surf, or playing volleyball with a net provided by one of the beach's long-time resident-users. The most harassment they've encountered is from these little green flies that periodically infest the place, and increasingly from the caravans of amateur and professional photographers who are having a field day snapping crotches and documenting the beach for posterity. For the most part, the beach scene is pretty non-sexual, as *Time* confirmed when it focused in on Truro's free beach, quoting from a Boston psychiatrist to the effect that "Most forms of nudity are not sexual. There is a difference between displaying genitalia and sexual behavior. Scientists who have gone to nudist colonies have repeatedly observed that when people take their clothes off, they are less sexual." Many of the folks lying on the beach say the same thing.

It's unlikely that Truro will eliminate its "nude problem" or that the free beach itself will disintegrate. If permitted, the para-institution will find its own ways to survive. There is a certain dynamic already towards self-policing, as when long-term users cart garbage off "their" beach or advise visitors of the ecological damage that too many people running on the dunes can cause. So far there's been no crime and less litter than one encounters on many public beaches which are heavily used by families and served by concessions. In the past some respectable residents have emerged as unofficial spokespeople for the beach's users, while the existence of an active and vocal liberation movement made the authorities think twice before singling out gays as they have in the past. As the beach gets more crowded, its users turn elsewhere. Already some residents fear a spillover onto other beaches, a factor which ironically undermines the argument that the beach will be overrun.

The free beach at Truro is an example—not something to read about, but something to duplicate. Its survival will be assured only as more free beaches spring up across the country. That will mean campaigning for free beach space in existing public recreation areas. Legally and spiritually, the beaches belong to the people. The only thing we have to lose is our suits.

Versions of this article appeared in the summer of 1975 in The Real Paper, a weekly in Cambridge, Massachusetts, and WIN, a magazine of non-violent action—both now defunct. I also covered the nude beach protests for WBCN, live from the beach, and in the nude, of course.

HOPES FOR THE FUTURE
1977

Slowly, a picture of the coming period is beginning to emerge: America glued to its television sets for a week straight watching *Roots*, a gas crisis, a fireside chat, a small tax rebate, and amnesty granted essentially to white, middle-class war resisters but not to those who are poor, black, or members of other minorities. As part of *Seven Days*' effort to make the picture clearer, we asked a number of friends and acquaintances to respond to the following question:

It's the beginning of a new year and a new administration, as well as a new magazine. We think that it is a convenient and natural point to reassess the lessons of the '60s and to gauge the opportunities for social activism and change—and the pitfalls—which may develop during the Carter era. What do you want to happen? What do you expect? We asked a number of writers and activists.

Danny Schechter: I want to feel hopeful again. I want to wake up in the morning to read a newspaper that doesn't depress me. I want us to happen again. I want to feel part of a social force rather than a subculture. I want to be surprised by acts of simple decency. I want a leader to believe in. I am already tired of Lyndon's ghost in blue jeans, Trilateral retreads and the resurgence of the '50s. I don't think politics go better with Coke. IBM is not "the real thing." I wish Jimmy Carter would be reborn again as someone Hunter Thompson could still respect. I want my "analysis" to stop making me cry. I wish I could forget to say, "Well, that's how the system works."

I want paranoia to stop being a rational response. I want free subways and enough parking places even for people without cars. I want junkies to get addicted to self-respect. I want every woman to feel alive and every man to nurse a child. I want kids to stop falling asleep in school. And could we throw in the abolition of nursing homes that imprison the old? Doesn't everyone want everyone to have heat in winter and eggs for breakfast?

I want a four-day week and work considered a vacation. I want workers' control and accountants with soul. I want all white people to get as tan as they can, and the ghettoes to become museums of historical crimes. I want "rip-off" to become a word of the past and the Pentagon a subject for nostalgia. I want science to find a serum to protect us from cancer-causing corporations, and the atom put back in the Bible with Eve.

I want Ed Sadlowski (an activist labor leader) as Secretary of Labor and Orson Welles managing Radio Free Europe. I want to see Johnny Carson on the *I. F. Stone Show*, and hear Dylan rewrite the "Star Spangled Banner." I want to see my old friend Abbie Hoffman again and I wish that Eldridge Cleaver would find a new trip. I want the left to bury sectarianism along with the term, "It's no accident that . . . " I want us to become as obsessed with Soweto as we were with Saigon.

And expectations? I expect I will go on wanting socialism to make America its home, and TV character *Mary Hartman, Mary Hartman* to be happy, really happy.

I expect we'll keep trying.

This piece originally appeared as part of a survey of perspectives on the future in Seven Days *magazine, April 1977.*

part two VIETNAM VET

passions, pieces, and polemics • 1960–2000

WAR CRIMES
1969/1999

As I write in 1999, two international tribunals are underway, one investigating crimes in the former Yugoslavia, the other the genocide in Rwanda. The international community is pressing for a third to try the Khmer Rouge leaders who carried out a genocide in Cambodia. In many ways, they are based on the model of the Nuremberg and Tokyo trials which passed judgement on a number of Nazi and Japanese war criminals.

Today, there seems to be a consensus about the need to insure accountability for atrocities, to guarantee compliance with international human rights standards and the rule of law. The United States is one of the leading advocates of this approach.

But is the United States prepared to apply these same standards to its own conduct? To date, it has opposed the creation of an international criminal court. Will the United States accept international scrutiny and intervention when there is a pattern of serious violations?

This was the question raised during the Vietnam War, not by any governments, but by an international panel of intellectuals convened by Britain's Lord Bertrand Russell, the eminent mathematician, philosopher, and statesman. He was also one of the most controversial figures of his time—and one of the few who accused the U.S. of war crimes. Russell, drawing on ideas put forth by American academic Norman Birnbaum and writer M. S. Arnoni, assisted by two American radicals, Ralph Schoenman and David Horowitz, came up with a plan for a Vietnam war crimes tribunal. (Schoenman would later be accused of manipulating Russell, and Horowitz, then a radical scholar living in London, would swing sharply to the right in the 1980s, denouncing many people he had been involved with, including me.)

I was invited to the preparatory conference in a London hotel. Russell, then ninety-four, shuffled into a press conference, made a short statement, and didn't take any questions. He looked like he was on his last legs, but what an impressive figure he cut. His flowing white hair and lined face were striking. The meeting that followed was a heady experience. There in one room were Jean Paul Sartre, Simone De Beauvoir, historian Isaac Deutscher, Yugoslav historian Vladimir Dedijer, Cuba's Amado Hernandez, Italy's Lelio Basso, the poet laureate of the Philippines, Cortland Cox representing Stokely Carmichael of SNCC, Carl Oglesby, president of SDS, David Dellinger of the American peace movement, and several other prominent figures from many countries. Plans were made to convene the actual tribunal, and to undertake investigations in Vietnam and elsewhere. Internally, there were tensions, with some questioning Shoenman's role as secretary-general. Externally, several countries refused to allow it to take place on their territory. They saw it, not totally incorrectly, as one-sided, and a body which had already made up its mind. The tribunal finally opened up shop in Stockholm, even though the Swedish prime minister disassociated his government from it, and the Swedish Parliament's immigration committee only granted visas to two Vietnamese witnesses by a vote of 4-3.

I went to Stockholm to report on the tribunal, and sent a dispatch to the *Village Voice*, dated April 29, 1967.

* * *

The tape recorder was switched on and soon the eerie thinning sound of Lord Bertrand Russell's voice began to resound through the giant modern auditorium at the Folkerts Hus—The People's House—half-occupied by members of the world's press corps.

"The International War Crimes Tribunal has been called into being because the United States is waging a war of atrocity," he began. He catalogued the uses and effects of U.S. military and economic power, speaking of "social forces," of the "world market as a major form of aggression," of the desperate need for social revolution, and the brutality of what he saw as a U.S. led and financed counterrevolution. The statement was long, somewhat polemical, but closely argued. It ended with the hope that the tribunal would "encourage people to look at world events the ways I have described them here." Russell doesn't euphemize; capitalists are not called free enterprisers while revolutionaries are not labeled subversives. Russell compares American behavior in Vietnam to Nazi behavior in Eastern Europe. That comment was the type of remark considered outrageous by the world press. It was reported widely.

Within the tribunal there was tension between jurists like Pakistan's portly senior Supreme Court advocate, Mahmud Ali Kasuri, who insisted that any verdict should be based on evidence, including testimony by the United States, and those who only wanted a forum to oppose the war. The U.S. government quickly denounced the whole idea while most of the American press falsely castigated it as a trial of President Johnson.

I watched Morley Safer of CBS, who had been tossed out of Vietnam for showing GIs burning down Vietnamese hamlets, do a stand-up denouncing the tribunal as North Vietnamese propaganda and worse. He was the classic liberal—criticizing tactics, but embracing the war's aims. [In 1998, Safer's program *60 Minutes* ran a report on the My Lai Massacre in which American soldiers who had intervened to save Vietnamese lives from fellow GIs suggested that the Pentagon should be tried for war crimes. CBS was not broadcasting reports like that when it mattered.]

As unfriendly as the American press was, much of the tribunal's evidence is based on dispatches carried in that same media, as well as extensive detailed testimony from Vietnam. Tribunal officials point out that many atrocities are widely reported. There is no lack of "legitimate" substantiated evidence, and the tribunal may have more trouble combating the hard callus of indifference and impotence that overexposure to atrocities has helped to create. This highlights at least one difference between America and Nazi Germany. Hitler advised his propagandists to lie big because immense fabrications are more believable. In America, the new credo is to report everything because people, after a while, can be conditioned to accept anything.

Mimeograph machines grind out copies of international statutes, legal briefs and press statements. (One of the documents from Vietnam War scholar Gabriel Kolko noted that the Tokyo War Crimes Tribunal unilaterally convened by the United States, the victor on the Pacific front, held the military brass to higher standards than the ones invoked in Nuremberg by the four allies—the United States, Britain, France, and the Soviet Union.)

Journalists from all over the world gather to cover the event, and uncover if they can—create if they must—false controversies, cleavages, gossip, and scandals. The tribunal has been found guilty by the very methods for which it has been condemned. It has been prejudged and attacked in a clearly non-objective manner. Not unfairly, it now asks time to do its work, to use its "intellectual power," to take a stab at pricking whatever it can of the world's conscience.

There are men who hotly challenge the convictions of the aging Bertrand Russell, now in his ninety-fifth year. That probing mind and combative spirit, however—the style which earned him condemnation and criticism in youth only to find later acceptance for many of his views— is still at it. By letter, tract, tome, or this morning on the well-amplified tape spinning a thousand miles away from his home in North Wales, his voice is arousing a whirlwind of controversy and, hopefully, change.

GOING THERE
1974

The author, Danny Schechter, is news dissector–director of WBCN-FM radio in Boston. He recently visited Hanoi with two other journalists on a visit arranged through the Indochina Peace Campaign, the anti-war organization identified with Jane Fonda and Tom Hayden. He then traveled to Saigon and zones controlled by the Provisional Revolutionary Government.

Saigon and Hanoi are both Vietnamese cities. That's about all you could say the two places have in common.

There are, in reality, three Vietnams today—one governed from each of the cities, a third ruled by the Provisional Revolutionary Government (PRG). The contrasts between them are striking, and only to be understood in the context of a polarized country into whose affairs the United States has continuously intervened.

For the North Vietnamese and the PRG, the current period is but a moment in a continuing struggle against foreign aggressors bent on dominating and dividing their country. For the PRG, it is a time of consolidating control over areas they deem liberated, and of winning recognition as the legitimate representative of the populace of South Vietnam.

For the Saigon regime of President Nguyen Van Thieu, it is a time of struggle for the survival of a stridently anti-communist government, which is under military assault on the battlefield and political attack in the streets by a mushrooming urban opposition movement.

Moreover, each of these situations is now developing within the framework of the Paris Peace Agreements of 1972, accords which all four principal signatories—the U.S., the PRG, Saigon, and Hanoi—claim to want implemented. Each side consistently accuses the other of frequent and deliberate violations.

Political conflicts either overshadow or give rise to everything else that happens in Vietnam. They are the reason you can still hear artillery fire from central Saigon hotel rooms. The reality is that the war is not over.

The war wears on, and with it political repression in the South and postponed development and reconstruction in the North.

Hanoi, capital of the North, is a clean, tree-lined city. Its streets are filled with bicycles and, with the exception of beeping cars and trucks, it is quiet. Its people appear spirited, orderly, well-fed, and disciplined. There are no beggars in the streets or prostitutes in the doorways.

General austerity is evident; goods are rationed and there are few signs of conspicuous consumption.

Saigon is the antithesis. Bustling and overcrowded, its boulevards are clogged with Hondas, foul-smelling cars, and military trucks. There's garbage strewn about and it is not uncommon to see small children picking through it for food or papers that can be re-sold. The social and economic classes are clearly recognizable. There were eight policemen and two M16-equipped MPs on the downtown street on which I took my first walk.

There was more firepower on this single block in Saigon than was visible in all of Hanoi. A single guard was posted at the Party headquarters where I met North Vietnam's Le Duc Tho. Other leaders are known to travel alone in the streets—perhaps an indicator of which government enjoys more popular support.

To be sure, the North is an ideological society. Its people share a political outlook, as confirmed by a Rand Corporation study which asserted that the North Vietnamese government is among the most popular in the world. Its leaders emerged during long wars against colonial rule. Many had been imprisoned like their mentor and guiding spirit Ho Chi Minh, who remains Vietnam's most legendary nationalist hero and communist revolutionary. Schoolchildren sing songs to him, peasants display his photo prominently in their huts—in the North and South.

Nguyen Van Thieu has outlived Ho, and a law now requires that his official photo be displayed in every store and office in Saigon-controlled South Vietnam.

But Thieu as a political survivor now faces his severest test. Demands for his resignation are mounting. He is scrambling to keep afloat. Trained by the French, a convert from Buddhism to Catholicism, Thieu increasingly models himself in the American political style.

I watched Thieu stage one of his rare public appearances on November 1, South Vietnam's National Day—the anniversary of the coup which toppled the despotic Diem regime in 1963.

He attended an afternoon mass at the Saigon cathedral. His troops had staked out the area hours in advance. The pews were packed with several hundred air force cadets in uniform and countless plainclothesmen. The president arrived in a motorcade flanked by nineteen security men in western-cut suits, all equipped with small walkie-talkies. They had reportedly been trained at the U.S. Secret Service Academy.

Thieu, his hair graying, his face beaming, spent a few moments shaking hands before sliding back into his Mercedes limousine with silver-coated windows. Despite Thieu's increasing skill at American-style political barnstorming, Vietnamese opposition to him has been escalating over the past few months. An anti-corruption movement headed by a conservative priest has attacked the graft which has become institutionalized in Thieu's administration.

In response, the president has purged his cabinet, including some of his closest friends, and reshuffled top echelons of his military command.

It is doubtful that Thieu will be able to run in the elections slated for next year, even if he is permitted to last that long. There is evidence that the United States is casting about for a replacement who would placate an American Congress which is hesitant to give aid to South Vietnam because it does not like Thieu's image. In an unusual statement issued in early October, the U.S. Embassy in Saigon denied any such intentions.

The PRG has charged the U.S. with manipulating Father Tran Huu Thanh's anti-corruption movement for political purposes. "He (Fr. Thanh) has spread the illusion that the Thieu regime can be reformed and that it is not necessary to overthrow it." charged Colonel Vo Dong Giang, a senior PRG spokesperson at a weekly PRG press conference at the former U.S. Army base in Saigon's Tan Son Nhut airfield.

In late October, opposition leaders in Saigon also were uncertain of U.S. intentions. Ho Ngoc Nhuan, one of Thieu's most vociferous and radical critics in the National Assembly, said that the Americans "are not behind the movement, they don't have a hand behind it . . . but the American hand behind Thieu is lessened. As that continues to happen, the people will rise up."

Demonstrations that never would have been permitted years ago are erupting almost weekly in Saigon now. The ones I witnessed in late October were quite unlike anything I had seen before.

The National Assembly building, which had been a rallying point for the protests, had been sealed off from the rest of the city. Streets had been closed with barbed wire barricades while jeeps packed with armed policemen and soldiers created an atmosphere of siege.

Prominent third force personalities like the lawyer Madam Ngo Ba Thanh had been unable to leave their houses. Plainclothes police had surrounded them as part of a strategy of isolating leaders from followers.

In the early hours of October 31, the Saigon Press Club was raided, and fifty journalists herded like cattle onto trucks. That was the day originally slated for the beginning of the trial of three newspapermen charged with violating Saigon's stringent censorship law by publishing an indictment of corruption in the Thieu regime.

The reporters were later released, but only after two opposition deputies had been beaten and hospitalized. When other members of the assembly tried to protest the beatings by carrying one of the injured men to the courthouse on a stretcher, they were stopped by police agents and surrounded. All the while, the Saigon police blasted shrill music and noise from loudspeakers stationed nearby on sound trucks, which drowned out attempts at press conferences.

Meanwhile, in another part of Saigon, followers of Father Thanh's anticorruption movement found themselves bottled up in a suburban church, unable to continue a nonviolent march into the center of the city. Clashes erupted when the demonstrators tried to break through police lines. Sixty persons were injured, including Father Thanh, who had his face punched and his glasses broken. A similar protest was reported in Saigon, December 1.

So far this protest movement has been primarily the work of Catholics of the right and the left. The powerful Buddhist Church has yet to throw all its weight behind the drive to overthrow Thieu. But Buddhist organizations have been formed. A National Reconciliation Force (NRF), connected to the influential An Quang Pagoda, is now headed by Senator Vu Van Mau, a former foreign minister under the late Ngo Dinh Diem. Mau told me his movement wants more than does Father Thanh's.

He said that for the NRF "it is stated firmly and openly that we want to put an end to the present war. All social evils are coming from war, so our aim is much bigger." Opposition leaders hint that the Buddhists are merely reorganizing in this period and will be playing a decisive role in the months ahead.

There are no signs of political turmoil in the North or the PRG zones. Criticism there has other, institutional, forms—within the party, mass organization, factory, or occasionally in letters to the editor.

Once the political line is established, it is implemented without debate. There is no anti-corruption movement in the North.

There are also none of the social problems which are so evident in Saigon where the misery is pervasive. Wells Klein, a member of a U.S. Senate subcommittee study mission who visited South Vietnam a few months before I did, testified to this in Congress.

"Vietnam," he noted, speaking of the South, "is in the midst of an economic depression compounded by an alarming and mounting inflation. More than half of Vietnam's workforce is not working or is unproductive in economic terms. Against this background, it is not surprising that malnutrition is increasing alarmingly in urban areas, as people are forced by economic necessity to switch from rice and protein foods to starchy substitutes." Even Willard Sharpe, chief U.S. economic adviser to the South's AID program, finds the situation "shocking" as real per capita income has plummeted twenty percent in two years. He's hoping that oil revenues will bail the economy out, but admits that that may be years off.

In the area of social services, health facilities, and educational opportunities, the North is far ahead of the South. Education and medical care are free. Adult literacy is very high—nearly one hundred percent—and everyone is encouraged to avail themselves of schooling and special courses. Many schools in the North are overcrowded; many were destroyed by the bombing.

In Saigon, the education system is quite different. Parents have to pay to send children to school. Literacy is between fifty and sixty percent. A USAID survey estimates that only twenty-five percent of those eligible are even enrolled in school. Recent press reports confirm that many parents, including those nominally considered middle class, have withdrawn their children from school because they no longer can afford to educate them.

The USAID program in Vietnam has sought to Americanize the Vietnamese educational system, a process many students and their organizations have resisted. The same is true of the medical system, which Dr. David French of Boston University—another recent Saigon visitor—says is in danger of collapse.

The physical contrasts between the three Vietnams today are not as striking as the human ones. A certain demoralization and fatigue has settled over Saigon. It manifests itself in desertions from the army, widespread crime, and drug use. The government's propaganda slogans consist mostly of crude anti-communist phrases.

The North Vietnamese and their allies in the PRG are anything but demoralized. Political education and popular mobilization are features of daily life. Even the American Embassy in Saigon acknowledges their determination, higher morale, and capacity to step up fighting to at least ten times its present level.

The people exhibit a spirit of optimism and confidence in victory. Throughout the countryside, one slogan of Ho Chi Minh's is emblazoned: "Nothing is more precious than freedom and independence."

This article originally appeared in Worldview, 1975. *Research for this article was partially supported through a grant from the Fund for Investigative Journalism, formerly the Phillip Stern Foundation of Washington, D.C.*

SAIGON CHRISTMAS
1974

Saigon, capital of South Vietnam, hasn't had a peaceful Christmas since 1947. This December, despite the Paris Peace Accords, things are as grim as ever in the most heavily policed town in Asia. Inflation has given an extra twist to the misery. Daniel Schechter, a news reporter for the radical Boston radio station WBCN, has just returned from a trip to the North Vietnamese capital, Hanoi; areas of South Vietnam administered by the Provisional Revolutionary Government; Phnom Penh in Cambodia; and Saigon. He talked to David Widgery about Saigon at Christmastime.

"Well, first of all the war is still going on strong. There have been a tremendous number of cease-fire violations. These have been mainly by Saigon, which has continually tried to get away with land-grabbing operations and moves to try to reconquer and bomb parts of the liberated zones.

In response to this, the Provisional Revolutionary Government of South Vietnam (PRG) engages in what were first angry replies and are now what they call 'efforts to punish the Saigon government,' which are direct attacks on their strong points.

But the economic depression is even more dramatic. The U.S. Embassy admitted to me a twenty-percent decline in the standard of living in Saigon over the last two years.

There's tremendous unemployment and under-employment and a lot of people whose jobs depended on the Americans no longer have any economic sustenance. The Americans pumped up and artificially transformed the whole economic basis of Saigon, and as they withdraw that whole structure is just collapsing in on itself.

You can see it on the streets. People are sleeping out all over the place. The price of rice has almost doubled this year. There are all sorts of shortages. There is actually a People's Front Against Hunger which has been organized because people are plain starving. People are taking their children out of school because they can no longer even scrape up the tiny fee.

American intervention has created a consumer market, with TV sets and Hondas and all the congestion and hubbub you associate with a modern urban area. But if you look a little closer you see things like little children rummaging through garbage cans, picking out pieces of paper that can be re-sold.

We sat by the Saigon river for a bowl of *fou*, a sort of noodle soup, and there were these kids begging. I left a bit of soup at the end and this kid came over and motioned towards it so I said: 'Well look, I'm finished.' The kid just grabbed the bowl of soup and gulped it down.

That really shook me because it was symbolic of the condition of large numbers of street kids, orphans, and other people dislocated by the war who don't have food or shelter or any prospect of finding employment.

On the surface, it appears that people have the right to organize, which they were guaranteed under the Paris Accords. There have been some demonstrations, but the government has totally penetrated the student movement. There are police agents on every campus and the leaders of the student demonstrations of 1971 are still in jail.

Every newspaper has a censor sitting in the office and if the paper is printed against the censor's advice the police charge into the office and seize all the copies. In one instance, the journalists rushed the newspapers out themselves and burned them rather than turn them over to the government. When we were in Saigon two newspapers had to close because they didn't have the financial reserves to fight the confiscations.

One night we saw fifty journalists arrested and packed into trucks like cattle.

The police are now mainly in plain clothes because Thieu wants to pretend they are no longer there. You can recognize them, however, because they all wear dark glasses and little pointed hats. Whenever we went to speak to opposition leaders, there were invariably secret police across the street reporting on everyone entering and leaving.

We went to the home of a woman who was organizing a demonstration for December 1.

Her street was roped off with barbed wire, and four jeeps sat outside her front door. She couldn't leave; nobody would visit her.

It's as if an army is occupying Saigon already, a real intimidating presence, even if you weren't already starving."

This article originally appeared in Socialist Worker *(England), December 21, 1974.*

VISIT TO A LIBERATED ZONE
1975

You may remember Quang Tri. It was the scene of one of the fiercest and "last" battles of that phase of the Vietnam war that ended when peace broke out in Paris. Eighty-five percent of the land in this northernmost province of South Vietnam is now firmly in the hands of the Provisional Revolutionary Government (PRG), the force which elements of the American press still call the "Vietcong" or just "the enemy."

The U.S. Air Force turned most of Quang Tri into a vast wasteland of shattered land and broken villages as its response to the PRG's offensive during the spring of 1972. The provincial capital of Quang Tri City, once a home for 86,000 people, is now a pile of rubble, totally uninhabited. A *Washington Post* reporter who visited the place described it as nothing more than a military outpost, a place of "eerie silence." He looked across the river at the other side and wondered who those people were; what they were so busy doing.

As their guest, I found out last October. I also saw the Saigon flag flying over what is left of Quang Tri City. But I saw it from another vantage point. I was standing in the middle of what used to be the runway of an American air base that is no longer operational. Scrap metal from its decimated hangars now provides walls for houses on which peasants hang photographs of Ho Chi Minh. This part of Quang Tri Province is in the process of coming back to life again. It is one of the "liberated zones" which the PRG is developing as one base in the revolution they expect will ultimately triumph throughout South Vietnam.

Traveling with two activists of the Indochina Peace Campaign, I entered liberated Quang Tri from North Vietnam. That is the only official port of entry. The frontier is as formally administered as any other in the world. Visitors need visas. There are immigration formalities and customs. Although the North Vietnamese firmly support the PRG, they show respect for its autonomous and independent existence. It has its own government, which is now recognized as the legitimate representative of the South Vietnamese people by forty-two different nations. Unlike North Vietnam, which is an integral part of the communist bloc, the PRG is a nonaligned state which does not play up the socialist content of many of its programs. It enjoys firm support from a number of non-socialist third world states, as well as from the socialist camp and some Western countries. Although the United States signed a peace agreement with the PRG, it still does not recognize its legitimacy, and throws all of its economic and political support to General Thieu's regime in Saigon.

Here in Quang Tri Province the diplomatic questions seem remote. Life for the people consists of reconstructing their lives and lands which had been totally disrupted. Nine months of systematic bombing pulverized the rice fields and leveled most of the buildings. That part of the farmland not riddled with craters could not be farmed safely because of undetonated mines, bombs, and other ordnance. Hospitals in Dong Ha, the center of the PRG-controlled Quang Tri, are filled with victims of U.S. antipersonnel weapons and other devices, casualties of the Vietnam cease-fire.

"We fully expect that the consequences of this war will be with us for another ten, maybe twenty years," Nguyen Phuoc, a veteran of battles dating back to the war against the French, told us. He is now a member of the Solidarity Committee which works with the American anti-war movement. He has met us at the border and is driving with us in two jeeps, one Chinese, one Russian, as we bump along at about ten miles an hour on what used to be a part of Vietnam's North-South Highway One. The area has been utterly destroyed. Bizarre sculptures of twisted steel and rusted tanks and vehicles still litter the fields. For miles there are no trees, a tribute to the deadly effectiveness of the defoliation program which turned this place into a no-man's land. It was on this flat expanse of land that former U.S. Defense Secretary Robert MacNamara erected his multimillion-dollar anti-infiltration barrier, a technological Maginot Line. We were later to find handbags in the market at Dong Ha woven with the bright-colored electric wires that strung this electronic battlefield together.

The Vietnamese ability to turn all of the gruesome reminders of war into useful products is symptomatic of what is happening in Quang Tri. The province is coming alive again as reconstruction brigades rebuild the roads and farmers reclaim their fields. Some of the craters are now fishponds. Slowly, rice and vegetables are turning a moonscape into a productive area. It is slow going, but the people are being fed and are restoring social life. This is in glaring contrast to life in the Saigon zones, where correspondents report squalid refugee camps, widespread corruption and demoralization, and actual starvation.

"We are a photo of our whole country," a member of the local revolutionary committee tells us with a heavy French accent. Geographically, you can see all the contrasts of Vietnam here. There are highlands, once prosperous coffee and timber country. These mountains border rice-rich lowlands famous for producing a tiny sweet banana. All of this sweeps to a fifty-mile coastline along the South China Sea, a center for fishermen and the site of scenic sand beaches.

As a photograph of Vietnam, Quang Tri has been blown up and over-exposed. Falling as it does across the seventeenth parallel, the DMZ, it has been hotly contested. U.S. troops occupied the area early in the American intervention. It became a testing ground also for the Vietnamization policy. It was on Highway Nine, which winds west from Dong Ha, that Saigon's finest units mounted their ill-fated "incursion" into Laos in 1971. Quang Tri experienced virtually every aspect of the war: pacification, strategic hamlets, search-and-destroy missions, defoliation, and carpet bombing.

Throughout this period Quang Tri remained a center of Vietnamese resistance. It had been a Viet Minh stronghold during the first Indochina war. It was one of the provinces most directly affected when the "temporary demarcation line" physically divided it in 1954. To this day the PRG considers the southern part of North Vietnam a part of Quang Tri, and, in turn, Hanoi administers it as a special zone. It was always a strong base for the National Liberation Front. Its guerrillas harassed U.S. troops while many of its peasants resisted attempts at pacification. Main force PRG units finally overwhelmed the Saigon army. On May 1, 1972, the province celebrated its liberation. Although the ARVN was in flight, moving south with thousands of refugees as their cover, U.S. military strategists plotted their counterattack. The PRG say their victory involved capturing twenty-four military bases and posts, routing 30,000 soldiers, and killing or wounding about 6,800 more. Although they did not release their own figures, it is reasonable to assume that casualties were high.

In Saigon the loss of Quang Tri was taken seriously. It was seen as a communist beachhead in the South, a base from which the North Vietnamese would mount their oft-predicted final offensive. (In several days of criss-crossing the province by road, we encountered no North Vietnamese army units.) The decision was made that Quang Tri would be better dead than Red. On June 28, less than two months after the province "fell," the air force and six companies of the best ground troops began the effort to retake the area. Half of the U.S. B-52 fleet joined in the systematic bombardment of Quang Tri, as did offshore batteries of the Seventh Fleet. It went on for 270 days—nine months. "We can say," a cadre who witnessed all this told us, "that the enemy used all kinds of weapons except the atomic bomb. They have dropped on our small ten square kilometers a quantity of bombs and ammunition equal to the power of seven atomic bombs. We have had our Hiroshima." When the smoke cleared, Saigon had regained only fifteen percent of the land.

Parts of Quang Tri resemble those photos of Hiroshima. Virtually every large structure was leveled. Of Quang Tri's 582 villages, only three were not totally destroyed. In all, some 50,000 homes were wiped out. More gruesome still was the ecological destruction. A team of American scientists warned that the bombing might make it permanently impossible to reclaim the land. The PRG is trying, however. There are plans to cut down what is left of the old trees, dig out the trunks, and replant the area in pepper and tea. The agricultural economy was totally disrupted. The irrigation system had been shattered, the supply of livestock depleted. A member of the local governing body ticked off the census of destruction. It included 95 percent of the cattle herds. Of 35,000 oxen they could find only 2,778 when the bombing stopped. Of 25,000 water buffalo, only 300 survived. Of 80,000 pigs, only 457. Elephants met a similar fate. (Our guide interjected to ask: Do you know what is an elephant?") There had been 300; now only 3 remained as beasts of burden. With the forests denuded, the rice fields destroyed, and the countryside a vast minefield and graveyard, there was not much of Quang Tri left to liberate. The last full-scale bombing raid on the province was on the very day that the peace agreement was signed in Paris.

The PRG had prepared as best they could for the liberation they knew would come. During the bombing many people lived underground. Others had been evacuated to the mountains and returned when the fighting subsided. Life was very difficult at first. A North Vietnamese journalist reported: "Meager were the first meals in freedom—rice, salt, wild vegetables; less often, powdered fish." Reclaiming the land and achieving self-sufficiency became a first priority. Today the market of Dong Ha, while not as prosperous as the one in Hanoi, is bustling. All the staples were in good supply, as were a wide range of fish, pork, chicken, vegetables, and some fruit. There were also imported goods, much of them shipped directly into the PRG's one functioning port at Cua Vet in Quang Tri. Shipments are received from mainland China, the Soviet Union, North Vietnam, and even some western countries like Italy.

In sharp contrast to life in the Saigon zones, social and educational services are being extended to the people. Free schools have gone up in all the towns and most villages. Adult literacy classes take place at night, and the local committee claimed that almost seventy percent of the people are now literate. We visited one small village school which resembled a one-room classroom in America of the last century. The school was built of thatch and bamboo with corrugated-steel walls, courtesy of the U.S. air base. It runs on a triple shift. We counted as many as fifty children in each of four classrooms. The students were clean and disciplined. They sang a song about Ho Chi Minh and asked us about the attitudes of American schoolchildren toward Vietnam. As we left, the orderly appearance broke down and the children chattered, laughed, and waved at these funny-looking foreigners, the first to visit their villages since American troops withdrew.

Social and economic life in Quang Tri has not been collectivized. Private enterprise is still practiced, and most land is privately owned, although much of it is cooperatively farmed with a clear socialistic spirit. The accent on cooperation is evident everywhere. A free health clinic in one village was built by the villagers themselves. Now some of them have been trained as nurses and assistant doctors. There are programs of preventive health education and inoculation. A doctor tells us that the most serious health problems are now found in those people who used to live in the Saigon zones and had allowed diseases and other health problems to go untreated. This was particularly true of women who could not afford to treat gynecological disorders.

In their own zones the PRG seems to be practicing the approach to reconciliation they want to see extended to all of South Vietnam. We met one woman who had been trapped in the PRG area when the fighting began. Her husband is still in the South Vietnamese army, and she feared that she would be punished because of it. Instead, according to her testimony, she had been welcomed, helped to find shelter and a job. "I feel freer here," she told us, "than I did under the Saigon side. There I was always being stopped for an I.D. card check and was restricted in every way. I was also hungry a lot. Here I have the right to go to school, to join any organization I like, to go anywhere." The PRG professes the belief that persuasion and example are the best methods for mobilizing the people and winning their loyalty. "If our revolution is to succeed," a cadre explained, "it will be because the people support it."

There were no visible signs that coercion is used to keep an unhappy population in check. There were no armed police in the streets, and no checkpoints except in military zones. The city of Dong Ha is in the process of being rebuilt. A Buddhist pagoda functions openly, as does a Catholic Church. The population is encouraged to join a variety of mass organizations, including a women's union, youth league, and a trade union. The people we met were animated, as curious about our impressions as we were about their experiences.

The reconstruction in Quang Tri is taking place in an atmosphere of continual hostilities. During our stay in the province one PRG soldier was shot while raising a flag. The shot was fired from the Saigon zone. In another incident, just a week before, an unarmed reconnaissance "drone" was shot down by PRG gunners. Officials here continuously stress Saigon's violations of the Paris agreement. The Thieu government has made similar charges, but the PRG has everything to gain and nothing to lose by "scrupulous adherence" to the Paris agreement. "Thieu's regime has no popular support," we are told by Le Hai, secretary of the PRG's peace committee. "The fighting in Vietnam is not just between our side and Saigon. It is within the Saigon zone as well. Thieu must continue to repress the people in order to continue the war, to continue as a stooge of the United States."

Although most of the population in South Vietnam lives in the Saigon areas, the PRG remains confident that they support the Paris agreement's goals of peace, reconciliation, and eventual reunification. "Thirty years of war is not a pleasant dream," Luu Quy Ky of the Vietnamese Association of Journalists had told us in Hanoi. But the dream of a free and independent Vietnam continues to be an inspiration. The confidence and optimism one encounters in Quang Tri is overpowering. It is clear that the PRG will never accept a permanently divided country. Its leaders stress the "provisional" nature of their mandate and continue to press for the full implementation of the Paris agreement, which is the mechanism they believe will return peace to Vietnam.

To American visitors they emphasize the U.S. role in continuing the war. They urge us to press our Congress to cut aid to the Thieu regime. "Your government is still financing attacks on our areas, killing our people," a youth cadre told us soberly in a small hut used by his village committee for meetings. "The American people can end this war. You must go home and tell them to do it."

Meanwhile, the Vietnamese will continue to fight, breathing life back into their own zones, and, if they must, fighting on the battlefield, giving and taking heavy casualties. They seem to have integrated a patriotic commitment into their lives. "We Vietnamese are not superhuman," a PRG minister told a gathering of Europeans who, she felt, tended to overly idealize and romanticize their struggle. "But we are well-organized and experienced. We have been fighting for a long time, and we know how to fight. The cause we fight for is also a just one. And we will win." It is hard to argue against that.

This article originally appeared in the Boston Phoenix, *February 18, 1975.*

SAIGON BRIEFING
1975

Who can still defend the U.S. role in Vietnam—after the Pentagon Papers or Watergate? At the embassy they can, and do.

Correspondents call it the Bunker. It's probably the most important building in Saigon, the place where the big decisions are made. After two weeks in North Vietnam and in one of the zones under the control of the Provisional Revolutionary Government, I am standing in the well-guarded lobby of the American Embassy. For the first time since arriving in Indochina, I feel like I'm in enemy territory.

I'm here to be briefed, although if they knew where I'd been they would want to reverse the roles. Availing myself of a service regularly extended to correspondents abroad, I'm about to expose myself to a series of encounters with some of the analysts and "experts" who serve U.S. policy objectives in this part of the world. I'm here to see how they work as well as what they have to say.

These briefings are arranged on request for "background" only, a part of the government's effort to win the hearts and minds of America's people through its press. They are a device which allows supposedly knowledgeable officials to impart information without being held accountable for what they say. The ethics of the journalistic establishment require that you play by the rules—rules which disguise deception and so often perpetuate fraud. As a partial compromise for the sake of those reporters who will have to deal with these people in the future, I will paraphrase and quote without direct attribution. The names are not important anyway.

The embassy was built as a fortress. Surrounded by a concrete wall with two prisonlike guard towers, it was designed to stop rockets. A private guard service watches over the front gate which is off limits to just about everyone. Taxis have to discharge passengers up the block. Armed marines patrol its small lobby, which prominently displays tributes to the bravery of those marines who lost their lives defending the place. That was on January 31, 1968, when "the Vietcong" sent some sappers inside to invite the ambassador to the Tet Offensive. Next to the plaques honoring the dead is a glass trophy case in which Marine Company E shows off the trophies it has received in interservice sports competition. It is the only personal touch in the whole place.

A reported 126 State Department officials keep themselves busy in

this six-story building. There are also an undisclosed number of CIA oper-
atives attached to such nondescript organizations as OSA, the Office of
Special Assistant to the Ambassador. All the people who work here also
apparently prefer the American lifestyle to the Vietnamese reality outside
their doors. They tend to live together in well-secured buildings or compounds, looked after by their servants, insulated from the desperation in
the streets. The embassy complex itself has its own swimming pool and
snack bar. The food is cheap, and only American money is accepted.

The Saigon embassy is being run these days as a "tight ship" by
Ambassador Graham Martin, a hard-line anti-communist by anyone's
standards. He is a veteran diplomat, a seasoned interventionist who used
to manage the U.S. military-political apparatus in Thailand. Martin's
vociferous defense of Thieu's regime has turned him into something
approaching a one-man lobby for more aid to South Vietnam. He has frequently locked horns with the peace movement. On one occasion he told
a prominent clergyman that he had blood on his hands because of his failure to condemn an alleged atrocity by the other side. He's categorically
denied the existence of thousands of political prisoners, dismisses well-
documented charges of torture, and praises the military stockade that is
Saigon as a "free and open society." He is said to run the embassy in a
totally authoritarian manner and has forbidden his underlings any contact with the press unless it has been cleared. He openly refuses to meet
with journalists he considers critical or negative toward "his" policies.

As a result, most of the resident reporters in Saigon feel frozen out by
the embassy. They dismissed my chances of actually getting in to see the
ambassador, something I had been able to do in Laos. "What's the point?"
one correspondent asked me. "He won't say anything. Even if he does,
you probably won't be able to quote him, he'll probably be lying and you
won't be able to check out what he has to say anyway." Compelling logic.
Nevertheless, seeing those people has more than curiosity value. Maybe I
could glean some factual tidbits about the covert maneuvers for which
this embassy is internationally infamous.

I was as interested in the psychology of these people as anything they
had to say. Who can still defend the U.S. role here—after the Pentagon
Papers, after Watergate, after the American people themselves became
disgusted with the war and the policies which spawned it? They can, and
do—as professionals, trained in the specialized discipline of diplomatic
apologetics. Ideologically, they are well-indoctrinated, although when
they talk to you they avoid rhetoric and tend to assume an agonized pose,

to pretend at "objectivity." After all, they reason, it is we who are acting out a responsible world role; it is we who defend the values of the free world against the dogma and violence of the communists. "They want to have this whole place," one of them tells me. "They are absolutely determined." He was speaking of "them"—the North Vietnamese.

They study "them" here, from Saigon. Their radios are monitored, and a CIA offshoot called the Foreign Broadcast Information Service (FBIS) translates and distributes everything broadcast over Radio Hanoi or the clandestine Liberation Radio in the South. An Indochina Peace Campaign delegation learned in Saigon that its visit to the PRG zone in Quang Tri had been announced—word of it is now on the desks of half-a-dozen spooks, news agencies, and computer banks. Undoubtedly, it is friendly embassies in Hanoi which send North Vietnam's newspapers, theoretical journals, and weekly reports on the price of bananas in the marketplace, an item that diplomats watch as an indicator of economic problems. These texts are studied, analyzed, and selectively used for intelligence and propaganda. Finally, documents are captured, or more usually "reconstructed," from the bits and pieces of information squeezed out of prisoners by the torture they called "interrogation."

The people here in the embassy are not torturers. They don't hear the sound of the electrodes which make possible the casual use of the phrase: "Information made available to the embassy indicates . . ." Made available how? But never mind. I am lectured about the evils of the "journalism of involvement," the kind of subjective reporting which certain newspapermen engage in these days. People like David K. Shipler of the *New York Times*, whose vivid series on the treatment of prisoners occasioned, I'm told, an apoplectic reaction by the ambassador, denials by the Saigon police, and cries of outraged innocence from the State Department. A foreign service officer, the ambassador has written, avoids "subjective emotional involvement."

Hanoi Watchers

My first stop is in the office of a man who calls himself "Hanoi-watcher." There are maps on the wall, maps of Vietnam. A finger points to the offices of the COSVN, the so-called Central Office for South Vietnam. That, I'm told, is VC Headquarters, their Pentagon. It was to have been wiped out during the Cambodian invasion of 1970, but our troops never found it. I'm told they've decentralized their operation now and keep it mobile. Today, two separate briefings locate COSVN in two different places.

The man talking to me just fell into his job, seems a bit bored by it now. He is earnest and authoritative, summarizing his perception of the North Vietnamese position, stressing their determination to "liberate" the South. The "so-called PRG," as the Provisional Revolutionary Government is called in these parts, is an extension of Hanoi, and the room is papered with diagrams to prove it. And then he pauses to add, "That's true, but it may not be relevant." He has plenty of facts to prove his case but this is a friendly chat, not an argument. Supposedly he has the information and I'm here to get what I can of it.

This Hanoi-watcher really doesn't tell me much, but his assessment is interesting. The PRG is not about to launch a new offensive although they "sure as hell" have the capability. They don't have to. As far as the North is concerned things are going the way they want. The military pressure—at approximately 1971 levels—is keeping the ARVN on the defensive, causing heavy casualties. Aid cutbacks are making things tougher for Saigon as well. PRG pressure discourages more foreign investment, keeps things unstable, and contributes to the economic crisis squeezing the South. They are also encouraged by the opposition movements, although they miscalculate their strength. I ask him if he agrees with my assessment, if he thinks things are going the PRG's way. To my surprise, the analyst in him says yes, although he's not to be quoted. I ask the expert jokingly if he thinks his research would enable him to be a good adviser for the other side or prompt him to convert, as Daniel Ellsberg did. "No" is his expected reply, although he won't deny a certain admiration for these people; they have "accomplished quite a bit."

On to the specialist on the domestic political scene. We have our coffee in the embassy bar. Looking out on the pool, we talk about the people who that very moment in late October were taking to the streets to challenge the regime. No one in the embassy takes them very seriously. What do these people want anyway? They have no real program. There's nothing Thieu can do to satisfy them without committing political suicide. To one embassyite, they're a bunch of prima donnas. To another, a growling but still ineffectual lot. To a third, an indication that democracy lives, however imperfectly. "They wouldn't be allowed in a real police state like Haiti or North Vietnam." Why then are there so many police in the streets; why the heavy intimidation? To protect property, of course; to prevent violence. "If these things grow," one press flack tells me, "there's a point where anarchy is approached and authority has to step in, as we saw in Washington during those riots in the Negro section. Now I'm not saying we've reached that point here . . ."

It turns out that this embassy is literally overflowing with Germans, just like the Nixon White House in its heyday. According to a knowledgeable embassy watcher, "There are at least fifteen old Germany hands or people of German extraction in important posts. They meet together and keep alive the spirit of the cold war. They even stage cultural events like a German beer festival called 'Oktoberfest.' This year they sent out invitations to it on embassy stationery. It was written in German . . . I'm not saying these people are Nazis; they're more like the crew that put West Germany together after the war. They accept the idea of a country being divided permanently as quite natural. They want to apply it here. They are every bit as fanatical as they imagine their opponents to be."

Saigon's CIA Station Chief Thomas Polgar is a Hungarian who used to have the same job in Bonn. Graham Martin's first major assignment was as an administrator for the Marshall Plan which rebuilt Europe after World War II. It also opened the European economy to U.S. corporate penetration and had among its political objectives the suppression of communist worker movements in France and Italy.

Vietnam may be the last frontier for these ideologues of anti-communism. They are mesmerized by the Red Menace, a posture which seems out of step in this age of détente and improved relations with the Chinese. While their experts concede that the government in Hanoi enjoys the support of its people, their propagandists reduce the enemy to barbarians bent on conquest. "Who is it that puts bayonets in the stomachs of children?" a propaganda slogan asks the citizens of Saigon. The answer: The Vietcong, of course. Until recently American advisers played important roles in this propaganda effort. It is this type of imagery, in subtler form, that the embassy continues to peddle.

Meeting the Press

Feeding the press corps with negative information about the enemy is not difficult. It is certainly easier than doing a public relations job for the Thieu government. Most of the effort these days seems to consist of denying that things are as bad as they seem to be. Ron Ziegler would be right at home. For example, an embassy official commenting on the institutionalized corruption that everyone knows is pervasive in the Thieu regime: "Sure, there's corruption, but this is Asia." On Thieu's announcement that he had purged his fourteen-member Cabinet of ten members in an attempt to appease the anti-corruption movement: "Well, we've had cabinet shuffles before. At least give him credit for being responsive and taking action." And so it goes. The reporter is advised to be positive, to avoid the temptation of overplaying the mushrooming protests. "Jesus," he is told, "one paper is playing these demonstrations as the biggest thing since the invention of sliced bread." All the embassy wants, to hear them tell it, is objective reporting.

To insure it, the embassy maintains its links with what remains of the American press corps. Favors are extended and favors are returned. There are occasional leaks to selected friends, special interviews, exclusives. The embassy monitors the press "product," influences it when it can, counters it when it must. Its accomplices are the lazy reporters who prefer rewriting official press releases to launching their own investigations. Its agents are those wire services that continue to function as virtual extensions of the government's information network. Its unwitting accessories are those reporters who basically share the values and outlook of those in power. Even the best of our newspapers fall into this category. The emphasis on hard news plays up the "facts," dubious as they may be, but offers no independent interpretation or historical context. The moment the reporter rejects the view that Vietnam is a nation in revolution, or that the ongoing war has an overriding political meaning, reportage inevitably assumes a conservative and distorted direction.

Reporters with another point of view are either denied access to Saigon (several were barred, others expelled in the last year) or find it impossible to gain access to official sources. Those who do manage to get around the obstacles face the prospect of government attempts to discredit them.

That is what happened to me after my return from Vietnam. My visit to the embassy was made possible because I was carrying credentials from the *Boston Globe*, one of the country's leading liberal and long-time anti-war dailies. The *Globe* had advanced me some money for the trip to Vietnam, and I visited the embassy to get the American point of view. When the embassy officials learned that I had first been to North Vietnam, and wasn't a run-of-the-mill reporter, they were incensed. The State Department protested officially to the *Globe*, while in Saigon the embassy inspired the next *Globe* reporter on the scene to attack me personally.

On December 17, the *Globe*'s Op-Ed page featured a column from its Asia correspondent Matthew Storin. Datelined Saigon, it asked: "Why does Hanoi merit support from Americans now?" It attacked an October 30 broadcast by Radio Hanoi on which I appeared—a transcript of which could only have been provided by the embassy. The column blasted me as a contributor "to the Hanoi government's propaganda machine" and echoed the Embassy line that it is the North Vietnamese who are responsible for fomenting the continuing war. People like me are called "simplistic" because we fail to insist that the communists massacre people and commit atrocities. As evidence, he repeats as fact the Saigon government charge that the "Vietcong" sent a mortar round into a schoolhouse in the town of Cai Lay in March 1974, murdering twenty-three innocent schoolchildren.

Curiously, this same incident was invoked, in almost identical terms, in a publicized letter from Ambassador Graham Martin to an anti-war clergyman implying that the blood of those children was on his hands. Several congressmen later rebuked the ambassador for using such offensive tactics. It was subsequently revealed that the facts of the matter itself are cloudy. There have been reports that Saigon forces accidentally destroyed the schoolhouse and then sought to turn the incident to propaganda advantage. But since Saigon never permitted an outside investigation, we will never come closer to the full truth.

But for the *Globe* reporter, as for so many of his predecessors, this controversy doesn't exist. There's only the Saigon and the U.S. government version. A day later, this same correspondent published a feature on the schoolhouse incident, once again treating it as a proven PRG atrocity. I have no doubt that the reporter's visit to the school was arranged with the help of the American Embassy and that the embassy's press counselor encouraged him to attack me by name.

This is a dirty business, a logical extension of a dirty war. Happily, it may be ending sooner rather than later. The defensiveness of the hacks in the embassy betrays a fatigue, a sense of the hopelessness of their own situation. There is none of the "turning the corner" optimism which used to flow from these same official sources years ago. Today they are a discouraged lot, bitter about the continuing opposition to the war and U.S. policies. What a contrast between them and their counterparts in Hanoi or the PRG. The revolutionary Vietnamese are optimistic and committed to a positive vision of the future. The official Americans have nothing to write home about, and know it. They want to keep the rest of us enmeshed in their own web of self deception. After meeting them and their adversaries, I know it won't work.

This article originally appeared in Ramparts *magazine, March 1975.*

LETTER TO THE EDITOR
1974

Boston Globe
November 15, 1974

Broadcaster's Reply

To its credit, the *Boston Globe* published the Pentagon Papers and crusaded for peace in its editorials, but its daily coverage of events in Southeast Asia remains deplorable. It persists in relying on wire service accounts which routinely accept Saigon and U.S. government interpretations. Just this past month, three separate front-page stories relied on hardly credible official sources for projections about an imminent North Vietnamese offensive, or so-called communist atrocities. All of these accounts invariably refer to the Provisional Revolutionary Government (PRG) as "the communists," a faceless and incorrect designation; "The Vietcong," a derogatory phrase which the PRG rejects, or simply "the enemy."

I have just returned from visiting the three Vietnams—The North, a "liberated" zone loyal to the Provisional Revolutionary Government, and Saigon. In a visit arranged under the auspices of the Indochina Peace Campaign, I met and interviewed Vietnamese leaders and ordinary people on all sides. Hanoi and the PRG zones are off limits to most Western correspondents.

Matthew Storin's December 17 Op-Ed column was an attack on me—not on anything I'd written, but on something I allegedly said in an interview broadcast over one of the North Vietnamese radio stations. While in Hanoi, I visited the offices of their equivalent to our Voice of America. As a radio journalist myself, I was curious about the type of work they do. After I interviewed their staff, they interviewed me about my impressions and feelings about my trip. Speaking as an individual, I criticized American policy in much the same way that I've done in the United States. Asia correspondent Storin attacks that broadcast. Relying evidently on a CIA-monitored transcript provided by the U.S. Embassy, he selectively uses it to attack me and certain unidentified anti-war activists whom he labels "simplistic" and locates geographically as "Boston-Cambridge circles."

Your correspondent calls me a propagandist after his Monday news report from Saigon devotes fifteen paragraphs to the theories and assessments of unnamed American and South Vietnamese officials while giving a PRG spokesman one unamplified quotation. I have my biases, to be sure, but I am explicit about them; Storin and the *Globe* are dishonest about theirs. His commentary camouflages them in a self-righteous denunciation of communist massacres for which he produces no evidence or documentation. He takes two instances which have been publicized time and again by the U.S. Embassy in Saigon, and repeats them as if they were the gospel truth.

In both cases—the so-called Hue massacres and the more recent incident at the Cai-Lay school—there are on-the-scene reports and scholarly studies which challenge U.S. propaganda claims. At Hue in 1968, the British photojournalist Phillip Jones-Griffith, who was there, writes that most of the victims "were killed by the most hysterical use of American firepower ever seen," and then designated "as the victims of a communist massacre." Gary Porter of Cornell University, who wrote the definitive study of the affair based on original Vietnamese sources, concludes simply that the massacres did not occur as reported.

At Cai Lay, "an atrocity" that U.S. Ambassador Graham Martin likes to use in speeches and interviews, there is also enough evidence to question the official version. First of all, both sides blame the other for the attack. (The PRG has firmly denied it.) Yet only the U.S.-Saigon charges are given an airing. Secondly, reporters on the scene from the *Washington Post* and the *Far Eastern Economic Review* were unable to confirm the Saigon version of the episode. John Spragens, a Vietnamese-speaking American reporter, went to Cai Lay and examined the evidence firsthand. His report raised the possibility that the schoolchildren were actually killed by a Saigon artillery round. It is hard to make a final determination because Saigon would allow no complete independent investigation.

The war in Vietnam continues to be a struggle between revolutionary nationalism and U.S. neo-colonialism. Both sides are not equally to blame. I find myself on one side—not as an apologist for Hanoi, but as an advocate of the right of the Vietnamese to determine their affairs and reunify their country without U.S. intervention. Matthew Storin may not feel comfortable being on the other side—his barbs at U.S. policy indicate that—but objectively that's where he stands. I am sure his article will win the State Department Award of the Week.

Daniel Schechter
Boston

HOW THE WAR WAS WON
or THE FALL OF WASHINGTON
1975

> *In Vietnam, spring is beautiful*
> *Because it is usually the season of national glory*
> *This land of braves was founded 4000 years ago*
> *In the springtime*
> *Since then,*
> *Its history has recorded resplendent pages*
> *Mostly in the spring*
> *Liberation fighter,*
> *Spring in Vietnam is ineffably beautiful . . .*
> *Liberation fighter*
> *Spring belongs to you.*
> —From *South Vietnam in Struggle*, newspaper of the
> National Liberation Front, 1972

> *"Peace is at hand."*
> —Unnamed "Vietcong" official quoted in the *New York*
> *Times* (on the Sunday before Saigon changed hands).

The American press was never much help in our efforts to find out more about those remarkable Vietnamese people who have now managed to out-organize, out-fight, and defeat a succession of U.S.-backed regimes. When the U.S. media did recognize the other side's existence, they often did so with disdain, distortion, and denigration. The victors in Vietnam have been systemically dehumanized in our press—called the enemy, the reds, the communists, the Vietcong. All of these terms were calculated to incite the enmity of an American population long conditioned by anti-communism.

This practice didn't change right up to the end, even after the U.S. government was forced to recognize the Provisional Revolutionary Government by co-signing the Paris Peace Accords. The officially inspired image of the PRG remains a faceless one; they are treated simply as an extension of Hanoi, an invasion army. Americans who wanted to know more about the political goals and perspective of the Vietnamese revolutionaries had to turn elsewhere—to the writings of the Australian journalist Wilfred Burchett, to the French press, to the histories of the

Indochina wars, or the publications of anti-war groups. This was a revolution that was televised, but never analyzed in terms that explained its context or strategy.

American policymakers at the highest levels always underestimated the size and popularity of the forces they were trying to crush. Since the government officially had determined that the war was a case of Northern aggression, it couldn't very well acknowledge that the National Liberation Front recruited its army in the South and enjoyed support from the people in the South. Instead, as former CIA analyst Sam Adams shows in a fascinating and detailed article in *Harper's*, this ideological faith led to systematic distortions in the intelligence estimates, which, among other things, understated the size of the NLF and its morale. This intelligence failure was as conceptual as it was statistical; the U.S. would never come to terms with the fact that it was defending a government which had no support, while attempting to crush one that did.

There will be plenty of postmortems to come on how and why the U.S. lost Vietnam.

It might be more interesting to think about how the Vietnamese people won Vietnam back—and how the anti-war movement helped them do it. Here are ten of the factors which I think have been central in that victory, and some thoughts of their meaning for our own society.

1. A Sound Political Strategy

Despite the fact that the PRG's final victory appeared to be military, it was actually the revolution's political strategy that was responsible for its success. By locating and defining the central political problems in the country, the resistance movement was able to mobilize for a combined political and military struggle. While military and political activity have always been interdependent in Vietnam, it was always the political analysis and vision which guided the armed struggle.

Politically, the Vietnamese revolutionary movement ignited and led the anti-colonial movement. It was able to focus the resentment of the peasantry and the workers towards foreign rule and then retain their allegiance when French colonialism was supplanted by American neo-colonialism. In the villages, the National Liberation Front won support by championing the class-based grievances of the farmer against the landlord and the absentee owner, of the worker against the boss. This political line not only helped people understand what was wrong but what to do about it. Most important, the movement offered a vision of a better society. In calling on people to take up arms and share risks in a common struggle, it was able to win the very hearts and minds that the American strategists always talk about but could never rally.

2. Military Strategy

Militarily, the NLF and the North Vietnamese out-fought and out-maneuvered the Americans and their "Vietnamized" allies. General Giap and the PRG command kept the initiative, forcing their opponents off-balance and on the defensive. The people's war strategy combined guerilla tactics and conventional approaches. Sophisticated SAM missiles were used alongside primitive weapons. Invariably these unorthodox techniques confounded and surprised their opponents. The Pentagon's projections and expectations were always found wanting. The offensives never came when they predicted they would. Battles were rarely fought when the PRG didn't want them.

From Dien Bien Phu to Xuan Loc, from the non-battles at Hue and Danang to the air defense of Hanoi, the Vietnamese refused to allow their movement to be defeated, or their country crushed. This is not to say that they were successful in every engagement, or that the technology introduced by the American military didn't take a horrible toll or have a genocidal impact. President Ford's rather glib after-the-fact admission that the other side's victory was "inevitable" was by no means always certain—except to them.

3. A Tradition of Resistance

One of our first stops in Hanoi (in 1974) was in a museum. I understand that Henry Kissinger was given the same treatment, although he was exposed more to antiquities, while we saw exhibits chronicling the long history of Vietnamese resistance to foreign invasions and repressive regimes. The Vietnamese revolutionaries of today see themselves as heirs to a 4,000-year legacy. They've appropriated and used their own history as a guide.

The English historian Thomas Hodgkin was struck by just how history-conscious the Vietnamese are. Writing in the English journal *Race and Class*, he notes that "in part no doubt this tradition is rooted in the structure of Vietnamese society, in the organization of the commune. But one important aspect of the tradition is the consciousness of possessing the tradition. Vietnamese peasants long ago acquired—and have passed on from generation to generation—a grasp of revolutionary methods, a knowledge of what to do in a revolutionary situation."

Our Vietnamese hosts told us in Hanoi that they were always startled by how alienated many of their friends in the U.S. anti-war movement seemed from their own society. This implication was that a successful movement has to link itself to its own traditions, and find inspiration in those moments in its own history with relevant lessons to offer.

4. Unity

The people in Vietnam have not always been unified, as in many societies, although the country was, up until 1956, always considered as one. There are ethnic rivalries, religious differences, and class divisions. From the outset, the Vietnamese communists sought to develop programs which could unite the different groupings in a framework of mutual respect and tolerance. The national minorities in North Vietnam enjoy a measure of autonomy and state support to preserve their own traditions and lifestyles. All are integrated in the military struggle and represented in the national government.

The U.S. strategy in Vietnam had sought to play groups off against one another as part of the strategy of encouraging Asians to fight other Asians. The CIA and the Green Berets drew on sophisticated ethnographic studies to deploy such ethnic minorities as the Montagnards in Vietnam or the Meos in Laos as shock troops against the insurgent forces. In the case of the Montagnards, who live in South Vietnam's Central Highlands, the policy backfired. It was this very group whose local uprising in the town of Ban Me Thout sparked the round of military activity which triggered Thieu's disastrous decision to order a strategic withdrawal.

According to the late Agence France Press correspondent Paul Leandri, whose dispatches led to his assassination by the Saigon police, these Montagnards belonged to the United Front for the Liberation of Oppressed Races (FULRO), an affiliate of the PRG. Leandri's reports showed the truly indigenous nature of the southern struggle, and confirmed the PRG's success in uniting the various forces in the society into a multi-racial and multi-national movement.

5. The Role of Women

Women played a major role in the revolution at every level. The PRG's Foreign Minister Madame Binh is perhaps the best-known symbol of the commitment to women's liberation; less familiar is Madame Dinh, the deputy commander of the PRG's army, and the many women who are conspicuously present at every level of leadership. The women's movement is not separatist, but firmly integrated into the total struggle. As Le Duan, the North Vietnamese theoretician and secretary of the Communist Party explains it: "If the nation and the working class are not liberated, the women will not be liberated. Yet if the women are not emancipated and do not yet share the role of masters of the country, the nation as well as the working class are not really liberated. A society cannot be considered civilized and advanced if women are still dependent and do not enjoy freedom" (*Some Present Tasks*, Hanoi 1974).

Women make up nearly a quarter of Hanoi's national assembly while the official Women's Union boasts a membership of five million. Women's liberation is firmly endorsed in Hanoi's constitution, and some women I met there quoted a dictum from Ho Chi Minh: "If the women are not emancipated, socialism is only half-established." It should be noted that several North Vietnamese leaders have admitted that their country has not yet fully created the conditions for socialist development. I am sure there are inequalities for women who always endured the greatest injustices in the old society. But the revolution's commitment on this issue is unambiguous, and undoubtedly a component of its success.

6. Organization

The Pentagon has long marveled at the Vietnamese insurgents' ability to move soldiers and equipment to the front in the most difficult conditions. A highly developed organization structure was required to direct the disciplined work of millions. But, for the Vietnamese, this is more than a question of logistical capabilities.

The Vietnamese revolution has adapted a classical Marxist-Leninist party structure to its own situation. That structure is able to transmit the Party's political message with the same efficiency as its military directives. It has created underground networks, mass organizations, and a system of cadre development which kept their movement moving. Any visitor to Hanoi has to marvel at the way this system functions, and also how it has institutionalized democratic procedures. Officials are regularly criticized in the Party's own newspapers in an attempt to correct against bureaucracy or too much top-down order-giving. I visited agricultural cooperatives in which the members elect officers. Workers are encouraged to have a say in how the economy functions. Membership in the Communist Party is not made public for fear that Party members would be accorded privileges.

Unlike many of the American New Left, the Vietnamese believe in the idea of leaders and practice the democratic centralist form of leadership.

Ho Chi Minh seems to have set the standard for those leaders in terms of his humility and close identification with the people. When I met Hanoi's Le Duc Tho, he was unguarded and quite informal in a non-interview situation. The same seems to be true of the country's other leaders. These are some of the reasons that a Rand Corporation study concluded that the North Vietnamese government is among the world's most popular.

The PRG leaders I met conveyed the same leadership style. Their behavior contrasted sharply with the Western-oriented leaders of the deposed Saigon government. General Big Minh struck me as a Francophile aristocrat when I met him in the courtyard of his posh villa in Saigon. Thieu was even more outrageous, cruising in an expensive Mercedes flanked by a coterie of security guards who I later learned were trained at the U.S. Secret Service Academy.

7. Serving the People

In its liberated zones, as in North Vietnam, the Vietnamese revolution constructed a network of human service programs. There are free schools and health clinics. North Vietnam states that there are six-and-a-half-million students in the country, a higher per capita percentage than in our own country. The Vietnamese were anxious to show us these programs—from day care for kids to adult education and scientific training sessions. By serving the needs of the people, the revolution wins their support. To the extent of its meager resources, it tries to practice what it preaches, and so transform daily life. Needless to say, there remain many problems compounded by an overabundance of authoritarianism.

8. Solidarity in Indochina

The victory in Vietnam followed the cease-fire in Laos, and the revolutionary triumph in Cambodia. Although the three Indochinese countries have different histories and cultural traditions, the Vietnamese worked closely with the Pathet Lao and the Khmer Rouge. As the United States expanded the war in Laos and Cambodia, the three movements achieved a united front which permitted them to assist and support each other militarily. An agreement forged by the three Indochinese movements in April 1970 provided a method for mutual aid and victory. [After the war, the Vietnamese and Cambodians quarrelled and fought each other. Vietnam intervened in Cambodia to topple the genocidal Khmer Rouge in 1979. DS–2001.]

9. Anti-War Movements

Throughout the war, the Vietnamese cultivated the active political support of peoples and governments throughout the world. They were able to walk the tightrope of the Sino-Soviet split, and receive aid from both the Russians and the Chinese. Worldwide protests helped isolate the U.S. government, and limit some of its strategic and military options.

Most important, the Vietnamese reached out to the American people, making a distinction between us and our government. For a people facing American bombs, this was a heroic, calculated, and principled gesture. I realized how heroic it was when I met some of the victims of our own bombing and heard them transcend blind rage in order to send greetings to the American anti-war movement. Politically, the Vietnamese always believed in the importance of the anti-war movement, small and impotent as it may have appeared to some of its supporters. They encouraged it as best they could, knowing that creating a climate of opinion hostile to the war would be one important way of ending it. In the end, their victory was accelerated by Congress's refusal to vote more aid. That refusal was a response to a climate of public opinion which the anti-war movement helped forge.

The Vietnamese were profoundly affected by the sacrifices of the American people on their behalf. In the early days of the war, virtually the entire North Vietnamese nation paid tribute to Norman Morrison, the pacifist who immolated himself in one of the first protests of the early '60s. In later years, they hosted a stream of delegations and journalists who returned to spread the word about the real situation in Vietnam. All of these Americans were deeply affected by those visits, while millions of activists throughout the world learned the meaning of "revolutionary internationalism" by watching how the Vietnamese applied it.

10. Faith

The Vietnamese are tough. They withstood everything concocted by the most criminal minds in the Pentagon. They never wavered in their commitment to the liberation of their country. Many Americans deprecated this steadfast determination as fanaticism or worse. But the Vietnamese didn't let that bother them. They weren't fighting for good PR in the United States. They had no truck with the schemes and maneuvers thrown their way by such slicksters of empire as Rostow or Kissinger and the stable of "experts" who did their bidding. The North and the PRG were responsible for the Paris Agreement on Vietnam, and all of Nixon's

B-52s couldn't change its essential structure. They sought to give the U.S. the decent interval it wanted and an honorable way out of the war. When Gerald Ford stubbornly held on, they kicked out the stops. Today they are in the Presidential Palace—to stay.

This has been a long struggle, one powered by their enormous confidence in the certainty of ultimate victory, and the justness of its cause. It was also characterized by an equal amount of patience. Despite all their setbacks, betrayals, and disappointments, they never gave up. They see their revolution as a process, as a series of stages. The North Vietnamese officials with whom I spoke conveyed a confidence that their hopes would come to fruition. But they seemed above all pragmatic realists at the same time. "The situation is excellent," they told me back in the fall, when it hardly looked that way from a distance. Even they were reportedly surprised by the rapidity of the collapse of the Saigon regime when it came this spring. They have now realized what often seemed to be the impossible dream of their beloved Ho Chi Minh.

Not everyone on the American left is willing to honor the Vietnamese, even in the moment of their triumph. A recent issue of *WIN* carried a symposium in which pacifists moaned about the Vietnamese reliance on armed struggle, while others lamented the coming of "benevolent totalitarianism" and "liberation without liberty." Others cynically consider "both sides equally at fault," while utopians belittle the strong nationalist and patriotic sentiments of the Vietnamese people. They demand nothing less than instant socialism, or an immediate end to the nation-state. The lack of humility and undercurrent of sectarian self-righteousness in all of this is unmistakable.

In a recent interview, the producer of the Vietnam documentary *Hearts and Minds* said he did not really delve into the dynamics of the Vietnamese liberation movement because he was more interested in the problem of "the liberation of America."

That seems to be the question we all have to turn to now. In doing so, we shouldn't cut ourselves off from the responsibility to continue to support the Vietnamese people as they consolidate their victory and seek to rebuild their country. We need to consider the many relevant lessons they have to teach us.

This essay appeared in WIN Magazine, *July 1975.*

THE UNTOLD STORY OF OPERATION BABYLIFT
1975/1984

This investigative report was based on a segment I produced for ABC's 20/20.

Plane crashes invariably make splashy news. So when the world's largest plane crash-landed in Vietnam—during a war that ended nine years ago this week—with a cargo of Vietnamese orphans destined for new homes in the West, it was front-page copy, and was featured on all the network newscasts. The incident became one more symbol of failure in Vietnam.

"The disaster was almost too unbearable to believe. It was laden with a sense that Americans were somehow cursed in Vietnam, fated to bring only tragedy even when trying to do good," writes Arnold Isaacs of the *Baltimore Sun* in *Without Honor*, a history of the war. Ninety-eight of the children who were being "saved" perished, and now there are claims that most of the 150 tiny survivors were brain-damaged as a result of a horrifying midair disaster and catastrophic landing that has since faded from public memory.

This tragedy has ended up in the courts with lawsuits filed on behalf of the surviving children. Their attorneys assert the young crash victims are being victimized again in what they characterize as a deliberately protracted legal "war of attrition" against the children by the company that built the plane (Burbank-based Lockheed Aircraft Company) and the Air Force that flew it. (The U.S. government is a third party.) Lockheed and the government deny the charges.

Court records now fill in many untold details of a shocking episode of the Vietnam War. They have raised new questions about the accident and its aftermath, about relationships between military contractors and the Air Force, about the legal system's ability to adjudicate.

Lockheed's lawyers no longer contest the role that defects in the plane may have played in the accident, even though they have contended that Air Force maintenance practices were the immediate cause of the crash. They have already stipulated before the court that liability per se is no longer an issue, in effect conceding the point.

But two questions are still hotly contested. Were the surviving children really hurt in the crash? And if so, what price tag should be placed on their injuries?

And there is another issue: that of collusion and cover-up. Lawyers for the children believe there had been a conspiracy between Lockheed and the government to suppress evidence, conceal the causes of the crash, and cover up legal misconduct. To explore this issue it is necessary to go back to a time that many Americans would prefer to forget.

* * *

Saigon, 1975. Suddenly it seemed as if there was a small child to lead the U.S. out of Vietnam. In Saigon, a number of child-care agencies were scrambling to find planes to fly the orphans in their care out of the country. The U.S. Embassy initially was of no help, because Ambassador Graham Martin reportedly feared any official evacuation would stir panic.

Enter Ed Daley, the late pistol-packing, sometimes sober president of World Airways, who offered the agencies a free ride out on one of his planes. But Daley's requirements turned his would-be benefactors off. "Among his indiscreet conditions," they revealed in a book published later, "was the obnoxious demand that the evacuation be 'performed' in an 'action-packed' manner for effective television coverage." Sadly, conforming to these egomaniac's demands was to be the only option after Pan Am and Air France showed no initial interest in providing airplanes, even as prepaid charters.

In desperation, officials of the child-care agencies agreed to Daley's offer. But the U.S. government declared Daley's plane unsafe, and prevailed on the women organizing the flights to let the Air Force fly the kids out. A bitter Daley denounced the women—"broads" he called them—for being ignorant about his safety record. Referring to both the embassy and the child-care workers, he thundered, "let it be on their conscience," prophetically as it turned out.

But if Daley had ulterior motives for staging the airlift, so did the agency that cut him out of the action. A highly publicized, officially backed airlift might stimulate a wave of renewed sympathy for the plight of South Vietnam, or so some U.S. policymakers hoped. The Ford Administration seized on the idea, christening it "Operation Babylift," a program that would bring the orphans to America, and in the process dramatize and humanize the attempt to save Saigon. "Marvelous propaganda" is how Ambassador Martin reportedly described it to an aide.

Several of the orphanages accepted Daley's offer despite the government's warning. Ironically, Daley's orphan flight on the allegedly "unsafe" DC-8 did get through without incident.

* * *

Anh Traer, born Bui Thi Kim Hoa, is eleven years old now. She's a pretty
girl who wears large glasses. She was one of the children brought to
America via Operation Babylift.

Anh has emotional problems. Her doctors have diagnosed them as
symptoms of a syndrome called Minimal Brain Dysfunction, or MBD. It's
not the kind of problem that shows up on an X-ray. It's an incapacitating
illness characterized by an often intense hyperactivity, serious learning
disabilities, and frequent emotional tantrums, including uncontrolled crying spells.

Through a process of intensive neurological and psychological investigation, doctors retained by the plaintiffs in the lawsuit have found that
virtually all of the crash survivors show some MBD symptoms. One is now
institutionalized; at least two are suicidal. Anh's story is one of 150. That's
how many children survived.

The plane arrived during the lunch hour on April 4, 1975. A big
plane, six stories high from wheels to tail, it had a 223-foot wingspan. "I
never saw such a big plane," one of the kids, Ly Vo, would say later. "We
didn't think it would get off the ground." "What a big mother," was one
of the nurse's reactions. The "big mother" was a C-5A. The C-5 is almost
as long as a football field, and capable of carrying 250,000 pounds. As
many as 50 Cadillacs could be flown in its giant underbelly.

C-5 number 80-218 had been flown in from the Clark Air Base in the
Philippines, its last stop on a flight that originated in California, stopping
in Georgia to pick up a load of Howitzers before flying west to Saigon to
drop them off and pick up a new cargo: babies.

Newsmen at the airport filmed the unloading, watching as the vast
rear doors swung open and a giant ramp clanked down into place.
Trucks drove right into the plane's belly to drag the artillery pieces onto
the runway. To open the doors, a loadmaster had to unlock a complex
system of fourteen interconnecting latches which had a tendency to slip
out of rig.

After the accident, the lawyers for the survivors would discover just
how dangerous this system was. It was so complex that many mechanics
couldn't understand or fix it. In 1971, an Air Force study called it a "monster system," which, if unrepaired, could lead to a "catastrophe." These
are strong words for a military study. But not much was done. There were
many subsequent malfunctions. Both Lockheed and the Air Force knew

about the problems, but there was no "fix" prior to the accident because of a quarrel about who would pay for it. According to pre-trial depositions, even Lockheed's own engineers had recommended improvements, but the company's management vetoed the work until the Air Force agreed to pay for it. The Air Force rejected one Lockheed proposal for a cost-plus contract for just such a fix because the military procurement officials felt it was Lockheed's responsibility to build a safe plane. This pre-crash skirmishing was low-key and bureaucratic.

Captain Dennis Traynor was the plane's veteran commander. He had received the order to pick up the orphans only a day earlier during a stopover at the Clark Air Base. In a statement incorporated in the accident report he noted that he was expecting to "combat load" as many as 1,000 children. He did his best to ready the plane for its new mission: he had containers of milk, box lunches, and baby bottles loaded aboard. Flight nurses and medical corpsmen were assigned to the flight, which had been designated a top-priority mission. In fact, the plane was dubbed "the president's plane" in honor of the man who would be meeting it upon its arrival in the U.S.

Much of the pressure to launch the babylift quickly was coming from the highest level in the chain of command. The Commander in Chief, President Ford, had unveiled Operation Babylift only two days earlier at a press conference in San Diego. In Palm Springs on a golfing vacation, Ford was preoccupied with the rapid-fire events in Vietnam. Only the president could authorize the use of Air Force planes to carry civilians.

Oddly, when Ford announced the airlift that day, he specified the precise type of aircraft to be sent: "I have directed that C-5A aircraft and other aircraft especially equipped to care for these orphans during the flight be sent to Saigon. It's the least we can do," Ford noted, "and we will do much, much more."

A contradiction went unnoticed. The C-5A is a cargo plane, not at all "especially equipped" to care for people, much less tiny babies. It was a plane that for years had been involved in controversy over massive cost overruns, design, and safety problems. Why this plane?

Lawyers who represent the surviving children put forth another hypothesis in their briefs: that the C-5 was also sent to rehabilitate the aircraft's image at a time when Lockheed was on the ropes financially and politically, a time when Congress was being asked to spend millions more to repair the plane.

A successful mission of mercy, they argue, would show the world how vital the Lockheed jet could be. They believe there was collusion between Lockheed and its friends in the Air Force to use the babylift to give the C-5 publicity. Lockheed has denied this.

I tried out the "conspiracy" suspicion on retired Air Force Col. William Gulley, who at the time acted as Air Force liaison in the White House. I was surprised when he didn't dismiss it outright. Could Lockheed and some of the C-5A's boosters in the Air Force have suggested that the president send the C-5, which after all was a symbol of U.S. power? Might they have wanted to "show off the plane" in the same way that the Pentagon "shows the flag" to project our presence abroad? Gulley said he had no evidence that it happened, but then cautioned me: "Don't be naïve."

When the government finally found an available C-5A to use, the aid workers organizing the airlift were uncomfortable with the hasty manner in which the operation was put together. Christine Lieverman, who was in charge of the evacuation of the children for some of the nurseries, recalls having second thoughts. She remembers embracing a co-worker while boarding the plane, wondering if they were doing the right thing. The crowded C-5A was a far cry from the Pan Am 747 they had expected.

Although the C-5A can be configured to fly passengers in its cargo hold, the optional seating modules were not available at Clark Air Base when the orders for the babylift came through. And no attempt was made to "jury rig," or improvise, an oxygen supply.

The boarding was a loud and noisy affair. The C-5 had two decks. The troop compartment upstairs had seventy-five seats and was filled first. The infants were strapped in, two to a seat. Lieverman and the others tending the children had to stand. Downstairs in the giant double-decker, the scene was even more chaotic. More than a hundred older children, some medical corpsmen, and U.S. Embassy personnel being evacuated under babylift cover were stretched out on the steel floor. Cargo straps were substituted for seat belts. There were no toilets and not enough air sickness bags, which would soon be needed. What's worse, there was no oxygen supply for emergencies.

"Try and picture a hundred children, screaming, hollering, carrying on—lots of confusion," Lieverman recalls bitterly. "Children aren't cargo. Children are people. They belong in seats. The don't belong on the floor of an airplane, particularly with luggage strapped in on one side of them."

Imagine: This was to be a twenty-hour flight. President Ford planned to greet the children when the plane arrived at Travis Air Force Base near San Francisco.

With the passengers on board, the crew prepared for takeoff. In the cockpit, they discussed a high-altitude flight plan, with a rapid climb up to 37,000 feet to get up over some turbulent weather. Incredibly, there were crew members with second thoughts about the safety of the mission. A cockpit recorder taped a discussion among crew members just before takeoff: "If we are up at thirty-seven and we have a rapid decompression, we're gonna lose someone," one man said. They noted the lack of oxygen below. "Those babies, they ain't gonna get 'em all out in time." Despite these recorded reservations, the operation continued. At 4:03 p.m., the seventy-five-ton machine lumbered down the runway and rose toward the clouds. In twelve minutes, the 80-218 would reach an altitude of 23, 752 feet, four miles high.

Christy Lieverman was filling up baby bottles in the rear galley upstairs when she heard the explosion. Susan Derge, who had volunteered to help out on the flight and was standing toward the front of the troop compartment, heard a more muffled sound. Medical technician Phil Wise was downstairs in the cargo area. He just happened to be looking toward the back of the plane.

The locking system failed. There was an explosive decompression. "We had no warning," Wise says. "It was just a loud explosion all at once, and I looked back and saw the doors falling off like they never were attached. There were blankets and debris flying, tumbling, and a lot of screaming."

In three-tenths of a second all the oxygen was sucked out of the pressurized aircraft. But not just air. Wise saw crew members standing near the door sucked out of the plane. Wise estimated that he passed out within twenty seconds.

Upstairs, a floor above the exploding clamshell-like doors, Lieverman remembers the plane getting cold, the children first becoming quiet, then passing out. The oxygen masks upstairs popped free of their compartments, but many didn't work. They were designed for adults and were too big for the infants' tiny faces. Most couldn't reach them, anyway, and had to be picked up and held close to the masks. Some were turning blue. Air Force personnel worked with the other attendants, sharing whiffs of oxygen with some of the babies. "Most of the children were unconscious at the time of the descent," Derge remembers.

Oxygen masks on, the captain and his crew faced a formidable task. Not only were the doors gone, but a flying piece of metal had severed the control cable. Their navigational capabilities were severely limited. Somehow Capt. Traynor managed to turn the C-5A around and head back toward the airport. By banking and rolling, increasing and decreasing power, he managed to get on an approach to the runway. But the 300,000-pound plane was losing altitude fast. Traynor had to keep the nose up. He applied power as it was going down, a risky and only half-successful maneuver. "I had to add max power in the dive," he reported afterward. "The nose pitched down rapidly and the addition of maximum throttle would not bring it back up."

They were at twice-normal speed when they touched down in an open rice paddy just two miles short of the runway. The plane was going too fast, and couldn't stop. It bounced back into the air and crossed the Saigon River, hitting an irrigation dike. The wings kept flying. The cockpit went one way, the troop compartment another.

The plane had literally come apart into four sections. Most of the crew walked away from the cockpit. The tail was torn off and the wings flew on by themselves until they burst into flame. The troop compartment filled with children slid at least a thousand feet, many of its occupants shaken, some hurt, but alive.

The downstairs—the huge, cavernous cargo hold—was pulverized. Only six children and a few adults miraculously survived.

Helicopters arrived on the scene first. The area was littered with parts, human and mechanical. Many of the babies had been thrown into the mud. Some were crying, most were abnormally still. Surviving crew members helped the child-care workers, including Christy Lieverman, load them onto choppers which rushed them to the airport. From there, they were raced by ambulance to a nearby Seventh Day Adventist hospital. Christy remembers being on the last helicopter out and yet arriving at the hospital first. She alerted the emergency room that a holocaust was coming.

UPI correspondent Alan Dawson reported U.S. Ambassador Graham Martin's reaction to the crash in *55 Days*, his book about the fall of South Vietnam: "Martin took a call telling of the crash in his embassy and he received the news calmly. 'The C-5A has crashed,' a U.S. official told him during a brief emergency phone call by embassy radiophone. 'Yes,' said Martin. 'Thank you.' Then he hung up."

Naomi Bronstein, a Canadian child-care worker who helped load the C-5A but decided not to take the flight, helped break the news worldwide, consciously inching towards the TV cameras because she thought that would be a way to alert her husband and friends in Canada that she was alive. Someone in the government had already suggested that the plane had been sabotaged, a Vietcong atrocity. Naomi refuted the story. She told reporters what the crew had told her about what happened. Nevertheless, Pentagon officials stateside would still be talking sabotage for weeks afterward.

It would take years for the children's doctors to understand what happened. Dr. Steven Feldman, a Rhode Island pediatrician/psychiatrist who examined some of the children and studied all of their records on behalf of the parents who were suing Lockheed, concluded that "the plane crash caused the Minimal Brain Dysfunction by exposing these infants to a variety of conditions: a degree of lack of oxygen; a degree of what's called deceleration or slowing down; a degree of explosive decompression; an impact, fumes, and a number of factors in the crash which we'll probably never fully understand, which caused damage and insult to their brains."

Often, pediatricians without special training do not diagnose MBD symptoms. One Colorado family was advised by their small-town doctor to just keep spanking their hyperactive, disobedient child. When they told him it wasn't doing any good, the physician asked, "How red is his behind?"

Larry Kitchen found out about the crash at 6:30 the next morning, Georgia time. He was then the president of Lockheed-Georgia, the principal contractor-designer of the C-5A. He is now president of the entire corporation. He was phoned by General P. K. Carleton, who was in charge of the Military Airlift Command. At 7 a.m., a half-hour later, Air Force General Warner Newby, the Air Force's one-time C-5A project officer, was named as head of the official and still-secret Air Force investigation. He knew and was well-known to Lockheed's executives. The appointment of Newby would later be questioned by the plaintiffs because his association with Lockheed led them to challenge his impartiality.

* * *

April 1975 was not the best of times for the Lockheed corporation. The company, which had faced bankruptcy in the late '60s only to be bailed out by the government, was having financial difficulties, surviving on ninety-day notes that were being rolled over by its bankers. Senator Frank Church was about to launch his probe into an overseas corporate bribery scandal that would eventually topple the corporation's top management and send shock waves through several governments. The C-5 itself was embroiled in heated controversy too. Cracks had appeared on the airplane's wings, indicating they were too light for the plane's load. They had to be replaced, at an enormous cost.

Once again the question was who would pay for the repair; who would finance what was called the "H-Mod program," Lockheed or the Air Force? Lockheed insisted it had met the government's C-5 specifications. The Air Force disagreed for the record, but was ultimately ordered to pay $1.5 billion for the repair, which included $150 million cost *plus profit* for Lockheed.

Although they were insured, Lockheed officials knew they could expect lawsuits and expected bad publicity because of the C-5 crash. The outcome of the accident investigation would be important for the company's reputation and its prospects for obtaining more contracts from the government.

The survivors had more immediate problems. After the crash, the dead, the dying, and the injured overwhelmed the capabilities of the hospital in Saigon. A triage system was set up to isolate the most serious cases. The broken bodies were treated, but little attention was given to trying to diagnose any broken minds. There was no time for neurological exams, even though observers reported that the children looked dazed. Those not requiring hospitalization were sent back to the orphanages where arrangements were being made to fly them out the very next day.

In contrast, the surviving crew members and some of the American passengers were flown to sophisticated medical facilities in the Philippines for intense observation. All of the surviving crew members would later be cited for heroism.

The following is from a transcript of a telephone conversation between Carleton and Newby on April 6, 1975. The subject was the initial accident report:

> Newby: I just got back in from Saigon (The investigators were likely afraid to stay in Vietnam so they based themselves in the Philippines and "commuted" by air each day) . . . we are not going to get one single instrument or panel out of the wreckage . . . it is just being carried away . . . the aircraft literally ground up into little pieces as it tore up. From the troop decks below . . . it's just flat out, not there, it's gone . . .
>
> Carleton: Worn off, huh?
>
> Newby: Yes sir, and I think there is a key lesson, boss, that we need to carefully consider and that's this, that this airplane ain't worth a damn for carrying people on . . .

You need a strong stomach to be an aviation accident investigator. Crash sites are heavy with the stench of death. General Newby's team was dealing with a particularly ghastly landscape in a country caught in the final spasms of war. The site was insecure; the investigators were afraid. The plane was being vandalized.

Crash investigators routinely photograph everything of relevance. These pictures later help analysts determine the force of the impact and the extent of the damage. According to briefs filed by the plaintiffs, the Lockheed representatives became nervous about the photos. At a later briefing for Lockheed, at which notes were taken that were later introduced into the court record, "there was discussion . . . that there should be no mention of pictures being taken and that the pictures retained by Lockheed should be marked 'legally privileged' and given to the legal department for filing."

Lawyers for the children sought all the photographs taken of the crash site, but surprisingly were given only a few that showed the condition of the C-5's troop compartment, which carried almost all of the children who survived. Although lawyers for Lockheed and the Air Force promised the court that all evidence would be preserved, vital photographs were destroyed by the Air Force, and that fact was concealed from the judge for many years.

When questioned, the Air Force officer involved in the destruction admitted burning "tons and tons" of pictures. In depositions he said he didn't know they had to be saved, and that he had acted in accordance with routine Air Force regulations requiring the destruction of non-permanent documents. In 1984 the trial judge called this destruction "intentional" and "questionable."

Although copies of some of the destroyed photos would be found years later, the fact of their original destruction would lead to cries of a cover-up and a demand that penalties be imposed on Lockheed and the government for misconduct.

* * *

The Traer family was living in California in April 1975. Bob Traer picked up his new adopted daughter at the Presidio, a huge parklike Army base situated alongside San Francisco Bay. The children were lying on mattresses stretched out on the floor—"just children everywhere," Mr. Traer recalls. Area doctors were examining the kids, but no effort was being made to separate the crash survivors from others transported out of Vietnam on subsequent airlifts. Many of the families who adopted the C-5 crash victims did not know what their children had been through.

At first Ann was quiet and withdrawn, but she clung to her new mother. "She didn't express a great deal of emotion or feeling for either my wife or me for quite awhile," Bob Traer says quietly. "It was only later, when some of those deeper emotions came out, as though she had locked them in. And when they came out (there was) sadness and grief. And fear and anger came out with them."

In Saigon, the investigation continued. Thirty-two people probed the site. The Navy billed the Air Force $50,000 a day for salvage operations that combed the South China Sea for the aft ramp and the pressure door that had fallen off the plane. On April 27, 1975, just three days before North Vietnamese tanks came rumbling into Saigon, they found a twenty-by-twelve-by-four-foot section. They hauled it aboard the search vessel. There, photos were taken, including one that expressed some of the sailors' feelings about the mission and perhaps the plane. It is now a part of the official investigation report. It shows the recovered wreckage, and in one corner is the lower half of a man's body. He is holding his penis, urinating on this object sought after by the Air Force.

Once on American soil, the Vietnamese orphans were a media sensation. Their plaintive faces stared out from the covers of newspapers and magazines. Special State Department phone numbers were flooded with calls from people who wanted to adopt a Vietnamese child. But a note of disquiet crept into the celebration, throwing the orphan agencies on the defensive.

First, critics pointed out there were many American orphans who were available, but going unwanted. Others questioned the assumptions behind this intercultural and interracial adoption. And finally, Vietnamese-speaking anti-war activists discovered that some of the children at the Presidio were not orphans. They later filed suit on behalf of these children, challenging the legality of their admission into the United States. In a class-action suit directed at Secretary of State Henry Kissinger, they in effect charged kidnapping. Sympathy for the crash survivors was dulled in the whirling controversy. The issues raised in the class-action lawsuit against Kissinger were never fully aired or resolved. Instead, the cases were dismissed on legal grounds, and then denied on appeal.

Meanwhile, on another legal front, families of those killed and hurt in the C-5 crash, and Friends for All Children, the relief agency that sheltered the children in Vietnam, began to find lawyers.

General Newby and his accident investigation board signed their report on May 23. That report is still classified under Air Force regulations designed to ensure that people questioned in connection with aviation accidents be granted confidentiality. A less comprehensive "collateral report" undertaken by an Air Force officer who was not allowed to visit the crash site in Vietnam was later released for public consumption.

While Lockheed's precise role in influencing the accident board's conclusions is not known, several documents in the court record indicate the corporation had an active interest in shaping its outcome, with one eye on the impending civil liabilities lawsuits and the other on how a negative report might influence Congress.

On April 28, 1975, Norman C. Apold, the Lockheed executive in charge of the C-5 program, phoned Newby to express his concern that accident briefings at the command level "appear to be placing excessive emphasis on C-5 lock-system design problems rather than focusing on the Air Force maintenance and cannibalization practices. I had further stated that improper inferences drawn by high-level government personnel could prove to be very serious to the C-5 and Lockheed relative to the H-Mod program and might be especially damaging in the event of liability actions related to the accident."

On May 29, General Newby called Apold, these same issues on his mind. It was six days after his secret report had been signed, but only one day after lawyers representing Friends for All Children had filed suit against Lockheed. This conversation was considered important enough for Apold to summarize in a memo sent to his boss, Lockheed President Larry Kitchen. The memo is marked "Lockheed Private Data": "General Newby reaffirmed that his purpose was not to impugn any one party; that Air Force maintenance actions . . . contributed to the events . . . He advised that AS A RESULT OF MY CONVERSATIONS WITH HIM (*emphasis added*), he has stated specifically . . . that the board does not consider this accident to be the result of a major design deficiency on the airplane."

Newby, according to the document, "added that he wants to do everything necessary to avoid a major confrontation" between the Air Force and Lockheed, and "that he is sensitively aware of the seriousness of lawsuits related to liability." Apold told Newby he would pass "his message" on to the president and chairman of the Lockheed Corporation.

Three months after the crash, there were still Air Force people probing into C-5 lock problems, and this prompted Apold to send another memo to Kitchen, this time in response to a question. Kitchen had asked, "Will it implicate [Lockheed Aircraft Corporation]—and why?"

"I feel that any verbal 'sparring' on the issue of what caused the ramp to unzip could implicate Lockheed because we can't be sure just how the Air Force would use our responses . . . " Apold wrote. "Even more important, of course, is the issue of avoiding any written analysis or position while the class-action liability suits are in effect."

When the lawsuits were first filed, it was unlikely that any of the parties expected they would be arguing over the same issues nine years later, that there would be 12 trials, 165 full-scale hearings, and several decisions by the court of appeals. In all, there were more than 150 separate cases to decide. One judge died while hearing the case. The current judge has called it "one of the most protracted, costly, and unpleasant litigations in the history" of his federal district court.

"It is a travesty that this case has not been settled even as of this date," charges Washington attorney Charles Work, who serves as the court-appointed guardian for the surviving children, and was a Justice Department official in the Nixon Administration.

"And these children, because of the delay, have deteriorated. These people have in effect perpetrated a terrible outrage on these children because these children could be better off for the rest of their lives if they had gotten treatment earlier."

Charles Work charges that Lockheed has pursued a "scorched earth defense," stretching out the proceedings in every way they could in hopes of wearing down the plaintiffs. Lockheed brought the Air Force into the case as a third-party defendant. Together they mounted an aggressive defense, spending an estimated $10 million, according to plaintiff's attorneys.

The Vietnamese orphans' cases were not the only ones to be filed after the crash. Another set of lawsuits involving Americans who were killed or survived were settled quickly. The Americans were taken care of—it was only the Vietnamese who had to slug it out in the courts for years.

Ten million dollars hasn't won Lockheed many acquittal verdicts in the courts, but public-interest military-watchdog groups say it has bought time with Congress, enough time for the crash to become a distant memory. The case never became a political issue, or a media cause celebre. Lockheed's ability to win new contracts from Congress was not impeded. As David Keating of the conservative National Taxpayers Union, an organization that has testified against military cost overruns, puts it: "Not only has Lockheed not suffered from this crash, but from what I can tell,

Lockheed has done very well with future contracts from the Air Force not only to fix its problems with the plane but, in fact, to get a new order for a whole set of new planes (the C-5B)."

In fact, after the crash, Lockheed stuck with its position that the C-5's locking system was adequate. The Air Force nevertheless ordered modifications, which Lockheed ultimately made on a cost-plus-profit basis.

"Everyone in the Air Force that flew in the C-5 knew the damn doors rarely worked as they should," one experienced airman said, recalling flights during which wet blankets were pushed into C-5 locks to try to keep the wind from whistling in. General Carleton was quoted in an internal Lockheed document after the accident as admitting that the Air Force should have known the plane had to be fixed. He cited constant noises in the locking system. "Even the plane was trying to tell us," he reportedly told a Lockheed representative.

Rather than concentrate on defending a plane that crashed, Lockheed's skillful defense team, headed by Carrol Dubuc, a lawyer who is also a pilot, focused on refuting the claims that the children who survived had been hurt.

Lockheed's contention is simple. (Lockheed and Justice Department officials declined to be interviewed on the record because the case is in litigation. The plaintiff's attorneys would not be quoted. The contentions of all the parties appear in court briefs and transcripts.) The children are not brain-damaged because of the accident. If the children have problems, they must have been preexisting, a function of cultural deprivation, malnutrition, wartime conditions, and the stress of intercultural adoption. Moreover, they argue, all of the kids are individuals and were affected differently by the crash. They can't and shouldn't be considered as a group or a class. The courts upheld that claim, thereby determining that each case would be heard on its own merits. This decision insured that the matter could go on for years.

The thrust of the defendants' legal case has been to show that the accident was not all that severe, that the oxygen loss was not serious, the descent was no worse than an amusement park ride, the crash landing was gentle. The defendants' legal briefs take all the horror out of the tragedy, referring antiseptically to the crash as "the erosion of (the plane's) structural integrity." They dispute virtually every "fact" put forth by the plaintiffs, and deny most contentions.

The plaintiffs have the burden of proving there is brain damage, and that's not simple. MBD is not a well-known disorder. Many of the kids don't look brain-damaged. Some have very high IQs, and are even per-forming well in school. Some of their own pediatricians can't identify the cause of their emotional problems. Even some of the parents denied at first that their children were affected.

It was only after the medical exams brought many of the children and their parents to Washington that the parents had a chance to trade experiences. Their doctors began to identify the symptoms shared by the children. They commissioned one study that showed that virtually eighty percent of the children shared symptoms, and their only common experi-ence was the crash. A second, independent study of all the Vietnamese orphans who came to this country indicated that only a small percentage of them had these same symptoms. It was statistical arguments like these that finally buttressed the medical case. Lockheed sought to discredit the methodology used in both studies.

In 1979, after losing several jury trials with average verdicts of more than $350,000, Lockheed entered into negotiations to settle the cases involving the children adopted by American families. Other children were adopted by European families, and these cases are just coming to trial. At first the children's lawyers declined the offers, rejecting them as too little compensation for a lifetime of medical problems. But once it became clear that the plaintiffs lacked the financial resources to keep fighting against a vastly more well-financed opponent, they reversed their decision. Months and months went by. Legal wrangling, disagreements between the par-ties, and appeals kept the lawyers busy and delayed a partial settlement for years. The case continued into the '80s.

The children's lawyers were not winning despite some minor courtroom gains and the evidence they had amassed. They needed a new issue, a smoking gun. Unexpectedly, they found one: missing crash photographs. In a new round of depositions in 1981, they learned that certain photographs thought to be missing were indeed available in Air Force archives, even though the defendants' lawyers insisted that they had turned over all the photos in their possession. Armed with these new disclosures, the plaintiffs threatened to argue that vital evidence had been suppressed or withheld.

At this point, on the eve of a new trial and faced with some explosive evidence, Lockheed and the government decided to settle the cases of the American families for a little more than $300,000 per child. They would not concede on the liability question directly, but in an acceptable legal flim-flam agreed not to contest causation if the plaintiffs promised not to press for sanctions for misconduct and punitive damages.

This time the attorneys who had been working on a contingency basis without fees accepted the out-of-court settlement with the parents' approval. It was a $13.5 million deal, with the government picking up a good part of the tab. Charles Work, the children's guardian, insisted on using a chunk of the money for a special trust fund for any children who would be eventually hospitalized or severely troubled. The children's lawyers split a $3.3 million fee from this settlement. Each family was left with little more than $125,000.

Commented Bob Traer: "The children were victimized by the long, drawn-out process. More money has been spent on lawyers than probably has been spent on any of the children, and there was no reason for that. Essentially, Lockheed just wanted to drag it out, in my opinion, and they've done that successfully because of their resources."

This multimillion dollar "global" settlement did not settle the case, nor was it global. Two groups of crash victims still remained. One group, the 98 dead children, has a less urgent claim. The second group involves 73 cases—ironically, the largest number of surviving children—who went to live with European and Canadian families. Medical screening conducted by the plaintiffs' doctors in Paris late last year indicated these children also may be suffering from the same problems. In fact, since many of these children are older now and in many cases went undiagnosed or untreated, their problems could be more acute.

Lockheed and the government have rejected an offer by the children's lawyers to settle the European cases on the same basis as the American settlement. So new trials must be conducted, and they will be heard as if nothing had happened before. There will be no mention of the out-of-court settlements, or the de facto admission that all the children were injured or are at risk. None of this will be admissible.

This time, the plaintiffs tried to escalate the conflict by asking Judge Louis Obodorfer to allow them to introduce the cover-up issue. They sought to have the judge advise juries hearing the cases to make an "inference" adverse to Lockheed because of the missing evidence—that is, to rule that the destroyed photos would have supported the children's claims for damages. Such an "adverse inference" ruling might encourage significantly higher monetary verdicts against the corporation.

The judge did not buy their argument, but he didn't totally reject it either. In a complicated order the court ruled that for now it will not allow the cover-up issue to be heard by the jury. Obodorfer's reasoning was convoluted. He agreed important evidence had been destroyed, and there

was a legitimate basis for crying foul against the Air Force, but not enough
evidence to have the charges aired against Lockheed.

A Personal Footnote

The babylift tragedy is now only a footnote to the Vietnam War—one of
those events that was bathed in publicity when it happened and then
promptly forgotten. Yet one can easily become obsessed with this "footnote" because it raises so many questions about humanitarianism in the
service of our foreign policy, the inter-workings of our military-industrial
complex, and the ways our court system can frustrate justice as often as
serve it. Would these children and their claims be treated the same if they
had been American and not Vietnamese?

But this is not a story that is widely known and therefore it is not yet
in the curriculum of Vietnam War courses that the *New York Times* reports
a new generation of students have demanded. In part that's true because
the most widely received media, like the *New York Times*, have barely
covered the story. When I produced a television account of this event for
the ABC news magazine *20/20*, I tried to interest other news media in
investigating and reporting the story further. I felt the case would become
a public issue only when more than one news outlet covered it. First I
thought some talk shows might want to explore the issue through interviews with the lawyers and parents, but *Donahue, Good Morning
America, Nightline, Freeman Reports (CNN)*, and others passed. They felt
that because the Vietnamese children who were still embroiled in litigation
live overseas, Americans wouldn't be interested.

I wrote a long article about the tragedy to expand many of the issues
which couldn't be compressed into the television report. Perhaps the article was too long, or too detailed, or not well-written enough. In any event,
it was offered to and rejected by the *New York Times Magazine,
Washington Post, People, Harpers, New York, Village Voice, Rolling Stone,
Washington Monthly, Mother Jones*, and the *Progressive*. None of these
publications chose to do their own reporting on the issue even though I
suggested it to some. No national columnists picked up the story either,
even though many were told about it in detail. I am pleased that the *Los
Angeles Weekly* and now *Intervention* have published part of it.

These children, victimized once by the war, again by the crash, and
a third time by the courts, deserve better at the hands of the media and
all who questioned the war and express concern about its aftermath.

One promising development: members of Congress and the Senate are writing to President Reagan asking him to intervene. Reagan has so far declined—but at least the issue is no longer buried in the courts. Perhaps, if pressure builds, he will follow the advice of the *Chicago Tribune*: "Forget the legalities and do what is right."

This article originally appeared in the LA Weekly *May 4–10, 1984.*

HO HO HO: HANOI FOR THE HOLIDAYS
Returning to Vietnam on the 25th Anniversary of the Christmas Bombing
1998

Curtis Sliwa is on WABC radio in New York, telling his listeners in thirty-eight states that I am heading to Hanoi for the holidays. He plays a country song that the GIs in 'Nam loved to hear back when the bullets were flying. It was about going home for Christmas.

Irony is his subtext, but I explain that I am going to Vietnam to help a Vietnamese-American filmmaker produce a documentary to encourage Americans to visit her native land. For me that is a double irony in light of nearly a decade spent encouraging the United States to leave Vietnam. But times change, and today the United States has normalized relations. Vietnam wants and needs dollar-rich Americans. The welcome mat is out. It is time for a second visit.

My first trip was in 1974, as one of a relatively small group of American journalists allowed into North Vietnam. The war was still grinding on, although most U.S. troops were gone. Hanoi City, as it is known, was a spartan capital then with soldiers in the streets, and the wreckage of American bombing still visible. There were no shops to speak of, and the wide avenues of this French-influenced town, with its colonial architecture and art deco touches, were deserted at night. By day, the only means of transportation were bicycles and the occasional jeep or Russian-made limo for officials. Two or three planes a week were the only link with the outside. If Hanoi had been a movie then, it was distinctly black and white.

Twenty-three years later, that movie is fully colorized. Capitalism has conquered the capitol of our ex-enemy, even though the flag of the Socialist Republic still flies and the Christmas decorations on a main drag sport a hammer and sickle with red lights casting an eerie reflection on a drizzly night. Christmas Eve there felt like New Year's in Times Square with packed streets and a celebratory spirit. Bizarre, I thought, in a land with no official religion and steeped in centuries of Buddhism. Bicycles are still pervasive, as they were twenty years ago, but today they seem to be outnumbered by Honda mopeds and motorcycles. It seemed as if every young person was on his or her dream machine, cruising the streets, American Graffiti–style. Some were three to a bike, with young lovers clinging to each other, many decked out with red Santa hats and blowing on noisemakers. The square outside the Catholic Cathedral was packed, as was the Church itself. Outside, the crowd seemed restless, waiting for something to happen.

And happen it did, at least on one nearby street where an unexplained altercation was reported between a mob of youngsters and the cops, resulting in arrests and a burned-out police vehicle. This is a generation with leisure time that its parents never had, where the old canons of obedience to authority are breaking down. A few weeks earlier, there was even a rock and roll riot when a Danish band, Michael Learns to Rock, played the Gian Vo Exhibition Center. Hundreds of teenagers who couldn't buy tickets stormed the arena, battling with fifty cops for forty minutes. Parts of the ceiling were destroyed, and windows were shattered, along with any notion that the Gen-Xers of North Vietnam are a conforming and compliant generation. Incidentally, the band, virtually unknown in the West, is popular in Asia because their songs go down well in Karaoke bars where they lend themselves to sing-alongs. Is this the rumbling of the next phase of Vietnamese revolution?

What, I wondered, would Ho Chi Minh have thought of "his children" who are quickly inheriting the land he spent so many years fighting for? Had he or anyone anticipated the time when seventy percent of the country's population would be under the age of thirty, most born after the end of what the Vietnamese call the American war? Ho is still there but not saying much even though every day, thousands line up to march single file through the mausoleum where his well-preserved cadaver sleeps in glass surrounded by a rifle-toting honor guard permanently at attention. The communist hammer and sickle sits behind him on the wall to his right; the country's red flag to the left. (I am told only four leaders have the honor of being so cured and pickled. There's Lenin, Chairman Mao, and, get this, Eva Peron, a.k.a. Evita, in Argentina. All of these bodies get an annual freshening up from an aging Russian mortician who doesn't make house calls. The *Lonely Planet Guide* to Vietnam counsels tourists against asking the guards if Ho is still dead.)

The late leader of Vietnamese communism passed on in 1969. He had asked in his last will to be cremated, but his final wish was not granted because his presence as a symbol remains too important. He is the link between the old Vietnam with its culture of struggle and sacrifice and the new which is pursuing an opening to the West. Ho Chi Minh's portrait is on every note of currency; his spirit invoked endlessly. While he may be dead, he is still around as a role model and example of fearless and fearsome dedication. You can get a sense of why he remains so loved by visiting the famous house on stilts where he lived simply, even monklike, alone in his last years writing and overseeing the armies that fought in his name. You can tour his command post in an open-air conference space under the two-room structure. The three phones that kept him connected to his colleagues and comrades are silent now. Everything is as he left it: simple, unencumbered, subdued. (Just before his death he was moved to a more secure concrete house with a bomb shelter, House #51, a name that was just a number.) A small government guidebook speaks of his daily routine, which included a mid-afternoon stroll to an adjacent pond, where he is said to have clapped his hands to summon the fish for their daily feeding. His hobbies included growing flowers, receiving delegations of children, and going to see movies in the Presidential Palace, which for years had been the headquarters of the French colonial governors who had signed death sentences for him in absentia. There was no mention of his favorite films.

Ho's most famous quotation, "there is nothing more precious than freedom and independence," was the rallying cry of the Vietnamese nation for many years. But as economic conditions worsened in the aftermath of the war's end, the slogan morphed into a standing joke, "there is nothing"— a reference to the hard times that followed the long fight for peace. For many, destitution followed the scarcity of the war years. Today, order is crumbling too as new economic policies usher in an outbreak of illegal street hustling, pervasive money changing, and the sale of counterfeit goods alongside legitimate business activity. The country's beauty remains staggering even if Hanoi's attractions now include a disco called "Apocalypse Now," a state-of-the-art video game parlor called "Magic," and one of the world's last publicly displayed statues of Lenin.

Ho's influence can also be seen in the posters that surround Hoan Kiem, one of seven lakes in the city. They commemorate the twenty-fifth anniversary of the Christmas bombings of Hanoi and Haiphong, those twelve days in December 1972 when Nixon and Kissinger sent in the B-52's to destroy the town in order to save it, to borrow one of the war's most telling quotes. Thousands died, but so did the American war effort, as the Vietnamese anti-aircraft gunners, armed with Russian rockets and courageous dedication, turned the sky into a shooting gallery. Many American planes were shot down, filling up more cells at the infamous Hanoi Hilton with scores of new pilots who parachuted into prison. The posters picture those giant bombers now as piles of junk against a background of construction cranes symbolizing a building boom that is propelling the country into the next century.

While the emphasis is on the future, the past has not been forgotten. I was told I was the first American to visit a new museum that had just opened to commemorate the defense of Hanoi. Outside this building, their holocaust-style museum, was rusted military equipment—giant radars, rockets, and MIG-21s. And next to them, a bizarre conceptual art piece, literally tons of twisted metal from a downed B-52 with its "Made in the USA" markings quite visible.

I watched as busloads of Vietnamese students were escorted through the exhibits by young guides who weren't alive when the bombs fell. They are being exposed to the horrors of wars not as victims but as victors. In the collection were photos and pins of American anti-war activists. There was no one I could recognize. The museum features a dramatic film, split on three screens, documenting the horror and the fear of the bombings and the frenzy of the fight against them. These were not images one saw on American TV. The sound still chills: the ack ack of the big guns, the terrifying whine of the bombs or planes exploding in midair. That battle is now referred to as "the Dien Ben Phu of the skies," named after the town where the French colonial army met its Waterloo, surrounded and decimated by Ho's guerrilla forces back in 1954. Hanoi's Madame Binh, who headed the delegation of the National Liberation Front to the Paris peace talks back in 1973, told a European TV show that they believe the war was won in the skies of Hanoi when that B-52 offensive was neutralized at great cost. Vietnam is a country whose greatest pride historically is marked by its defeat of foreign armies—the Mongols, the Chinese, the Japanese, the French, and, most recently, the Americans. Clearly the Vietnamese don't take kindly to foreign invaders.

Two days later, I met one of the flyers who dropped those bombs, a veteran who had returned with a delegation of fifty Americans, a group called World Team Sports, in Hanoi to participate in what was being called "The Vietnam Challenge." It is a bicycle ride from Hanoi to Ho Chi Minh City, formerly Saigon, in the South. 1,500 miles along Highway One! Like many enterprises in Vietnam these days, this was a joint venture, bringing together our vets with their Vietnamese counterparts. Many are disabled. All are tough and seasoned athletes. "We Ride the Same Road" is the slogan for this initiative in reconciliation. There are tears and cheers as the two sides meet over dinner, sharing war stories across the boundaries of language, ideology, and culture. It is a thrilling moment for onlookers as well as the participants. One of the Vietnamese organizers is a small guy in suspenders, who speaks English with great style and is nicknamed Elvis.

Who woulda thunk years ago that an event like this would take place, or for that matter, that it would be sponsored by big American companies like FedEx and MCI who want in to this emerging market. You will be able to see it in all of its glory, in living color, on NBC, when a film about the Challenge made by the crew that did *Hoop Dreams* airs on TV as a *Sports Illustrated* special. I watched as the ride began from a park next to Ho's mausoleum after a ceremony punctuated by a martial arts demonstration, enlivened by the drumming of a band of young people wearing red scarves—a contingent of the communist Young Pioneers movement. They are like our Boy Scouts and Girl Scouts, only they still pledge allegiance to Karl Marx's dream.

Helping to organize the event are members of the Vietnam Veterans of America Foundation led by an old friend of mine, Bobby Muller, a wounded marine who has fought for peace ever since a bullet left him paralyzed in Quang Tri thirty years earlier. Bobby, in his wheelchair, is the force behind the international campaign against land mines that was recently recognized with the Nobel Peace Prize. It was Bobby's story that inspired Bruce Springsteen's song "Born in the U.S.A." as I reported in a segment for *20/20* ten years earlier. Muller is there with a delegation of his own, including a former American general who had served in the South, as well as his new wife, who turns out to be Doctor and philanthropist Solange MacArthur. They have come bearing gifts to Vietnamese hospitals including Bach Mai, which was partially destroyed during the bombings that defiled "the season of peace" in 1972. After the bike ride begins, Bobby will go back for the first time to the battlefield where his life almost ended—to show his wife and pay respect to his private ghosts.

For many of these veterans, Vietnam was a defining moment, a turning point in their lives. They lost buddies here, but also their innocence and childhoods. Now they have come back, wearing cameras, bringing smiles, offering a form of personal witness—some to help rebuild what they helped destroy, others to find closure and a kind of inner peace from a war that traumatized so many of our generation. I realize that I am a Vietnam veteran too, although I never served in the military. I was in the army on the other side—opposing the policy, feeling vindicated when it collapsed. Vietnam for me became a country as well as a conflict half a lifetime ago, when I came here to see it for myself and write about it, which I did for at least five publications as well as the radio station I worked for then.

I am in Vietnam working with Tiana, the Vietnamese-American

director whose documentary *From Hollywood to Hanoi* recounts a personal story rich in the contradictions of this Vietnam drama. Tiana was born in the South, the child of an anti-communist official who moved to America and hates her coming back. The communists will get her, he has warned her repeatedly. She is a hurricane of activity, bursting with energy in three languages, as she maneuvers through walls of bureaucracy and protocol. Tiana is making a new film chronicling the transformations of Vietnam, shooting the scenery as it changes, talking to people about the evolution of the country and its culture. She helps me see Vietnam through Vietnamese eyes, with more shadings, nuances, and absurdities than I could have understood on my own.

For example, even though Tiana's film featured interviews with such Vietnamese leaders as General Giap and the late Pham Van Dong, the former defense minister and prime minister respectively, copies were seized by customs in Hanoi. Since I had them with me, I was taken into a small room with a VCR where the guard asked me if the video was "sexy." It takes a week to get the dubs back, as they circulate through various layers of bureaucracy, all seeking to stop the flow of pornography and other so-called social evils. The old hard-liners are still in power and there is a continuing tension between the modernizers and free marketeers. The Communist Party apparatchiks fear that what happened to their old ally the Soviet Union could happen to them. When I was in Vietnam, the Party named a conservative military politician as its new chief.

The country remains committed to a one party state—to blocking political pluralism and western-style democracy. Human rights are a problem for dissidents and others who run afoul of well-enforced rules. When I asked a government official if the United States has raised human rights concerns, I was told that in light of all that was done to the people during the war, Washington is in no position to lecture Vietnam on that issue. Who could disagree, even though I knew of repression and political prisoners. I understand where he's coming from, but I can't buy it fully in light of the sufferings of the boat people and the abuses committed in the name of reeducation after the war. Yet, as an American, I don't feel like I have the legitimacy to debate the issue, although to this day I regret not having spoken out unequivocally against human rights violations committed by Hanoi after the war ended.

While the propagandistic Voice of Vietnam blares from loudspeakers in the streets, it is not clear who is listening. A new Vietnam is emerging within the bowels of the old, for good and for bad. The mixed economy is delivering benefits that the old state-run system couldn't. Yet, I was told about growing corruption both within the Party and in the business sector. In late January, the government reportedly held a public execution to make an example of a few symbols of corruption. Crime is on the rise, and drugs are rampant too, another by-product of the market system.

The power struggle at the top has produced a contradictory set of policies, welcoming foreign investment, while at the same time making it difficult for most foreigners to make money. International companies have to take the state in as a partner, yet regulations, customs rules, and red tape force costs up. This is very frustrating for many entrepreneurs who wanted Vietnam to be a new get-rich-quick environment. The bloom is now off that rose. They complain that it takes too long to get approval for their projects, and that it is hard to meet deadlines. Some companies have run into other problems. A Nike factory was exposed for unfair and abusive labor practices. Strikes take place with regularity in joint ventures. The Vietnamese are not servile workers. The Ford Motor Company has built a plant, but most of the people I spoke with fear the day that cars become more common on crowded streets that were never built with them in mind. They worry that Hanoi and Saigon are on their way to becoming overcrowded Bangkoks, teeming with too many people and far too many traffic jams.

The economic troubles besetting the region are also affecting the country's growth. Investors in neighboring countries have already started to pull back on promises and new deals. For example, all work has stopped on a new Sheraton Hotel being financed through Singapore. Vietnam, still one of the world's poorest countries, had a relatively high nine percent growth rate last year. It is expected to grow less in 1998, caught in the crunch of the Asian financial crisis, trying to balance state control and private investment. I experienced just one small aspect of the problem when I tried to check my email. I learned that while Vietnam has the Internet, the government is trying to restrict its use. It is now hard to gain access, but that could change soon. [And it did! DS–2001.]

There are tensions too among the people, many of whom are rooted in a culture deep in tradition and geared to political mobilization. I visited a teacher's college and asked an English class what their aspirations were. One young man said he wanted to get rich. When I asked who shared his view, only two hands in a class of thirty went up. The others spoke idealistically and articulately about wanting to help the next generation and build the future. They are proud of their country and say they want to retain its progressive traditions of solidarity and working for the common good.

As I listened to the debate, including their collective curiosity about the outside world, I was struck by their sense of hope. Having visited Saigon in the last days of its degradation years earlier, I was impressed with how different Hanoi feels today. It is the optimism of a society that still reveres its old, and respects its past but is focused on the future. At the same time, I know it will be hard for its special character to survive as the engine of globalization sweeps in. It may prove to have been easier to defeat foreign armies than their corps of businessmen, and an even bigger challenge: sustaining a burgeoning population that will hit one hundred million in the next century.

Despite all of these problems, Vietnam is now, thankfully, a country at peace, coping with the same pressures as many of its third world neighbors. The war is now a memory, although its legacy in lost years of development and scattered memorials for the millions who died are evident. Yet despite the pervasive poverty, the living carry on with an awesome humility and determination. The new buildings rise among streets still packed with pedaling cyclo drivers, farmers in conical hats selling an exotic range of vegetables, and young kids on the move. In all these respects, Vietnam projects a power and charisma that continues to exercise a hold on the world's imagination, as it has on mine for all of these years. Think of how central a role Vietnam has played in influencing the last half of the twentieth century. I think its voice will still be heard in the next.

A version of this essay originally appeared in Z Magazine, *March 1998.*

Author's Note, 2001: As I review these accounts, I'm struck by how Vietnam has disappeared down America's memory hole, but not its subconscious. Now, on the twenty-sixth anniversary of the war's end, the question of U.S. war crimes is back in the *New York Times*, this time with an account of a barbarous act committed by a Navy SEAL unit in Vietnam on February 25, 1969 in which a number of unarmed women and children were allegedly slaughtered—led by former U.S. Senator Bob Kerrey. Says Kerrey, who covered up the incident for decades: "It's going to be very interesting to see the reaction to this story . . . because basically you are talking about a man who killed innocent civilians." "Interesting?" If ever there was a word demanding prosecution and an American Truth Commission, it is "interesting."

part three I-SPY

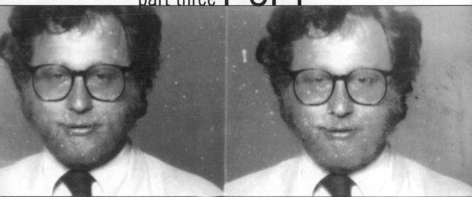

passions, pieces, and polemics • 1960–2000

THE CHAOS CAPER (GETTING MY FILES)
What Freedom of Information Act?
1975

I want my files.

I know they know who I am. I was part of the "chaos" of the late '60s, a *bonafide* "dissident." I was a staff sleuth for the CIA muckrakers at *Ramparts* magazine. I visited some of those commie countries planning our destruction. I protested against the war. If they were doing their job, OPERATION CHAOS must have my number.

That name is really incredible. CHAOS—an acronym that outdoes SMERSH of James Bond fame, or the invention of any novelist. The Rockefeller Report on the CIA, which Art Buchwald correctly likened to a Don Corleone report on organized crime, outdoes our every expectation. Tim Leary will be amazed to learn that the CIA was into LSD years before he was turned on. Seymour M. Hersh of the *Times* will take solace in its confirmation of the essential details of his story on domestic spying, although the Commission sought to downplay it while Hersh called it "massive." What I was most fascinated by was the concept of an operation named CHAOS. It was something for the conspiratorial imagination.

CHAOS was a super-secret operation, even within one of the agency's most secretive divisions. It quite literally operated out of a "vaulted basement area." Fifty-two full-time staff officers and thirty field agents took part in the activities that Rocky's Commission say "unlawfully exceeded" the CIA's charter. Significantly, the panel, whose report has been branded "responsible" by most political and journalistic opinion makers, considered the "declared mission" of the domestic spy program proper. ("We agree with your ends but not your means.") In its six years of operations, the Chaotics compiled a list of 300,000 names, of which 7,200 were the subjects of "personality files."

Since I think I was one of those "personalities," I've been trying to find out what the CIA knows about me that I don't. For months now, I've been engaged in a game of verbal Scrabble, seeking out my files before the paper shredder gets its orders. It's been frustrating.

Back in March, the *New York Times* reported that the CIA had admitted keeping track of Congressperson Bella Abzug for twenty years. William Colby told her that she could request her files just like everyone else. Just like everyone else! At that point, I had only the thinnest recollection that the Freedom of Information Act had just become relevant to the problem at hand. And sure enough, Bella had had a peek at what they had on her. So I decided to do the same.

On March 6, I mailgrammed (it's cheapest) the CIA, directing a Freedom of Information request to Director William "Pianowire" Colby, at the CIA home office in Langley, Virginia. ("Pianowire" is the nickname Colby was given by anti-war journalists for his role in the Phoenix assassination program in Vietnam). Western Union sent the wire back marked "Addressee Unknown." I was amazed, but tried again, this time sending off the inquiry to Washington, D.C.

On March 18, I received my first overt response from the CIA. It was a letter advising me that "it is impossible to make a search of our records" with just the information I had provided. It informed me that, at a minimum, the agency needs a date and place of birth, as well as any other information I thought could assist the search. The letter was signed by Robert S. Young, Freedom of Information coordinator.

On March 21, I wrote Mr. Young a chatty letter telling him about my problems in locating the agency's secret address, and telling him a little about myself. It was cutesy, intended to establish the authenticity of my identity and to express my faith in the retrieval capability of his computers. "I am who I say I am," I wrote. "This request is . . . an effort, in a sense, to establish who you are." Since the law requires a response within ten days. I thought that I would soon have file in hand.

But no such luck. On March 26, Young answered with a two-liner saying my request was being processed. I shot back a query asking how long it would take. On April 8 he responded with a letter telling me about his troubles. It seems that my letter was but one of hundreds of such requests received by the agency in the last several weeks. He then explained that the mighty CIA was not up to the task:

> Since each individual request requires a thorough search of our records, and a thoughtful review of any material located, we find ourselves faced with a backlog of requests and resultant delays in our responses. Even though we have temporarily reassigned a significant number of personnel from their regular duties to the handling of these requests, we nonetheless are unable to provide a comprehensive response to your request at this time.

I was shaken. Could my request—and requests like it—be creating tumult, perhaps even chaos, within the Central Intelligence Agency? Young told me I could appeal and "could of course" consider his letter a denial of my request.

Now that sounded suspicious. Here was an overt reassurance coupled with a covert contradictory meaning. Back at my typewriter, I asked that the mystery be unraveled and that the CIA send along a copy of the relevant regulations. This time, a weary Mr. Young passed my letter on to a Mr. Charles Savigi, who wrote back, enclosing the text of the statute and reassuring me once again that a response was in the works. This time I was told that several "components" were being queried and that some had not yet responded.

On May 8, I thanked him but confessed that "it is difficult for me to conceptualize a component's response."

That was more than a month ago. Since that time, the CIA has been mum. On May 23, the *Globe* reported that between January 1 and May 8 the CIA received a total of 1613 requests for access to files. The story mentioned my efforts, in brief, but focused on a Dartmouth College professor, Jonathan Mirsky, who did obtain some CIA files about his work as an Asia scholar and war critic; apparently a congressman's intervention was responsible for his speedy success. The files turned out to be incomplete and heavily censored, although they contained information on him dating back to a job he held as a camp counselor in the 1950s. Among the more startling disclosures was mention of a 1967 CIA memorandum alluding to "a CIA contact" on *Ramparts* magazine. I've seen nothing more about that since. I worked for *Ramparts* during that period.

I am still waiting to see what if anything the CIA is holding on me. On May 15 I had a letter from FBI Director Clarence Kelley, with whom I had also filed a request, advising me that the FBI needs more time "because of the need to consult with another agency having an interest in the determination of your request."

And what agency, Clarence, could that be? Fish and Wildlife? The Strategic Air Command? Or perhaps an agency so secret that even the FBI prefers not to use its name? I asked Kelley about that, but so far, to no avail. I am wondering if the FBI has a mail cover on the CIA.

Under the law, everyone now has the Freedom to seek out Information. The FBI and the CIA apparently have the freedom to keep you from finding out what they don't want you to know. If you are interested in writing for your file, drop a line to Robert S. Young at the CIA, care of their secret zip code: Washington, D.C. 20505.

You may find out whether the man from CHAOS was watching you.

This story originally appeared in the Boston Phoenix, *June 17, 1975.*

EDITED CIA FILES TELL A LITTLE TO HIDE A LOT
1975

They came in an official-looking brown envelope distinguished by the logo of the American Revolutionary Bicentennial and the slogan, "An Equal Opportunity Employer." The return address was the ominous giveaway: Central Intelligence Agency, Washington, D.C. 20505
At last, here they were! My CIA files!

I had been after them with letters and telegrams for over four months, trying to use the provisions of the Freedom of Information Act (FOIA) to pry open the secret computer banks which, I knew, knew about me. The correspondence had been classic: the demands in my letters had been alternately angry and cute, their responses unshakably bureaucratic and form-letter precise. In late June, I sent the CIA a copy of my recent *Phoenix* tirade against their procrastination and delay (*Phoenix Forum*, June 17). I even invited their reply. Perhaps it put the fear of CIA critic Congressman Michael Harrington in them, because within two weeks an expurgated selection of their info was in my filing cabinet.

Not all the files, understand—just the ones they decided I could look at. By their own admission, the CIA has located 145 different cables, dispatches, memoranda, internal memoranda, and one name-check pertaining to me. Of these, they released a mere 19 blotched Xeroxes marred by as many deletions as the White House tapes. CIA officials apparently consider the law that is supposed to insure government disclosure and accountability as just so much Swiss cheese. It is so full of holes in the form of amendments, exemptions, and overriding Executive Orders that the CIA can use it to withhold more information than it provides. According to their interpretation, the FOIA has to do with protecting the freedom to inform more than the freedom to obtain information.

The documents I have received reveal that the CIA had been on my trail since 1968. That was the same year I got on theirs, as an editor and researcher for *Ramparts* magazine. I was then based in London and looking into a whole network of covertly subsidized organizations we had uncovered.

According to the first of twelve censored agency cables, CIA headquarters was alerted to my journalistic sleuthing: Dated February 29, 1968, the version supplied to me reads:

(WORDS DELETED) VARIOUS REPORTS HAVE
BEEN RECEIVED CONCERNING ACTIVITIES

HERE OF DANIEL SCHECHTER, YOUNG AMERI-
CAN WHO RESEARCHING (DELETED) EXPOSÉ
BOOK WHICH RAMPARTS HOPES TO BE PUB-
LISHED BY MCGRAW HILL.

And so it began, the first of a series of cables chronicling my European travels, reporting on my whereabouts, schooling, and background. None of the information released is very detailed. Censored, it certainly doesn't inspire too much confidence in the CIA's research abilities. But, of course, there is more—much more.

The CIA seemed very interested in *Ramparts*. A March 25 cable from Headquarters refers to "OTHER RAMPARTS PERSONALITIES KNOWN TO HAVE BEEN IN LONDON." No names were listed next to the letters A through G on the form supplied to me, but there I am, listed as H. Two days later, a short biography was cabled noting, "HAS BEEN INVOLVED PROTEST GROUPS IN U.S. AND LONDON." The next line bears the curious instruction: "(DELETED) INTERESTED ALL ACTIV-ITIES (DELETED) SCHECHTER."

In the meantime, a "Memorandum for Chief" and a "Memorandum for Record" were prepared in early March 1968 presumably detailing my activities. The CIA will not let me see these documents because they contain other names and "to release them would constitute a clearly unwarranted invasion of their personal privacy." It was not until reading that passage that I recognized the agency's deep commitment to civil liberties and personal privacy.

In the cover letter—an apt term—the office of the CIA's Freedom of Information coordinator lists various categories of information which they've collected on me over the years. Each category also contains appropriate legal references to regulations and statutory authority explaining why I can't see what they have. In one case, information was received "from our liaison relationship with a foreign government." Hence "FOIA subsection (b) (1)" applies. In another instance, the CIA says it must protect "the identity of confidential sources" and "investigative techniques and procedures." And on and on.

It turns out that the CIA has also been collecting and sharing information with other government agencies. I found this out rather inadvertently when in response to a separate FOIA request I submitted to the FBI, Director Clarence Kelley informed me that the G-Men first had to consult with "another agency". It sounded so mysterious that I wrote back wondering what agency that could be. (Fish and Wildlife?) Kelley has since replied, advising me that there are classified CIA documents about me in the FBI's central file. In its letter, the CIA doesn't cite the FBI by name, but admits to having sent twenty-two memoranda "to another government agency containing information relative to your anti-war and other activities abroad." The CIA then cites a mass of subsections and rulings to circumvent disclosure. Incidentally, the FBI is still "processing" my request but does promise to make some documents available.

Supposedly, all of this information is restricted to my "activities abroad." In the eyes of the Rockefeller Commission and many CIA apologists, that would make the CIA's curiosity legitimate and quite legal. I am afraid I cannot take comfort in these distinctions. First of all, the CIA has been claiming that all of its meddling abroad was legal—which is quite possible. As newspaper reports make clear, the CIA helped shape the laws which guide its operations, and has quite successfully undermined and co-opted efforts by Congress to assert any independent control. I do not think that spying on journalists or legal protesters is a legitimate function of government, here or overseas.

The CIA's interest in me did not diminish when I returned to the United States. One of their dispatches plainly links me to a publication supporting the Harvard student strike of 1969 and makes reference to the now defunct *Old Mole*, described as a "militant biweekly underground paper." There are also references to anti-war groups in the U.S. All of this suggests that I may have been one of the 10,000 Americans who came to the attention of the CIA's domestic program Operation CHAOS.

The sanitized files I have received are slim pickings, I know, but they have confirmed my suspicions about CIA surveillance. I now know for certain that at least some of my paranoia has been justified, and that the CIA is concerned about people who are concerned about them. The folks at *Ramparts* were watched. There's even a dispatch offering a "Who's Who of the *Ramparts* staff as of November 1, 1970." The information may even have come from an agent on the magazine's staff. According to a recent *Boston Globe* report, there was a reference to a "CIA contact" at *Ramparts* in a memorandum supplied to Dartmouth College Professor Jonathan Mirsky by the CIA. We still don't know who that person was.

There may never be any way of getting all the facts about the sordid allegations of the CIA. Michael Harrington's ouster from the House committee investigating the CIA shows Congress's attitude, and the Church Committee in the Senate has already limited the scope of its inquiry. The Rockefeller Commission report was an example of telling a little and hiding a lot.

I am still going to press for full disclosure from the CIA; the FOIA allows for an appeal. The only catch is that the appeal goes to an Information Review Committee composed of CIA brass with a chairman appointed by Agency Director William "Operation Phoenix" Colby. In other words, the CIA reviews itself.

If, as I expect, the bureaucracy rules in favor of itself, the next step is to take the CIA to court. A number of people are already doing that, some to demand more information, others to protest CIA interference in their lives and livelihoods. A presidential apology last week to the family of the scientist who committed suicide after unwittingly ingesting agency acid does not seem to have headed off their suit, and there are others. A Rhode Island man is suing because his mail was tampered with. In New York. Grove Press has filed a $10 million damage suit against the CIA, accusing it of having participated in the firebombing of the firm's office back in 1968. The Rockefeller Commission revealed that Grove was a target of CIA attention. Publisher Barney Rosett says the agency tapped its phones, infiltrated its staff and intercepted its mail, and he says there is evidence suggesting that the CIA supplied anti-Castro groups with bombs. One such group attacked its offices. Grove published the writings of Cuban revolutionary partisan Che Guevara and French leftist Regis Debray.

I don't seem to have been firebombed or materially damaged by the CIA's comparatively minor interventions directed my way. I am angry, though, about what the files suggest—and determined to find out more about what they found out.

Who knows? Maybe they know more about me than I do. I also want to know if their files on me are as good as mine on them.

This column originally appeared in the Boston Phoenix, *August 5, 1975.*

CIA FILE: INFORMANT'S REPORT
FILED 1967/RELEASED 1975

Central Intelligence Agency
Washington, D.C. 20505

Danny Shekter—about 25, believed to be U.S. citizen. Shekter speaks poor French. He is at the present time a student at the London School of Economics, where at least two of his friends (name unknown) are Cuban students.

Appearance: Funky. He is about 6ft. tall, with a round face and a very white, pimply skin. He wears his hair in a sort of bouffant hairdo more commonly seen in women. Appears to be in good health and to be an energetic person, with organizational skills (he was able to fill the auditorium of the London School of Economics.)

He speaks rapidly, with authority, but does not give the impression of being bossy.

I have not seen him drink nor smoke. I know nothing of other habits. Around him one is comfortable, he is friendly and has a warm manner. He is carelessly dressed and his appearance is strange, but once over the first surprise one can find him amusing, good-natured, and happy.

Politically, he is far left, Marxist. He is in constant touch with groups inside the U.S. and is at the present time engaged in an inquiry on [CIA] activities in Europe.

His main characteristic is that of an odd but friendly person who is strongly devoted to a cause.

LETTER FROM THE MASSACHUSETTS CIVIL LIBERTIES UNION
1982

From: My lawyer
Re: My CIA Files

Date: April 15, 1982

Dear Danny:

I have been reviewing old files and discovered that this office has a rather extensive dossier concerning your activities in the late '60s and early '70s. As well-written and exciting as they are, I have no real interest in keeping them.

The question is: What should I do with them? I can send the entire file back to you. I can throw it away, OR I can send it back to the CIA-FBI-NSA and let them decide what to do with it.

Please advise.

Sincerely,
John Reinstein

G-MEN ON MY TAIL
1973

Like most kids growing up in the '50s, I was exposed to the exploits and glories of our G-Men, the FBI, which like the Mounties in Canada always got their man. I used to see their Most Wanted posters in the Post Office, and was taught to admire the Bureau's effectiveness at crime fighting. Remember the adventures of Efrem Zimbalist Jr., and countless other TV shows which the FBI itself encouraged, lobbied for, and consulted on?

It was only later, in college, that I realized what a dupe I had been, and that, for decades, J. Edgar Hoover ran an agency that spent as much time spying on Americans as any real or imagined enemies elsewhere. America's top cop was an authoritarian hypocrite, who kept dossiers on every politician, actively deploying covert strategies like the infamous COINTELPRO program, to divide and destroy the civil rights movement. Back in the early '60s, I heard firsthand stories about FBI agents in the South who stood by and counted blows while civil rights workers were assaulted in front of them. I knew about Hoover's wiretapping of Martin Luther King to try to entrap him for sexual infidelities; it was only after Hoover's death that his own sexual bizarreness and proclivity for cross-dressing was exposed.

I was a target of FBI spying too, as I learned when I obtained some of the files in which my name appeared. The first one documented an anti-segregation protest when I was a student at Cornell. I am including that document here, as well as excerpts from two other encounters that I wrote about for the weekly *Real Paper* in Cambridge, Massachusetts.

FBI File

October 8, 1962, item concerning a picket of Howard Johnson's in Horseheads, New York, to protest alleged discrimination policies of the chain's southern restaurants. DANIEL I. SCHECHTER, class of '64, is identified as the spokesman for the picketing group which was organized by the CLU as part of a national demonstration conducted by CORE.

May 10, 1963, item concerning rally held by the CLU on 5/9/63 to protest Birmingham Police brutality. DANIEL I. SCHECHTER, class of '64, identified as a CLU spokesman, was one of the speakers. He called the deprivation of the rights of Negroes a "cotton curtain".

November 12, 1963, item concerning various Cornell students aiding in the civil rights movement which states that DANIEL I. SCHECHTER, class of '64, has left school for a year to work in Harlem and that recently six families there, encouraged by SCHECHTER, withheld rent payments because of the decrepit status of their housing.

May 22, 1964, item concerning a speech given at Cornell on that date by WILLIAM STRICKLAND, Director of the Northern Student Movement. DANIEL I. SCHECHTER, class of '64, is listed as the moderator of the program, co-sponsored by the Cornell Forum and *Dialogue Magazine*.

The CLU and Cornell Forum are officially recognized student organizations at CU. No information has been received or developed that they are under communist influence or domination.

It's My Agent Calling

Two years ago, my WBCN colleague and *Real Paper* staff writer Andrew Kopkind published a review of two books assessing the FBI program of domestic surveillance. The piece was cutely titled "See My Agent."

In late August, one of my agents came to see me. A disaffected Boston-area FBI informant, he turned my tiny studio into a confessional over the next few weeks, revealing information on the FBI's massive illegal intelligence-gathering operations in Boston.

At first, Ulick A. Mahoney, known on the streets as Yule and in the FBI's security informant files by the pseudonym Hari Seldon, wasn't sure if he wanted to disclose his real identity. He had decided to tell his story because of personal torments. He had come to me, apparently because my news broadcast on WBCN had long been a primary source of information he passed on to the FBI. He told me that he respected me, and that I seemed to know a great deal about what he called "CIA-FBI stuff." I was also one of the people he had informed on; yet he trusted me to help him tell a story which he had bottled up for years.

Mahoney's revelations confirm, for the first time, the existence in the Boston area of a network of government agents and informants who have been burrowing around virtually every citizens' movement for at least the last five years.

Since 1971 he has spied on more than thirty-three New England–area organizations, informing on or identifying at least 900 persons. And Mahoney thinks he was only one of ten such informants in the Boston area.

Mahoney told me that he was urged by the FBI to infiltrate several media organizations, including WBCN, the station I then reported for. He told me that he considered our news programs the best sources of information on dissent, and that he would listen regularly and then phone in a summary to the FBI. "They pay well," he revealed. Thanks Yule, so that means I was working for the FBI without knowing it—unpaid of course.

* * *

In 1973 the FBI made a little house call to my own home to arrest my housemate, Bill Zimmerman, who had been involved in organizing a dramatic and successful airlift to American Indian Movement activists under siege in a protest at the site of a massacre of Indians in the last century at Wounded Knee in South Dakota.

Wounded Knee Airlift: The Boston Arrests

UPI might have broken the story but it woke me up. Or at least the presence of six well-scrubbed FBI in our front hall at 8:30 a.m. on Saturday morning rather abruptly disrupted our domestic tranquillity. With three unmarked cars staking out our days, these G-Men were doing what actor Efrem Zimbalist Jr. celebrates weekly; only this morning they had come for my friend. While the man who was being charged with conspiracy to feed people was looking for his glasses, and trying to get his teeth brushed, the rest of us were trying to deal with our uninvited "guests." The feds ordered all of us to identify ourselves. We demanded that they identify themselves (they did—rather nervously), show us their warrant (they had none), explain the charges (they wouldn't), and tell us how the Watergate investigation was going (no comment). Just for the record and to their aggravated discomfort, I tape-recorded the event. FBI agents are used to doing the bullying. Apparently the training manual is a little weak on how to deal with people who know their rights, much less with those inclined to turn an arrest into a bit of a happening.

They had been knocking for quite awhile before Zimmerman let them in, in the process letting himself in for his first big surprise of the day. Busted before breakfast! I was downstairs within minutes, Sony cassette machine at the ready, welcoming them with the announcement that they were on the air. "And who are you, sir," asked a man who later identified himself as Bill Smith of the FBI. "I'm Danny Schechter covering this arrest for WBCN." The response produced a momentary pause before a chorus queried, "Let's see your identification."

And that was the game we played. I'll tell you if you tell me. They were more nervous than we were. I tried to pepper them with some questions but the responses ranged from a muted "Get lost" to warnings that I was interfering with justice. They really called it that. Their threats to arrest me for interfering worked; I stopped interfering. We parried some more, but I knew that the interview was coming to an end when they put cuffs on Bill and started to take him to the door. My interaction with the federal agentry was ending; Zimmerman's was just beginning

"What impressed me about the arrest was the feeling of total absurdity," he told me later. "No one seemed to know what was going on, or cared. Every one of the FBI agents was filling a bureaucratic function, acting like automatons. I came away with the sense of them as complete functionaries, and not at all the super-competent investigators they have been pictured as."

This story originally appeared in the Real Paper, *May 2, 1973.*

Author's Note, 2001: The charges against Bill Zimmerman were ultimately dropped when it was discovered that, as I had suspected, there was no legitimate warrant on file. Bill wrote an informative book on the topic, *Airlift to Wounded Knee.* Today he is a well-known political consultant in California.

SPYING ON THE FBI
1976

Investigative reporting may still be fashionable in post-Watergate America, but as every muckraker knows, the muck you rake only gets results when it is taken seriously by institutions other than the one which first blows the whistle.

The reaction to the disclosure in last week's *Real Paper* of FBI surveillance directed against radical groups in the Boston area seems to confirm this view. What was most significant about it was the lack of other coverage. No other media outlet, except WBCN, picked up or amplified the first confirmed account of local bureau spying. Although I personally called a friend at the *New York Times*, UPI, WBZ, WGBH, and WNAC, no one to my knowledge sought to follow up. A friend at one local TV outlet quoted his boss as dismissing it because the FBI informant named in the piece also admitted to being a drunk and, hence, was clearly unreliable.

I doubt if any conspiracy is at work here; a more likely explanation is that the media, which barely covers the activities of protest groups in the first place, couldn't get excited covering how the government was covering them. Now, if that informant had only spied on Teddy Kennedy . . .

If the establishment media was not interested, the community certainly was. WBCN's switchboard was flooded with calls after the interview with ex-FBI informant Yule Mahoney was broadcast. A number of individuals wanted more information about Mahoney's surveillance of their organizations. A local group of dissident Iranians was fascinated by Mahoney's admission that he had targeted them; they say that the FBI is working with the Shah's secret police (SAVAK) and this disclosure might help confirm that relationship. Radical lawyers in Cambridge told me that the story is important because it proves what many people had been suspecting. "It helps people understand how they work," commented attorney David Rockwell. One law commune is now planning to seek more information under the Freedom of Information Act about Mahoney's disclosure that he stole confidential information from their offices. This may lead to a suit against the FBI.

I received at least two threatening calls as a result of the piece. One came on Tuesday afternoon from an anonymous but gruff-sounding voice who said he didn't appreciate the attack on the FBI, and had "no use for me." "Get your head on straight," he growled. Two other calls from the National Caucus of Labor Committees or U.S. Labor Party, one of the groups that Yule Mahoney spied on, did not contradict my description of them as crazoid. One caller attempted an obscure joke, advising that he could arrange an exclusive interview for me. He implied that I was an agent, although I am not sure for whom. Another NCLC message phoned into the 'BCN listener line was transcribed in our comment book this way: "To Danny: 'I read the article in the *Real Paper* and I just wanted to tell you to stay away from NCLC. He'll get the picture.' (click)". The volunteer, a terribly nice but naïve high school student, asked me who they are. I couldn't begin to explain.

As for Yule Mahoney, he liked the article and the broadcast, although he felt they should have focused more on the FBI than on him. He claims that the FBI followed him the day after the piece appeared, but says he is not afraid of them. At this point I am worried more about him than them. In some ways, the FBI was his crutch and now that that's gone, I am not sure where he will go. He is a troubled young man whose life is complicated by alcoholism. There is not that much of a community support network for ex-informers who have ostensibly seen the light. He doesn't have the skills or the opportunistic bent to write a book or go on the lecture circuit. Moreover, he now has to live with the fear of retribution from both the FBI, which he betrayed, and the left, which he surveyed. It is not a happy place to be.

In fact, it reminds me of a story about spies written by Doris Lessing. She relates the horrid dilemma faced by a police agent who inadvertently gets converted by the people he's watching. He gets turned on by a communist leader who, after long hours of interaction, comes to trust the agent's sincerity and anguish. Soon the cop becomes a communist, and decides to confess to the Party secretary. He's tired of informing, he says, he hates being in the secret police. He wants to serve the revolution. But what does the Party do but order him to remain in the secret police, but now to inform on them for the Party. The man is trapped in the logic of an impossible situation. He has nowhere to go.

Has the FBI really cut back its domestic surveillance? Last Tuesday, FBI director Clarence Kelley testified before the Senate Select Committee on Investigation that it had, substantially. There were only 626 individuals and organizations being watched now, Kelley said, and all were being handled by the general crimes section of the Bureau, rather than its intelligence division. Kelley said the FBI had had 21,414 active cases just three years ago.

This story originally appeared in the Real Paper, *October 2, 1976.*

HARVARD AND THE CIA
1967

I was involved in several investigations of university complicity with the CIA. This selection appeared in How Harvard Rules, *a collectively written publication of the Africa Research Group.*

> *America's new role of Free World leadership, an accelerating technology which has shattered traditional time-space relationships, the new reality of warfare fought not on the battlefield but by means of espionage, propaganda and economics: all combine to require a kind of intelligence preparedness which in the past has only been mobilized in times of shooting war.*
> —Harry Howe Ransom, Central Intelligence and National Security, *Harvard, 1958. (This book, which justifies and supports the CIA, was published as part of Harvard's own Defense Studies program.)*

Harvard and the CIA

The CIA, like so much of official America, appears to have special affection for Harvard. It ought to; Harvard men were the backbone of the wartime intelligence effort, the Office of Strategic Studies. The OSS, whose covert research operations were transferred to the State Department after the war, was also the predecessor of the CIA. William Langer, of Harvard's history department, helped in the formation of the CIA, and has served as a civilian on a number of intelligence supervisory boards. After the war, many of Harvard's "best," who had served in the intelligence agency during the war, kept up their ties and membership in this secret gentlemen's fraternity.

Now there is irrefutable evidence of links between the university and the CIA on a number of levels: (1) At the very top of the governing structure, several influential Overseers have direct and indirect associations with the CIA; (2) Several faculty members are consultants to the CIA; (3) Contract research for the CIA is done at Harvard; and (4) Harvard itself has been directly involved in sponsoring and actively cooperating with CIA programs based in Cambridge.

Contrary to its public statements, Harvard has gone to great lengths to hide its relations with the CIA. The evidence we have represents only a fraction of what we cautiously estimate to be the extent of the connections between the CIA and Harvard men. It is important to understand that these connections with the CIA—covert as they might have been—are no more odious than many of Harvard's quite open links with the Defense Department or the great Foundations. Within the logic of the men who run the government, business, and Harvard, the CIA is only one component of an indivisible system. Hence, programs backed by the CIA might just as easily be supported by the Ford Foundation or vice versa—and often are.

And now, the evidence:

Harvard and the CIA: The Links at the Top

On the most direct level, Harvard's Board of Overseers is graced by the presence of Robert Amory '36, the CIA's former Deputy Director of Intelligence. Amory was a law professor at Harvard before he signed up with the CIA for a ten-year stint, from 1952-1962. While he was with the agency, he served as a representative to the National Security Council, the highest level decision-making body for the American strategists. Former Harvard Dean McGeorge Bundy was JFK's representative to this key inner council; now Harvard man Kissinger is Nixon's link.

Two other Overseers, Francis Taylor Plimpton Jr., a lawyer and diplomat, and Amory Houghton, Jr., of the Dow-Corning Company, were both involved as directors of the Foundation for Youth and Student Affairs (FYSA), the CIA's principal mechanism for organizing and funding international youth activities.

George Cabot Lodge, Director of the Harvard Business School's Division of International Affairs, and Henry's son, has been directly involved in channeling CIA money into Harvard-related programs. Along with Associate Dean of the Graduate School Richard Hunt, Lodge sits on the Board of the Fund for International Social and Economic Education, a CIA conduit. Through the Fund, grants have been made to the Business School and some of its students.

Harvard Professors Serve the CIA

Among Harvard's "consultants" to the CIA is Arthur Smithies, a conservative economist and Master of Kirkland House. Smithies admitted to a "connection of ten years duration" in a letter to Dean Franklin Ford, dated December 7, 1967. He, as one would expect, minimized its importance: "I wish I could add that there is something subtly interesting or sinister about it." Harvard found the admission definitely sinister, however. Dean Franklin Ford scribbled on Smithies' letter: "Acknowledge. Should we have a confidential file on such relationships outside personal folders?" Other professors perform for the CIA on a contractual basis. Take the case of Professors Anthony Oettinger and Ivan Sutherland, both computer whiz kids, who sought over $100,000 in CIA funding for intricate computer experiments and a three-dimensional display device. Since all external contracts require the corporation's approval, the matter was bounced around all sorts of bureaucratic channels, discreetly of course! No one objected, in principle, to doing work for the CIA, but there were certain delicate problems. It was March 1967, and certain Deans were jumpy because *Ramparts* had just published its CIA expose. They feared that Harvard's fair name might be smeared in the growing national indignation against CIA practices.

A rationale to steer Harvard around these dangers was proposed to Dean Franklin Ford in a confidential memo from Dean Harvey Brooks:

> There is a difficult problem involved here. As I told you on the phone the other day, none of the conditions of this proposed contract have the features which were so objectionable in the publicized cases. The work is unclassified and in an area which is politically neutral. The terms of the contractual agreement which will be between Harvard and the navy will be a matter of public record. On the other hand, it is true that the work to be done will result in the development of a new technology which will be valuable to intelligence collection and interpretation, although not as far as I can see, in connection with clandestine-type activities.

These incredible distinctions illustrate the corporate mentality's need to rationalize acceptance of the monies while somehow exonerating themselves from the political responsibility of association with U.S. intelligence operations.

Other Harvard professors were among those whose political and ideological views were fed by covert subsidies from the CIA. Leading liberals Arthur Schlesinger, Jr. (now in exile at CCNY) and John Kenneth Galbraith were deeply involved in such CIA-supported organizations as the Congress for Cultural Freedom (CCF). Galbraith also administered the "transmigration of the CCF from the CIA to the Ford Foundation" as he admitted to Franklin Ford in a confidential letter.

Countless other professors, we are sure, consult with the CIA, or groups which have their noses in the agency's trough. Even foreign policy whiz kid Henry Kissinger took CIA conduit money for an annual summer seminar in international affairs he ran at Harvard. The seminar, which brought third world mandarins together to exchange trade secrets and discuss world issues, got money from the American Friends of the Middle East and the Asia Foundation, both CIA pass-throughs. And then there is Richard Pipes, a Harvard historian, who is a consultant for the American Committee of Liberation, a CIA-riddled group that sends radio broadcasts from Germany, Spain, and Taiwan into the USSR and China. Mr. Pipes says he edits radio scripts for this group, which he says is "a private organization with close ties to a government agency." He also says the group has ties to Radio Free Europe, which is the USIA-CIA propaganda arm headquartered in Munich. And then . . .

Harvard's accessibility to the CIA may have something to do with the disproportionate number of Harvard grads who have occupied key posts in the CIA and its predecessor, the OSS. In addition to Overseer Amory, the following Harvard men occupied key posts in the CIA (most of the others are Ivy League men as well): Archibald Bullock Roosevelt Jr., CIA London Station Chief until 1966; John Adams Bross, CIA Deputy Director; Ray S. Cline, replaced Amory as DDI May 16, 1962; the late Desmond Fitzgerald, Harvard AB and Harvard Law Graduate, was Deputy Director of Plans. Harvard's Coolidge Professor of History William L. Langer went from top posts in the wartime OSS to the State Department, and then back to Harvard from 1954-59 as director of the Russian Research Center. President Kennedy named him to the five-man Federal Intelligence Advisory Board charged with coordinating and supervising the CIA and the rest of the intelligence community.

Harvard's Own CIA Programs

Harvard professors have been active in at least two programs, covertly helped by the CIA, concerned with grooming strategic elites in the third world.

The International Marketing Institute

The IMI is a spin-off and yet a part of the Harvard Business School. It was organized in 1960 by James A. Hagler, one of the Business School's more dynamic faculty members, ostensibly to "increase worldwide understanding of the dynamic aspects of marketing and distribution and to spur greater use of sound marketing practices." Its high-powered training courses for international management elites received grants from the Department of State, AID, the Ford Foundation, and the CIA.

American policymakers use the IMI as a prestigious training ground for what they hope will be an enlightened managerial infrastructure which can make the world safe for American capitalism. Its program consists of seminars, specialized research, and training. It also makes available a stable of globetrotting consultants. In its proposal to the Ford Foundation, IMI stressed that its program for shaping more effective commercial activity and "commercial intelligence" had been discussed with the CIA and apparently had its approval. Between 1963 and 1964, the Independence Foundation of Philadelphia, a CIA conduit operated by Paul Helmuth, a Harvard grad, pumped over a hundred thousand dollars into the IMI.

One of the IMI's most interesting programs was its effort on behalf of women's liberation in Saigon. Well, not quite women's liberation. IMI Director Hagler, in consultation with CIA officials and other government agencies, put together an extraordinary program for training Vietnamese women in managerial techniques.

In December 1966, Hagler applied to and received $40,000 from the CIA's Asia Foundation for some of the expenses connected with the largely AID funded program. In his proposal to the Asia Foundation, he outlined how Harvard's managerial skills could be put to the service of American imperialism.

The IMI's program in Vietnam was similar to the programs it conducted elsewhere in the "developing" world. At all times the objectives, given official sanction by the Harvard Business School, remained the same: (1) to train a managerial class wise in the ways of private enterprise, and (2) to increase U.S. economic control of foreign markets.

The Trade Union Program
Harvard's work with international trade union leaders was and has been somewhat more insidious. You expect a business school to be propagating business ideologies. But what is a well-endowed business school doing helping to shape and mold working-class leadership?

Harvard's concern with improving international business prospects for the U.S. required some programs aimed at controlling and manipulating the one potential oppositional group which stands in the way. Hence, an international trade union training program was organized under the direction of our old friend George Cabot Lodge. Lodge helped organize both the IMI and the Trade Union Program. That's like training Israeli pilots in the morning and then, in the afternoon, teaching Arab anti-aircraft gunners to misfire. The Trade Union Program was also supported by Dean Hunt's Fund, a pass-through on whose board Lodge also sat.

The two Lodge Business School programs were not the only Harvard activities that had CIA support. A report submitted to the faculty in April 1967 revealed that thirteen programs and activities between 1960 and 1966 were financed to the tune of $456,000 by the CIA.

The money backed programs ranging from the International Seminar of the Summer School (conducted by Henry Kissinger) to the research of individual professors in the departments of Psychology, Philosophy, and Social Relations. Fifteen different conduits supplied the University with funds. The *Harvard Crimson* (April 14, 1967) reported that none of the conduit donations "had strings attached."

The CIA does not have to attach strings to its help to Harvard. The agency's many friends on the faculty and governing bodies know what needs to be done, and are doing it. Or should we say trying.

The Brooks Memo:
On the One Hand, We Need the CIA; On the Other, It Needs Us

> *MEMORANDUM*
> *CONFIDENTIAL*
> TO: Dean Franklin L. Ford
> DATE: March 20, 1967
> FROM: H. Brooks
> SUBJECT: Sutherland and Negotiations with CIA
>
> The technical section of the CIA is continuing to express interest in a research proposal which Sutherland has made to them, and he is continuing negotiations, but with the full realization that the University might ultimately be unwilling to become involved in this sort of contract. If a contract were worked out, the funds would be supplied probably via the Office of Naval Research, so that the contract terms, including freedom of publication, would be the same as for all of our

unclassified contracts with defense agencies, which have been entirely acceptable to the University for so many years. While the CIA would not like the source of funding to be blazoned in the newspapers, the fact that the University was receiving this support would not be considered as classified information, as it was in all the publicized instances of CIA support. Sutherland has made the additional suggestion that the terms of the contract could be written so that the support was for equipment and supplies only and no salaries would be paid from this source. The amount of the contract might be of the order of $100,000.

There is a difficult policy problem involved here. As I told you the other day, none of the conditions of this proposed contract have the features that were so objectionable in the publicized cases. There is no attempt to conceal the source of the funds. The work is unclassified and in an area which is politically neutral. The terms of the contractual agreement will be between the navy and Harvard, and will be a matter of public record. On the other hand, it is true that the work to be done will result in the development of a new technology which will be valuable for intelligence collection and interpretation although not, as far as I can see, in connection with clandestine-type activities. One could argue that since intelligence is a legitimate and accepted function of all governments, there is nothing wrong in principle in having the University accept funds from this source, provided the terms and conditions are the same as for any other unclassified contract. On the other hand, one could argue that in view of the present sensitivities in this regard, the divisive effect within the university community of having it accept support from this source may outweigh any benefits to be derived for a particular educational program. Karl Willenbrock thinks that the University should not get involved at the present time. On the other hand, Arthur Maass and Don Price apparently did not feel there was anything wrong with this, although I don't believe they were discussing the wisdom of the policy as opposed to its morality.

I am laying out all this information before you because you may wish to use it in discussion with some of our colleagues.

HB:ef

Harvard's IMI Writes the CIA's Asia Foundation with a Plan to Save Vietnam

December 9, 1966

Mr. Jack E. James
Deputy Director of Programs
The Asia Foundation
550 Kearny Street
San Francisco, California

Dear Mr. James:

The material accompanying this letter answers most of the "operational" questions but does not go into a sharply focused rationale needed to justify this grant. The following attempts to answer the subtler questions, as well as the obvious.

1. Unlike most countries, Vietnam has a business and institutional infrastructure which is largely under the direction and domination of extremely energetic and capable women. These women are North and South Vietnamese, Chinese, and partially Chinese.
2. We must assume that in the future there will be an armistice, cease-fire, or negotiated peace. When the non-military period occurs, the United States and its allies must be prepared to develop another "showcase" country similar to the economic successes in South Korea, Taiwan, and Japan.

3. The opportunity to prepare a "management base" exists. This is apparent as a result of my trip to Vietnam at the invitation of the Department of State. The proposed project is described in the attached material.

Objectives of the Project
1. The immediate objective, of course, is to professionalize the management techniques of the first group of Vietnamese women. They are all in the top management of their companies or institutions. Experience at Harvard clearly indicates that unless the highest levels of management endorse executive training, it is almost impossible to make any progress at lower levels.
2. With an initial group of fifty women coming to the School, the way will be prepared for the development of management training courses at the University of Saigon and the National Institute of Administration.

Smithies to the Dean: "The Central Intelligence Agency Has Instructed."

Dean Franklin L. Ford
5 University Hall

Dear Franklin:

The Central Intelligence Agency has instructed its consultants to inform their official superiors of this connection with the agency. I hereby inform you of my connection of ten years duration. I wish I could add that there is something subtly interesting or sinister about it.

Yours sincerely,
Arthur Smithies
Master

* * *

Professor Arthur Smithies
Kirkland House

December 13, 1967

Dear Arthur:

Thank you for informing me, in your letter of
December 7, of your connection with the Central
Intelligence Agency.

Sincerely yours,
Franklin L. Ford

THE CIA AND JOURNALISM
Informed Sources (Off the Record)
1977

For about a year, I cowrote a media watch column with the writer Sidney Blumenthal, who later worked as an assistant to President Clinton.

Even before Carl Bernstein's story was published in *Rolling Stone* about how four hundred American journalists worked in one capacity or another for the CIA, newspaper editors were issuing flat denials.

It seems doubtful whether the public will ever know the full extent of CIA-media collusion. This latest revelation received scant interest in the dailies and was consistently downplayed, relegated to back pages. When the Senate Intelligence Committee was looking into these charges over a year ago the papers also dealt with the story skittishly.

The *New York Times* reported on the Bernstein story: "Much of the information in the article about purported relationships between reporters and the agency . . . has been reported previously by the *Times* and other publications." The *Times*, however, dropped its investigation after the CIA assured it that none of its reporters was on the agency payroll.

Actually, Bernstein does present new facts. A dismissive attitude on the part of the *Times* and other publications will not make them evaporate. One of the incidental consequences of Bernstein's story is that the *Times* has renewed its request to the CIA for names of its reporters who might also have served the agency. Does this sound like the *Times* is taking Bernstein seriously? Perhaps its attempts to publicly diminish the significance of his report shows that it does.

The importance of the inquiry is not necessarily to expose the names of CIA-sponsored journalists, but rather to detail the nature of the CIA-media relationship. Names are important, but the name of the game is even more illuminating. The intelligence community is deeply involved in monitoring and influencing the news received by unwary readers. Stories in *Time* and *Newsweek* citing "Western intelligence sources" as the only sources in foreign reports indicates a glimmering of what this relationship is about.

Part of this shrouded CIA-media alliance is rooted in shared perspectives, social worlds, and even expensive lunches. Many top executives float in and out of high government posts—John Chancellor of NBC was chief of the Voice of America, for instance—helping to create a seamless point of view.

Controlling the flow of foreign news is not difficult since it comes to the American audience from a narrow number of sources. "Approximately seventy-five percent of the news most Americans read (and hear) is provided by Associated Press and United Press International," the *Los Angeles Times* reports. Both UPI and AP are listed by Carl Bernstein as being CIA-tainted. Only the hierarchies of these operations and others need be penetrated or influenced in order for the agency game plan to be effective.

Outside direction is probably superfluous since almost all media are already supportive of the essential multinational corporate strategies for dealing with and reporting the world. The *Christian Science Monitor*, in a recent stark example, editorialized in favor of capitalism. "The honorable fruits of capitalism are the best defense of what is still the soundest economic system the world has devised," the paper baldly stated.

This column was originally published by In These Times, *October 26-November 1, 1977.*

part four ENGAGING AFRICA

passions, pieces, and polemics • 1960–2000

AFRICA JOURNAL
1967

White Lives

Durban is their Miami Beach with long sandy beaches, surrounded by giant hotels and apartment buildings, all fronted by black watchmen guarding them against themselves. The town feels like the 1950s even though the Jefferson Airplane is on the radio singing "Somebody to Love." The exchange rate is seventy cents to the dollar although one man tells me dollars are better in the poorer countries. Not here, I ask? Oh no! We are a rich country. [They were rich then, under the "stability" of apartheid rule. In 1998, the rand fell to fifteen cents on the dollar, a disaster.]

I am meeting people, mostly white people. A young man at supper tells me why he hates "Kaffirs." I listen. He got fired for punching one. They are so stupid. He asked one to bring him something. The poor black didn't know what it was. "They work for nothing and live at a low standard. There are bloody millions of them. If I was the government, I'd step in with bloody birth control so quickly." He doesn't like Cape Town. Too many coloreds. He once met a colored girl there; asked her out and then realized she was colored. The most embarrassing moment in his life, he calls it.

I meet Stevenson, a pipe fitter from Holland. A real Dutchman, 28–32, hair slicked back on each side. He has been here four years. He worked most of them in the mines, which for whites really means being a supervisor. Says the Africans earn three dollars a month in the mine. They are from Congo and elsewhere and don't know about money, he claims. They get board and clothes. It is ninety-five degrees underground. I ask him why he doesn't leave.

"For me it's the same all over. The same! I work. Period! Spend it today." He talks about his pleasures. Friday night, boozing and dancing in the Carleton Hotel; Saturday, the Races, Sunday, soccer; Monday, work. He works for Shell. He is impressed with Americans. "Very clever, very efficient," he calls us. His job is tiring although he admits the Africans do much of it.

Two fell off of hundred-foot furnaces and were killed the other day. What? I interrupt at his matter-of-fact detail dropped into a monotone description. Yes, dead, he repeats. One died the day before. "It's always like that," he says with a slight pause. He tells me about his girlfriend. She looks white, he swears, but confides that she doesn't have white registration. You'd be surprised, he chuckles, about how many colored girls have white boyfriends, even husbands. He was caught with a colored girl in Cape Town once. He drew a suspended sentence He then stops and looks at me, changing the subject back to THE subject. "Oh it will come. It has to. I tell you something. I won't be here when it does. Oh no."

[How was I to know that I would be there when it did? Twenty-seven years of pain later. May 10, 1994, Pretoria, when Nelson Mandela is sworn in as President. Baie Dankie Suid Afrika. Thank you South Africa.]

I meet two white girls. I am turned on, until they open their mouths. One says "You don't know our bantu? They haven't a care in the world." The other: "Don't you have apartheid in America? What do you call it—segregation?"

Arithmetic

Cape Town '67
Who is in control, who?
It is the black man says my friend Susan:
75% of the laws are written to keep him in his place.
79.4% of the propaganda explains away his condition.
51% of the neurosis stems from the fear of his wrath.
In short, the country revolves around him. His labor propels it; his passion defines it. The potency of color causes sterility among the colorless. The former are oppressed but the latter suffer. He will be here if anyone is left.

Farewell to the Chief

I am in a church. The village is Groutville, in the countryside where he grew up, was banished, and died in a mysterious accident. His name is Chief Albert Luthuli, president general of the African National Congress, Nobel Prize winner. The church is divided into three sections: native, press, diplomats. Security men all over, all Afrikaner. A handful of whites, mostly foreign guests, the majority blacks, working people. Aisles are filled. There is a black and gold banner of the ANC. Men, some bearded wearing black berets, black ties, white shirts; women in green with black collars. One man stands, his fist clenched in the air, for hours. They are singing African songs. The preacher concludes: "Let us pledge ourselves never to abandon what he struggled for, freedom and equality of his own people in their own land."

Alan Paton, author of *Cry the Beloved Country*, is next. I am scribbling furiously, trying not to miss a word. "I am not allowed by some foolish law to tell you what he said, but I can tell you what he did. He stood up for the rights of his people, for the rights of all people, for the rights of the dispossessed, the poor . . . They took away his chieftanship but he never ceased to be the chief; they took away his freedom, but he never ceased to be free . . . He had a voice like a lion, and because he spoke in a lion's voice, he had to be silenced. The real tragedy, which is the tragedy of us all, is that those great gifts could not be used and that that great voice could not be heard in the service of our great country, South Africa."

The building is sweltering. You can hear army planes circling overhead. The man in the ANC uniform still has his fist up. Everyone is steely quiet. The eyes of the security force dart from face to face. Paton continues: "We shall never reach the solutions we deserve as long as we give in to silence . . . There are some people who think that his life was a failure. Some will think that he went too far; others that he didn't go far enough. The real story of his life was his fortitude. And if you go on, whether you win or lose, you have more success than failure. You keep your own soul. Luthuli lost the world but he kept his soul . . . The sun rises and the sun sets and tomorrow it rises again. Nkosi Sikeli Afrika. God help Africa."

There are other speakers. A young Gatsha Buthelezi bringing greetings from the Zulu king. Margaret Marshall, twenty-two, with long blond hair, represents the National Union of South African Students with eloquence and defiance. And it is here that I see the passion and resolve of the South Africans' struggle. What a privilege to be present, what a historical moment to treasure. With Luthuli dead, the leadership of the ANC passed on to the next generation, to Mandela and his comrades, Mandela who in that moment was just beginning his long prison sentence on Robben Island clear across the country.

To the world, with Luthuli's death, this revolution appeared over; to me, at that moment, in that church, it had just begun again.

Dar Es Salaam, Tanzania

It is the lunch hour. The town will reopen at 2 p.m. And then bake throughout the afternoon. I have spent the day walking on these streets, past the open shops with their Indian merchants and sometimes African assistants, up dirt-caked roads and the occasional sign that asks in English (not Swahili) that people not litter the streets. Unlike Nairobi, this is not a European city. It lacks those pretensions. Its streets are often winding, set at odd diagonals. They also shout at you: Nkrumah Street, a literal revolutionary arcade is lined with offices of the would-be liberators of Southern Africa. The ANC of South Africa; FRELIMO, with its plans to transform Mozambique; ZAPU, envisioning the rebirth of Zimbabwe from the ruins of Rhodesia; and on and on in alphabetical procession. And also as one would expect, the Chinese Association and nearby bookshop featuring every word the Great Helmsman Mao Tse-tung ever wrote.

Yesterday, there was an incident. I had just left the small two-room National Museum with its wall displays of Mr. Stanley's historic expedition to find Dr. Livingtsone, I presume. And also—still even in this land of socialism—charts depicting the brave explorers who came to DISCOVER what many people knew existed anyway. African history here is still being told by colonials. When I left the museum, I walked passed a small nicely groomed house fronted by a big sign and a bigger hope:

ORGANIZATION OF AFRICAN UNITY
LIBERATION COMMITTEE
FOR SOUTHERN AFRICA

I casually photograph the yellow placard as a revolutionary memento. A young man runs up at me and taps my shoulder, saying excitedly there is a man in the bush up the road calling after me. I squint in the sunlight, barely see him, and stroll on. But the chap is insistent, running after me with the news that the man is a policeman, and that I'd better see what he wants. When I get closer, all I can see in the bright sunlight is a very small beard at the tip of a very black face, and only then, a rifle aimed at my head. He is pointing at my camera and asks if I took that picture. He is not amused.

Journal entries, 1967.

FROM A CLOSED FILING CABINET
The Life and Times of the Africa Research Group
1969/1970/1971/1991

I blame it on the CIA.

The Africa Research Group (ARG) was formed as an outgrowth of an investigation I had undertaken as a *Ramparts* magazine reporter to flush out some tentacles of covert U.S. intervention south of the Sahara. It turned out that identifying CIA involvement was simpler than evaluating its underlying political thrust or gauging its impact. This sort of assessment required a fairly sophisticated understanding of African political economy as well as U.S. foreign policy. It was clear that a group effort would be a more productive way of studying this phenomenon than any individual enterprise.

The Africa Research Group was an independent organization with a radical perspective on the impact of imperialism and revolution in Africa. When we organized the group in the fall of 1968, American bombs were falling on Indochina. The founding members were convinced that the policy objectives and strategic interests which led to war in Asia could involve the United States in wars elsewhere in the third world. America's alignments with apartheid and counter-revolutionary forces in Africa seemed to us particularly pernicious and destined to suck us into another explosive confrontation which the American people knew little about and would not support if they did. We saw the overt and covert U.S. interventions in Africa as an international dimension of a racist society which was under attack at home. We decided, as we noted in an original declaration of purpose, to try "to put the problem of African liberation on the map of American political consciousness."

The political crisis and moral outrage provoked by the disclosures of massive covert U.S. involvement in Angola became in one instance a confirmation of the essential validity of the Africa Research Group's prognosis. CBS newscaster Walter Cronkite's introduction to a series of nightly specials about the origins of the "Vietnamlike" intervention recalled concepts and language that our group had advanced years earlier. It was as if history were catching up with us—although the Africa Research Group was no longer around. We had dissolved in 1972, in part out of frustration with the seeming political marginality of our work.

The reports of U.S. involvement in Angola dating back to the early '60s, the fact that the CIA and South Africa found themselves on the same side, for us underscored the importance of this work. The government was pursuing secret policies that we were trying to expose. For example, in this same period, the National Security Council was considering a secret staff study advocating covert intervention and an alliance with the apartheid state. Henry Kissinger's report on southern Africa, prepared for the National Security Council in 1969 proposed a closer alignment with South Africa. That report also postulated that the U.S. had major (although not vital) interests in Angola. The full text of the report was published in England as *The Kissinger Study of Southern Africa* (Spokesman Books).

Since African affairs are barely (and badly) reported in the United States, we felt that research and educational work was needed to arouse interest and inspire action on behalf of Africans struggling to end apartheid, colonialism, and neocolonialism. As college students or graduates ourselves, we sought to fuse our own academic skills and intellectual interests with a political commitment. Our framework was explicitly anti-imperialist: that is, we viewed American intervention in its global framework as the instrument of a small ruling class advancing its own special interests. While this analysis itself is not particularly original, we felt that in the case of Africa it needed a more up-to-date, empirical foundation and a non-rhetorical popularization.

At the outset we found that although millions had been spent on African studies in the United States, very little of it illuminated the growing American penetration of Africa. Despite the involvement of hundreds of American companies and nonprofit organizations on the continent, few writers and researchers had examined their impact. There were more books and monographs available about the "communist threat" than there were about the U.S. presence. So we became pioneers in the uncharted field of imperialist studies. Our first task was developing a research methodology with our own sources of information and an accessible database. This meant a systematic monitoring of published material ranging from American newspapers to specialized reports by corporations; from the publications of African movements and governments to documents exposing the essence of official American thinking. Slowly, the Africa Research Group put together our own files and library with a host of technical studies and reference materials.

We concluded early on that Africans needed this information as much or more than we did. It turned out that there is more information available about Africa in American universities than there is in most African institutions. This form of scientific neocolonialism is one way of fostering dependency and mystifying Africans about the real thrust of U.S. policy. Consequently, we developed our own contacts with progressive African forces and newspapers. We tried to make available material to which they might otherwise have little access. We did what we could to provide material assistance in this form to liberation struggles. For example, we were able to get American scientists to undertake some research on the American-made herbicides which the Portuguese Air Force was using in Angola. The request for this information had come from the Popular Movement for the Liberation of Angola. We helped publicize the cause of African liberation by reprinting and distributing publications and communiqués issued by various movements.

The purpose of all our work was to popularize African issues. We wanted to encourage, if not inspire, political action. I argued in an unpublished working paper prepared for a January 1969 conference of radical researchers that specific information about Africa can have political implications and action consequences. Here was a chance to marry Marx to Malcolm among anti-imperialist whites; and introduce some specific radical political content to a widespread (and extremely co-optable) cultural-psychological interest in Africa among blacks. Synthesis: possible joint action projects and international campaigns.

While these hopes proved somewhat idealistic, the group's work did play a role in a number of campus struggles and anti-corporate fights. Our work did achieve some impact, and as my own CIA files—recently made available to me under the provisions of the Freedom of Information Act—indicate, the CIA was keeping tabs on our work.

The Africa Research Group was best known by what it produced in its four-year existence. The output was prolific: books, pamphlets, reprints, newspaper and magazine articles, leaflets, and posters. The topics ranged from "power structure" studies of African class structure, to more superficial agitational propaganda. Circulated at academic conferences and through the underground press, distributed by mail and through bookstores, these publications stirred some controversies, provoked debate, and provided information which seemed consistently missing in most writings about Africa. In some cases, these materials were translated and printed abroad. In one instance, an ARG exposé triggered banner headlines and a diplomatic flap.

The Africa Research Group was an attempt to forge a radical alternative to conventional styles of intellectual work. We were a diverse group, and most of us were without specialized academic training or research experience. There were about ten of us who formed the core of the organization. Some worked full-time on subsistence salaries raised through the sale of literature, contributions, and small grants. Others were part-timers. A few of our members had studied and taught about Africa. One had been a business consultant; others included a former member of the Peace Corps, a divinity student, a graphic artist, and several journalists. Some were more theoretically oriented than others. We worked closely with a number of academic supporters and at the height of our activity spawned affiliated groups in New York, Washington DC, and the University of California at Santa Barbara.

We were as concerned with how to insure impact for what we wrote as we were with the content itself. Our research projects reflected intensely discussed political priorities, and hence our biases were always quite explicit. Our own interests shifted as the group membership developed. Some of us, for example, were more interested in detailed investigations of U.S. government and private aid programs; others stressed the need to publicize and organize support for the liberation movements in southern Africa.

Some of our work was primarily directed to others in the field of African studies. We published critiques of conservative scholarship and attempted alternative studies in the Marxist tradition. Much of our work aimed at introducing African issues to political activists, and to the public at large. Group members spoke at university forums and political meetings. We helped design high school curricular materials and provided concrete assistance to organizations such as the Polaroid Workers Movement, which was challenging their corporation's involvement in South Africa. The group also took part in demonstrations and often worked with other organizations active in similar regional research, such as the North American Congress on Latin America (NACLA), the Committee of Concerned Asian Scholars (CCAS), and the Middle East Research and Information Project (MERIP).

This rationale and choice of audience had implications for the style and content of our work. We decided early on that we would try to avoid a dry and dull academic style as well as the rhetoric and jargon which had come to typify too many Marxist journals. We tried a more popular approach, integrating graphics, documents, and even cartoons into our publications.

Like many organizations identified with the American New Left, the group sought to abandon a hierarchical and alienating work style. Learning to work collectively was a difficult but positive accomplishment.

A few people had set the group's initial direction, assigning tasks and developing contacts with other people and organizations. This was especially true in my own case and led to resentment, political discussion, and restructuring. Collectivity may have sacrificed efficiency in some areas, but it fostered significant personal and political growth in individual members. Collective writing helped individuals temper their own ego-involvement; it helped group members be self-critical without being self-destructive. It also gave us a method and structure for dealing with each other's work in critical and constructive ways.

Collectivity also had its problems. Group members sought to explain some of them in one draft of the statement released when the group decided to disband in June 1972. "We recognize with hindsight that we emphasized collectivity to an extreme degree. Group decision-making became cumbersome because it was applied at all levels. We let collectivity prevent experimentation with division of labor and undermine individual initiative. By emphasizing process over product, we were never as productive as we hoped to be."

The Africa Research Group disbanded for a number of reasons. Many of the original members had begun to tire of research and educational work. Some were simply burned out. Others wanted to move directly into a more activist type of political engagement. As one group statement put it:

> Research work which is separate from action and organizing can often lead to isolation and academic detachment. In our own group, many of us felt dissatisfied with merely servicing a broad and diffuse audience with information. As the demands for our literature increased, and as mail requests for information became overwhelming, we felt ourselves turning into bureaucrats and found our energy drained away from research and writing. This reinforced our sense of distance from the political realities of America. We decided that this situation was not healthy.

After several years of poorly funded but intellectually and politically charged work, the core of the group began to dissolve. Some of us went into academic life, others into activism, and some, like myself, into journalism and the media. It was a time when the student movement seemed to be sputtering out. Africa had become a symbolic reference for black identity politics more than for political solidarity. By the early '70s, as the war in Vietnam seemed to wane, the student movements of the left began splintering into a subculture. In South Africa activism was suffocated until the students rebelled in Soweto years later in 1976. [That country would not become a democratic state until 1994. With the ARG's dissolution, I took a break from Africa work, although I would return to it periodically as a writer, and then, intensely, as a filmmaker and TV producer in the late '80s and '90s.]

The quiet dissolution of the Africa Research Group did not mark the demise of the work we deemed important. Individual scholars and activists have pursued, amplified, and improved upon the type of "radical" analysis we advocated. In the United States, African studies institutions changed, and publications like *Issue*, linked to the once conservative African Studies Association, opened up to articles like this one. New magazines sprang up, spreading radical ideas about African problems.

Over in England, a group of intellectuals, at least in part encouraged by the ARG's example, began to meet in the early '70s. The *Review of African Political Economy* (RAPE) emerged, publishing the work of Africans, and of non-African Marxists who examined problems of economic underdevelopment and class conflict in an Africa dominated by capitalist relations. The exiled South African writer Ruth First, a close friend of mine, admired ARG and was a moving force in this new journal. In their editorial statement of purpose the *Review* put forth a framework very much in our spirit, which should be a challenge to all serious scholars:

> We must seek to comprehend African reality at a number of levels. We must reject the orthodoxy of bourgeois social science which sees each national economy, state, and society, and often each of their separate problems in isolation; in this view international forces are at most the "context" for national development and never the source of exploitation and dominance. However, we must not simply see Africa as the reflection of imperialism. There is a need to develop theoretical insights into the specificity of the social formation that underdeveloped capitalism gives rise to, in response both to the pre-capitalist history of Africa and to its integration into the international capitalist system. Such an approach sees the dynamic of African societies as a

complex result of internal and external forces which distort and limit the development of the forces of production under capitalism.

Africans themselves are still dealing with these questions and struggling to define their answers. At the same time, the type of intellectual and educational work that the African Research Group attempted remains more urgent than ever. Southern Africa is still destined to explode into a conflict of international dimensions. Africanists who have been studying these issues for years—and who presumably most actively sympathize with African struggles—have a responsibility to educate the American people about the complicity and responsibility of their own government. Liberation is very much on Africa's agenda in this century, and in our lifetimes. Our lives can be enriched—and will at the least be judged—by how we relate to this exciting and historic human drama.

From Issue *(African Studies Association) 1971, updated 1991, 1994.*

Africa Research Group Publications

Some excerpts from the Africa Research Group's work offer the flavor of our approach, collective writing style, and political agenda. The first target of our work was African studies itself—a field of academic inquiry that was all too often a training ground for government specialists, intelligence agencies, and corporations. As we looked into the funding and focus of America's Africanists, we identified them as a tribe unto themselves. While many U.S.-based African research institutes monitored Russia's Africa policy in the name of the Cold War, we decided to monitor them. The result was a study we called *The Extended Family*, which purported to offer a "tribal analysis" of one ideologically twisted branch of international studies. We released the report at the 1969 Montreal convention of the African Studies Association. Some students there cheered—especially black students who were challenging the white domination of the field. But many of the professors became defensive and aggressive, denouncing us as McCarthyites and worse. The pamphlet blended well-documented conclusions with the language of an ideological broadside. It stirred a debate that went on for years within the field.

The pamphlet also stirred some minor controversies by naming institutions and individuals linked to CIA and Pentagon research projects. It also offered a mass of empirical data to show how the specialized African studies programs were coordinated and funded by a relatively small number of foundations and scholars, whose research priorities and brand of liberalism tended to enjoy the government's stamp of approval.

Excerpt From the Extended Family

The African studies industry in the United States is a child of the American empire. It developed to meet the needs of ever-expanding U.S. corporate and governmental penetration of Africa. The industry is managed by an extended family of interconnected and incestuous "experts," who, while living off Africa, serve a system pitted against Africa's needs. They are American social scientists, comfortably ensconced in the institutional architecture of the American intellectual environment. Nurtured by foundation and government grants, they operate under cover of the false neutrality of academic scholarship, which permits them to camouflage their ideological biases and the strategic policy implications of their work.

In the fifteen years or so since the white power structure wholeheartedly "discovered" Africa, these researchers, through well-financed jet-setting safaris, have amassed a mountain of information for filtration through the research apparatus of corporations and government agencies. There it is translated into the languages of consumption or counter-insurgency, or both, and used to formulate strategies aimed at "mobilizing" Africans and controlling their societies. Like the missionaries who "opened up" Africa for subsequent exploitation by a now atrophied colonialism, the West's intellectual missionaries and intelligence-gatherers have, through their research and publishing efforts, training programs, and control over the means of ideology formation, helped shape and perpetuate a new framework of neo-colonial rule and imperialist domination.

The activities of most U.S. African scholars cannot be understood outside of the context of the role they play on behalf of the American Empire. It has become fashionable, for example, to attack U.S. scholars as CIA agents, as covert representatives of the "invisible government." It would be more correct to see them as servants of an "indivisible system" where the source of the funding is less important than the function of the work. African peoples are not unaware of what is going on. There has been a growing chorus of protest against cultural imperialism and ideological penetration, although too often it has lacked a deeper analysis of the strategy of modern imperialism.

From The Extended Family: African Studies in America, *1969–1970*.

MEDIA MYOPIA
1977

Is Soweto a "suburb" of Johannesburg?

Like predators on the veld, journalists are quick to smell blood—and they smell it these days in South Africa. As the increasingly repressive white minority cracks down on the increasingly frustrated black majority, Western reporters are arriving almost daily in Johannesburg. In recent months, all three U.S. television networks have opened bureaus in the troubled country. Media stars like Walter Cronkite and Harry Reasoner have added Soweto and Pretoria to their international itineraries.

South Africa provides the type of neat, cut-and-dried story that American journalists love: four million whites, led by a neo-fascist Afrikaner government, exploiting and degrading eighteen million blacks cooped up in Bantustans and ghettos. Out of this sorry equation comes all the stuff of conventional news: political drama, confrontation, violence.

Predictably, that's how most of the media have covered the story. With a few exceptions—the *New York Times*, the *Washington Post*, and the *Christian Science Monitor* among them— the complexities of South Africa's conflict have escaped or been ignored by the media.

"The South African story has come down the tubes so fast," says Tim Leland, a *Boston Globe* editor who has reported from South Africa, "that the American public has no background information on it. The press, by and large, has not covered it with any sophistication."

Jim Hoagland of the *Washington Post*, who won a Pulitzer Prize in 1971 for his reporting from South Africa, agrees with Leland's assessment. He recalls that during Vice President Mondale's trip to Vienna last spring for talks with South African Prime Minister John Vorster, "Most of the reporters on the plane didn't have a basic understanding of the policy issues or choices. Most of the time they asked questions for purposes of getting a lead, rather than for eliciting information that they could put into context."

This lack of sophistication and understanding has led to a number of serious omissions in U.S. press coverage of South Africa. These omissions fall into four categories and give rise to the charge that crucial aspects of the story are being distorted.

The Reporting On Apartheid
Apartheid is more than just a perverse system of racial discrimination— although it is that with a vengeance. Despite surface similarities, it is not

a South African version of the racial segregation that was practiced for years in the American South. Invariably, correspondents identify apartheid as South Africa's "system of racial separation or segregation," and focus on its most visible practices of racial differentiation and domination. This conveys a simplistic image which obscures an understanding of some of the worst features of apartheid.

At its core, apartheid is an organized and highly structured method of controlling and exploiting black labor. Most American journalists, by and large, have yet to discover and fully report the economic underpinnings of apartheid.

South Africa runs on cheap black labor. More than 200 apartheid laws exist to keep it that way. "These laws, and the system of migrant labor which they are designed to regulate, have long provided the foundation for South Africa's industrial and agricultural development," explains Andrew Silk in an article he wrote for the *Nation* this fall after spending ten months in South Africa. Silk's pieces were among the few to have appeared in the American press that discussed apartheid as an economic system.

By regulating movement and restricting the number of Africans who can live near white areas, the National Party government attempted to tightly monitor and regulate a hideously underpaid and captive workforce. Virtually an entire population was turned into a migrant labor force. An additional series of anti-union laws prevent Africans from organizing to improve their working conditions. Unemployment—now estimated at forty percent of the black South African population—is disguised by shunting workers off to rural "homelands." This is the heart of the "separate development policy," which at present assigns thirteen percent of the land in the republic—the worst land—to eighty-seven percent of the population.

A few reporters, like Silk, have tried to explain this complex system of domination. But most focus instead on the jim crow surface manifestations of apartheid. "It may be because many journalists just don't understand economics," guesses Silk. "After all, the race problem is also a class problem. And because most American journalists are not well-versed in looking at class issues, it's difficult for them to see it. For most of them, the stress has been on covering day-to-day events. They don't understand that a lot of the fervor in South Africa is because of the discontent of a working class."

"Protection of white economic privilege has become perhaps the main product of apartheid," writes Jim Hoagland of the *Washington Post*. Hoagland agrees that this central characteristic of apartheid tends to get lost in the imagery of racist whites against segregated blacks. "The whole economic story," he says, "has not been done well."

A recent overview of apartheid in the *New York Times* by Jim Darnton, for example, began with an anecdote about the first black woman to win a multi-racial beauty contest. The woman was not allowed to stay at the resort hotel in which she had won a vacation. Not until the ninth paragraph of the piece did Darnton explain that it was the exploitation of black labor that led to apartheid laws. He spent three paragraphs discussing these laws, but his emphasis was on how poorly these laws work and how hard they are to enforce. Darnton's piece touched many of the right bases, but it failed to convey the economic foundations of apartheid.

The American Economic and Political Role

Not only have American reporters had problems untangling and explaining the complexities of the South African economic system, they have also failed to grasp the crucial U.S. economic relationship with South Africa.

In recent years, the United States and South Africa have become important trading partners. The U.S. imported nearly a billion dollars of South African exports in 1976, while South Africa imported $1.85 billion worth of American products. Moreover, investments by more than 350 U.S. companies have nearly doubled over the last ten years to nearly $1.7 billion. U.S. banks have an estimated $2 billion in loans outstanding to the South African government. In addition, the U.S. has an important political and economic stake in safeguarding Britain's $7 billion economic investment in South Africa.

While total U.S. economic involvement amounts to only one percent of all U.S. corporate assets abroad, the tie to South Africa is hardly an insignificant one. Yet, the American press has been reluctant to explore these ties or to explain U.S. policy as an outgrowth of this economic relationship.

Opponents of apartheid believe that Western economic involvement helps prop up the South African regime, while enabling multinational corporations to prosper. (In 1974, the return on investment in South Africa was 19.1 percent, compared to a world average of 11 percent.) For years, at the UN and in other forums, African states and black South African organizations have crusaded for economic sanctions against South Africa. They've argued against the view promulgated by the Western powers that foreign investment will ultimately erode apartheid and transform South Africa.

Most press coverage of the economic sanctions debate reflects the U.S. government's view that such sanctions would be counterproductive.

Few newspapers or newsmagazines gave the pro-sanctions African perspective any substantive hearing.

In its report on the UN debate in October, *Time* magazine wrote extensively about the U.S. vote in favor of a mandatory arms embargo, but devoted only one line to the resolution calling for economic sanctions which had been vetoed by the U.S., France, and Great Britain. Such sanctions were dismissed categorically by *Time* as a "step that would have caused real damage not only to South Africa but also to the Western powers and many small nations that trade with it." The *Time* article quoted South African government sources and a prominent white liberal—but no Africans. One week earlier, *Time* articulated its thinking on sanctions in a piece headlined "Embargoes May Sting, but They Don't Really Hurt."

Newsweek's coverage was similar, quoting unnamed economists to the effect that South Africa could withstand economic sanctions. In its October 3 edition, *Newsweek* stated that a world embargo on arms to South Africa was already in effect when, in fact, only a UN resolution for a voluntary ban had been passed.

John Burns of the *New York Times* was one of the few journalists to seek out and report African views—those of a worker in Johannesburg who would be hurt by sanctions but who favored them anyway, and Chief Gatsha Buthelezi, the moderate leader of South Africa's 5.8 million Zulus, who has changed his position and now favors sanctions, as does virtually every other black South African leader. But even Burns' backgrounder of November 6 cited only one reason for sanctions, and then enumerated seven against. His sources were "many economists" and unnamed "white liberals."

One of the few mildly dissenting views in an American newspaper appeared in the last paragraph of reporter David Ottaway's news analysis in the *Washington Post* of October 28. In an article devoted to explaining why an arms embargo was too late, he noted that "More effective measures against South Africa would be such things as an embargo on loans and other economic steps. The (South African) economy is already in a recession and facing an eleven percent inflation rate, so this sector is more vulnerable than the country's military establishment." On the same day, the *Post* carried a column by Stephen S. Rosenfeld, writing from Johannesburg. Rosenfeld favorably quoted the views of white industrialist Harry Oppenheimer, who argued that the U.S. should pressure South Africa with understanding. Rosenfeld also criticized the one man, one vote standard as "alien to the Afrikaners and, I believe, to many South African blacks." No South African blacks were cited.

Few papers explored what other economic options, short of a total U.S. embargo, might be employed to exercise leverage on the South African government. In mid-November, the Carter administration hinted that it was considering other outside economic pressure. But such measures—including a possible cutoff of Export-Import Bank credit, or limits on future investment—were hardly discussed in the press. It seems as though the media was waiting for the government to act so that it might react.

The issue of economic sanctions only began to receive publicity after President Carter was reported to be considering supporting them, says Mzonke Xuza, a staff member of South Africa's Pan Africanist Congress (PAC) office at the United Nations. "It is as if the whole issue had to be made legitimate by white leaders before the press will seriously discuss our demands. For months, we have been trying to get our position on this out to the press, but they refused to print it. Yet, after Carter's press conference which raised this issue, we saw the television crews come crawling around us, with their people asking if we didn't think this was a positive step."

Reed Kramer, who edits *Africa News*, an alternative news service published in Durham, North Carolina, believes that "sanctions are considered a non-issue in the press because it is considered an unrealistic demand." Kramer agrees that there is not much press coverage about the strategic role American investment plays in such key economic sectors as oil, computers, electronics, auto, rubber, and communications. "What coverage there is," he says, "usually focuses on employment practices of U.S. companies rather than on how important U.S. investment, trade, and bank loans are to the South African economy."

"The British press, which is consistently more informative about South Africa than the American press, is also disarmingly frank about the role that self-interest plays in its rejection of sanctions," says Reverend Kenneth Carstens, a white South African exile who directs the North American branch of the International Defense and Aid Fund. "But your government tends to camouflage the significance of your trade and investment, and the press reflects this."

Jennifer Davis, research director of the American Committee on Africa, echoes this view. "I find press people very uncritical of government sources," she says. "They seldom consult groups like ours, perhaps because the conclusions of our studies challenge U.S. government policy and the impact of the corporations."

Davis was critical of the questioning of President Carter during his October 27 press conference, when he announced U.S. support for a UN arms embargo. "The reporters didn't even know what to ask," she says, "and the questions they did ask showed unfamiliarity with the issue."

During the press conference, ABC's Anne Compton asked Carter if he was worried about dictating domestic policy to South Africa. In his response, Carter denied that the U.S. was meddling, and then made a revealing statement about the need for the U.S. "to decide when we should and should not invest in another country." But Carter's opening provoked no follow-up questions on how the government could or might regulate investment.

A few newspapers have carried informative reports on U.S. economic involvement in South Africa. The *Christian Science Monitor*, whose South African reporting frequently outclasses its competitors', carried a well-researched report by Harry Ellis the day after Carter's October 27 press conference.

Ellis's article disclosed that American steel and chemical industries are dependent on South African chromite ore and other metals. The paper also suggested that U.S. exports to South Africa have grown so rapidly that 50,000 jobs could be affected if trade were cut off.

One story conspicuous by its absence from American papers was covered by the *Rand Daily Mail*. In late September, South Africa's Prime Minister John Vorster was given a standing ovation by 600 guests at a dinner of the American Businessmen's Luncheon Club in Johannesburg. The speech that drew so much applause was a blistering attack on U.S. "meddling" in South Africa.

Reporting Black South Africa

The American press has consistently slighted the black resistance movement in South Africa. "I don't think they want to show that there is a struggle going on," says Thami Mlabiso, the UN representative of South Africa's African National Congress, the country's oldest liberation movement. "The uprising of *our* people has been portrayed as a riot, or a series of riots. This has presented a distorted picture of the whole black struggle."

A survey of some press coverage during the Soweto rebellion in June 1976 bears out this charge. In its front page headline and lead paragraph on June 17, 1976, the day after the township erupted, the *New York Times* called the protests against the compulsory teaching of the Afrikaans language in African schools a "race riot." A day later, a *Times* editorial spoke of "outbursts of racial hatred just ten miles from Johannesburg."

Newsweek reported that, "In the days that followed, black students and many adults roamed through the streets, burning buildings, wrecking buses, and trying to find and kill whites." Curiously, a backgrounder on Soweto, written by John Burns and carried by the *Times* on June 17, indicated that white Americans received a friendlier reception in Soweto than in Harlem.

Time magazine, like many newspapers, featured more information from government sources than from blacks in its "riot" reports. In trying to explain who initiated the violence, the newsmagazine noted that police officials *insisted* that they fired in self-defense, while some witnesses (in this case black reporters) *claimed* that police had provoked the conflict.

"Exactly how and why a student protest became a killer riot may not be known until the conclusion of an elaborate inquiry that will be carried out by Justus Petrus Cille, Judge President of the Transvaal," intoned *Time*, not bothering to note that blacks scoffed at an investigation headed up by a pro-apartheid Afrikaner.

As for black viewpoints on the Soweto events, few publications knew where to turn. *Newsweek* featured an interview with the aging, white liberal writer, Alan Paton, hardly a spokesman for the new generation of militant blacks.

Michael Kaufman of the *New York Times* could find no spokesman at all by June 24, complaining that there were no black South African groups to articulate "the feelings and motives of mobs and looters . . . There are no counterparts to the National Association for the Advancement of Colored People, or the Congress of Racial Equality. There are no Malcolm Xs or Sonny Carsons or James Baldwins who can publicly speak for the street people." Kaufman was apparently not able to locate student leaders who were communicating quite well with their own people.

Four days later, Kaufman visited Soweto to interview witnesses who contradicted the thrust of many earlier reports by suggesting that African violence had an organized political character and was directed largely against government buildings, banks, and other symbols of the apartheid system. No residents expressed "get whitey" attitudes.

The *Washington Post*'s Jim Hoagland, whose in-depth pieces in the late fall of 1976 did much to explain the dynamics of the Soweto uprising, agrees that the press did an inadequate job covering Soweto. "When I arrived in late October, I realized that it had been an essentially unreported story. Part of the problem was vocabulary. It may not be accurate to call what happened riots. That in itself conveys a false impression. I am not criticizing people on day one or day two—you know, there were physical problems, and access to

Soweto was blocked. But there was no follow-up. I asked wire-service people if they had ever gone into Soweto, but they hadn't." Hoagland also noted that no American newspapers, to his knowledge, employed black stringers who might have had greater access to the townships.

"I remember when the police riots first rocked Soweto," recalls *Africa News'* Tami Holzman. "Robin Wright of CBS had her cameras behind the police lines, reporting on wisps of smoke rising above Soweto. We had contacts in the township and were able to telephone people directly to get their eyewitness accounts. Other news outlets could have done the same thing, but they tend to have more contacts among whites than among the country's black people."

Holzman also criticized the media for referring to Soweto, the largest urban concentration of blacks in all of Africa, as a "suburb of Johannesburg."

"You can hardly call it a suburb," agrees James Thomson, curator of Harvard's Nieman Foundation and a one-time South African correspondent. "It's much more like a concentration camp or an Indian reservation. The images of South Africa, as conveyed to an American audience in 'language they can understand,' can be obscenely inaccurate."

The Liberation Movements

South Africa's liberation struggle did not start or end with the Soweto uprising or with the death of Steve Biko. A bitter fight against white domination has been underway for many decades.

In 1960, two of the country's principal black organizations, the African National Congress (ANC) and the Pan Africanist Congress (PAC), were banned, their leaders arrested, and many of their most militant members driven into exile. These two movements are now involved in organizing underground actions against the apartheid system. Both groups train guerrillas and claim credit for an escalating series of skirmishes, acts of sabotage, and guerrilla attacks inside South Africa. These actions have led to a series of trials throughout the country, few of which have been reported on.

Both movements maintain representatives at the UN and send delegates to third-world conferences. They issue publications and release position papers on a variety of South African questions. For some reason, perhaps because their approach is thought to be too radical, their political perspective is seldom acknowledged in the American press.

This failure to report on black liberation movements might be rooted in the structure of contacts that American correspondents have in South Africa. Most U.S. journalists are middle-class whites with liberal sympathies who tend to seek out their counterparts in South Africa. Thus, a few white South African liberals, who are relatively ineffectual politically in their own country, often receive inordinate attention in the American press. Until recently, only a handful of blacks were part of this elite group, and usually they were people who were considered "moderates."

"Take Steve Biko," says the American Committee on Africa's Jennifer Davis. "They made a fuss about him when he was dead, but barely covered what he actually stood for when he was alive. Perhaps because he wasn't, in fact 'moderate' enough to their terms."

If the press doesn't do a satisfactory job of covering black South Africa, its stance toward the country's white minority is schizophrenic. Despite a clearly pervasive anti-apartheid bias, the dictates of professional neutrality often appear to lead to reports which equate the Afrikaner position with majority claims.

One recent example of this was an October 24 broadcast by ABC's Harry Reasoner from a white South African farm. Reasoner interviewed an Afrikaner who was pictured as "honestly paternalistic" and quite sophisticated (he "quotes Shakespeare"). Of the Afrikaner, who employs thirteen black men, Reasoner said, "He would say his men are happy and he's probably right."

This type of all-too-common reporting reinforces the notion that the South African situation can be boiled down to a tragic clash of competing nationalisms, each with its own legitimate claims.

"If you are able to write a story which 'balances' these viewpoints, you miss the point," says Robert Maynard, formerly the only black national correspondent for the *Washington Post*. "And a lot of journalists are missing the point."

Improving Press Coverage

How can press coverage of South Africa be improved?

1. Better briefings for correspondents.
"I spent a year studying at Columbia University before I went to South Africa," says the *Post's* Jim Hoagland. "It is essential that reporters do more reading."
2. More utilization of South African journalists and stringers.

The *Boston Globe* maintains an exchange program with Johannesburg's *Rand Daily Mail*, which suggests the possibility of more collaboration between American newspapers and South African or British journalists, whose reporting is often more in touch with black aspirations.

3. More interaction with the black press in South Africa.

Harvard's Nieman Foundation has a long history of sponsoring visits by South African journalists, although it was only in recent years that blacks became fellows. Two great South African writers, Lewis Nkosi and the late Nat Nakasa, were among them. Percy Qoboza is the most prominent South African Nieman alumnus. The United States-South Africa Leader Exchange Program has financed other black reporters as interns on American papers. Perhaps when black Africans are working for American newspapers they can have a role in coverage.

4. Consulting specialized sources and news services.

Media outlets need to be made more aware of specialized African publications and should consider subscribing to *Africa News*, a professionally written, alternative news service in Durham, North Carolina. The research departments of such institutions as the American Committee on Africa, which has a wide range of academic resources and contacts in the African diplomatic community, should be consulted more regularly. Paul Irish, ACOA's associate director, says that the only media outlets which regularly tap the group's expertise are the alternative press, college papers, and some broadcast outlets such as Black Mutual Network News.

5. A team approach to coverage.

Newspapers often don't effectively coordinate their stateside coverage on a particular issue with the work of their foreign correspondent. As a result, coverage often lacks cohesion. Any serious investigative reporting about U.S. corporations in South Africa, for example, would require interviews and research in both South Africa and the United States.

6. Recognizing the liberation movements.

The ANC and PAC are often major sources of information about underground activity in South Africa. It's about time the U.S. press recognized their existence.

Implementing these six suggestions will hardly transform the nature of the American press, but it might help some news outlets improve their deeply flawed coverage of the escalating crisis in Southern Africa.

Writing in this magazine at the end of the Vietnam War, Frances

Fitzgerald said, "After fifteen years of reporting the war in Indochina, the news organizations appear to have learned almost nothing, and their policies to have changed rather less than Henry Kissinger's." Will a similarly harsh indictment be necessary in the aftermath of the war in South Africa that seems on its way?

This article originally appeared in MORE, *December 1977.*

VISITING THE NEW SOUTH AFRICA
1996/1999

When I was finally permitted to revisit South Africa in November 1990, I was only allowed to stay for ten days with the proviso that I do no reporting. When I handed over my passport for inspection at the airport, little men, all white, came running to question my motives for being there. My name must have been on some list that demanded closer scrutiny. I was relieved to be let in after an exhausting sixteen-hour flight.

In February 1996, I breezed right through. No one in authority seemed at all interested in my history of hostility to the old regime. All the immigration officers, now black and white, wanted to talk about was the victory of "Bafana, Bafana," the national football team that has just won the all-Africa soccer cup.

I was met at the airport by a white driver with a white Mercedes, a status symbol, no doubt, and welcomed to the country in a manner to which I had never been accustomed. I was back at the invitation of MNET, the pay cable TV station, to promote a documentary I had directed on a reunion a year earlier on Robben Island, the prison where Nelson Mandela and other political prisoners had spent so many years. That event was probably unprecedented in history—1,250 former convicts returning to the place of their incarceration for a reunion and as a gesture of reconciliation. Even the victims of apartheid wanted to confront their past and move beyond it.

The film *Prisoners of Hope* was shot in just three days on a slim budget as an Anant Singh production. Anant, the country's leading black film producer with such credits as *Sarafina* and *Cry the Beloved Country*, wanted to document the event. Barbara Kopple, who had won two Academy Awards for documentaries, came with me and directed one camera. MNET had agreed to screen the "doccie," as South Africans call documentaries, on the sixth anniversary of Mandela's historic release from prison.

As we traveled to that prison, you had the feeling of being part of the wave of liberation, a force of history that had overthrown an evil system. The victims had become victors. The new South Africa had arrived, and was destined to succeed in a world where the miracle of a peaceful transformation had turned the country into a successful model.

I wanted desperately for that to be true, but as I looked around, and spoke with graduates of the long anti-apartheid struggle, new questions and concerns emerged. I would return to South Africa in '96 and '98, and of course was following developments in the South African press, which is easily accessed through the Internet. In 1998, I also covered Mandela's farewell visit to the United States, traveling with him to the White House and Capitol Hill when he was lionized as a real lion king should be, by American institutions which for years ignored and demonized him. (One amusing moment on the trip was my first encounter with President Mandela in two years. He walked over to me, smiled, put out his hand, asking: "Remember me?")

Even though I have made several films with and about him, I know that he had by then become a titular head of state, an icon on the top of a society that was trapped in a vise of forces larger than itself. Mandela spoke often of the need to transform South Africa, but transformation is easier said than done, especially in a global economy in which all emerging markets play a secondary and subordinate role. I haven't studied all the economic issues closely, but the people who have are not optimistic. The gap between the rich and the poor inside South Africa has broadened, not narrowed. I documented that in a film about globalization and human rights that reported on speculators in Europe who drove down the price of gold in hopes of making a quick profit leading to massive unemployment in the mining industry. One hundred and fifty thousand workers were affected.

These are not the issues that most American journalists write about. South Africa tends to get in the news these days with stories about crime and violence or the drama of the Truth and Reconciliation Commission, one of whose hearings I attended. Yet the post-apartheid system is ushering in a deeper conflict that demands attention. Hein Marais, a respected political journalist, writes about this in his sophisticated analysis of the structural issues in a must-read book, *South Africa: The Limits to Change* (Zed Books). "The key objective of the liberation struggle became the seizure of state power in order to work its levers in the interests of the majority," he explains. "Of course, this did not happen. Instead of seizing power, the democratic movement negotiated its partial transfer. Instead of taking over and transforming the state, the movement found itself assimilated into it."

"What has changed," complains the Australian-born, British-based journalist John Pilger in his new book *Hidden Agendas*, "is the inclusion of a small group of blacks into this masonry, a process of co-optation that was well underway during the latter, 'reformist' years of apartheid. This has allowed foreign and South African companies to use black faces to gain access to the new political establishment." This is called black empowerment—but it is not clear if black people as a whole are benefiting, or only a tiny upwardly mobile elite. Pilger, who spent years covering the struggle, says the government's neo-liberal macroeconomic policies are betraying the poor.

Larger forces of free market "liberalization" are at work at the same time, undercutting the government's reconstruction and development plan which had been, until it was dropped, central to its nation-building strategy. The question is: Will privatization advance that strategy or cripple it? The "logic" of the marketplace invariably insists that citizens be treated only as consumers. And when you are living in desperate poverty, even that status is not within reach. In this world of the so-called "free market," commercial values tend to rule, and nothing is free. Can you transform a society by relying on institutions that reinforce the status quo? Lurking in the background are the international players, the Goliaths of globalization, who want to get a foothold in a market long closed to them thanks to apartheid laws and sanctions.

New York Times editor Joseph Lelyveld, who wrote a Pulitzer Prize–winning book on South Africa some years ago, recently returned and shared his impressions with a magazine published by the Institute of Advanced Journalism at Wits University in Johannesburg: " . . . the mood of the South African press ought to be buoyant . . . bubbling with excitement and new-found possibilities...Instead...the mood seems to be anxious, perhaps a little sour. The new leadership...isn't happy with its coverage in the press. It thinks its accomplishments are being played down, even overlooked; its problems magnified; its serious ambitions for social justice underdeveloped."

He is right—they do feel that way. And they are often right to feel it. Much of the mainstream media in South Africa still reflects the interests of the white upper-class elite, but bashing the press doesn't help. The government's own lack of leadership and clarity about its strategy, or candor about articulating it, often compounds the problem. There seems to be a lack of consciousness and vision on this question. Economic realities do need to be examined more openly, with more debate and disclosure by the ANC and the larger movement it created.

And the truth is, these issues don't get discussed fully in the local media. The American freelance investigative journalist Jeff Stein, who recently visited newsrooms in South Africa, toured the South African Broadcast Corporation, concluding afterwards that there was very little investigative reporting going on. He said that the journalists he met were satisfied to get information via the fax machine and showed little desire to look for alternative angles and more in-depth explanations. He blamed it on the legacy of apartheid. For all South Africans, the past is still present, or as James Baldwin once put it: "People are trapped in history and history is trapped in them."

There may be a deeper corruption of the spirit going on as South Africans who want more fundamental change begin recognizing that they are also trapped in a world economic system that favors the rich countries over the poor, and is, despite Western rhetoric and occasional praise, investing relatively little in the country's new democracy and economy.

I was told that in 1998, when South Africa's finance minister visited the IMF-World Bank conference in Washington, there was little interest in his delegation's proposals for reforms that might promote more equity in the financial relationships between emerging economies and the more developed ones. When told about the legacy of apartheid, a prominent international financial official reportedly said dismissively, "that was a long time ago."

What I see as a "consciousness gap" may also be reflection of a much deeper gap that is reinforcing a battle between two economic visions of the country's future—one pushed by business, the other by labor. That debate is central to South Africa's future.

In April 1996, two months after the South African Broadcasting Corporation launch, the organizations representing the country's workers released a study arguing that two years after the arrival of majority rule, gross inequalities remain, with economic power and high incomes favoring whites by a large margin.

"As the white population had to give up its monopoly of political power in order to usher in the new democracy, so the economic elite should now be challenged to share the wealth and resources of our country to the benefit of all," argues a report on "Social Equity and Job Creation."

An independent study by Pretoria's Human Services Research Council confirmed their case, revealing that the gap between the total income of the thirteen percent of the population who are white and the eighty-seven percent of the country's forty-one million people who are not white is the largest in the world. Sam Shilowa, then leader of the Confederation of South African Trade Union (COSATU) said, "Under the captains of capital our economic ship in sinking. We need to shift the emphasis." He was referring to an unemployment rate that hovers around forty percent.

Business is trying to shift the emphasis too, with demands for a two-tiered system which would create a deregulated, essentially union-free, labor-intensive market to function alongside the present "high wage, low employment sector."

COSATU rejects this, arguing that already there is an enormous difference between salaries received by workers—the average was $73 a week—while directors at the stock exchange take home $17,000 a month. Top executives in South Africa receive giant salary hikes while workers are being cut back or laid off.

So, South Africa, which burst onto the world stage as a racial clash, is rapidly becoming a class and economic conflict

The business community is pushing for a "well-handled privatization program which would serve as a performance catalyst for the economy and help government escape the looming debt trap." The unions want to go slow and oppose total privatization. This issue has surfaced in the telecommunications area, where the country's main phone company, Telkom, is being privatized. Industry wanted it done quickly while the former Minister Pallo Jordan, still an independent Marxist, wanted the process to move more slowly. Newspapers reported that President Mandela was unhappy with his inclination to placate the unions more than the company. Jordan was later fired from his post—for a number of reasons—but then reappointed to the cabinet as environment minister.

For many who worked in and for the struggle, there is an inevitable sense of disillusion, even disorientation. When that happens, some get cynical, and others turn on their past and themselves. That's what produces defections and conversions to the other side. Many more stay the course, still believing, but in a way that is more understanding of the need for compromises and deferred gratification. Others just tune out and turn off to all politics.

Perhaps expectations, including my own, are too high. Maybe it is just not realistic to expect everything to change in a few short years. This is also an age of cynicism, and, alas, of retrenchment, when "winning" may mean just being able to get up to fight another day. Multinational corporate power seems resurgent in so many parts of the world, so perhaps it is enough that South Africa is even there, keeping hope alive in its own way, even surprising us again and again. When one sees all the other conflicts tearing African states apart, South Africa looks very advanced.

In April 1996, the weekly *Namibian* carried an article about an autobiographical novel by Pepetela, the nom de guerre of an Angolan freedom fighter. It's about the liberation war and its discontents. It includes a fictionalized but well-imagined exchange between a guerrilla commander and a commissar of the new revolutionary government.

The guerrilla is speaking: "We don't share the same ideas. You are the machine type. I am the type who can never belong to the machine . . . what I want you to understand is that the revolution we are making is half the revolution I want. But is it all that is possible? I know my limits and the country's limits. My role is to contribute to this half-revolution. So I go to the end in the knowledge that in relation to the ideal I have set for myself, my action is half useless, or rather half useful."

For many years, I considered myself a mole in another machine, the media machine. I tried to use it to bring these kinds of issues to public attention. In relation to the ideal I have set for myself, I am not even halfway there. On some days I feel I am getting around the contradictions of change; on others, they are constraining and overwhelming me. I traveled 10,000 miles, halfway around the world, to visit the new South Africa. What I found, in part, was an echo of the questions I keep asking myself and struggling to answer right here, even though the journalist in me tells me there are no answers, only more questions.

In the end I have to agree with my Angolan colleague: a "half a revolution" is probably better than none.

Being "half useful" does have some satisfactions.

February 1999. Parts of this essay originally appeared in Z *Magazine July/August 1996.*

MBEKI'S MUDDLE
South Africa's AIDS Debate
2000

Durban, South Africa, May 10, 2000
What was Mbeki going to say? That's what the press and the crowd packed into the Kingsmead cricket stadium were buzzing about as they waited on May 9 under an African sky threatening rain for South Africa's second democratically elected President Thabo Mbeki to address the opening ceremony of the thirteenth international AIDS conference.

The ten thousand strong AIDS "community" had been outraged by earlier comments attributed to the head of state now hosting the first world AIDS meeting ever held in a non-Western country. Was Mbeki with them or against them? It was a question that grew out of a simmering controversy that began a month earlier when the South African president spent a few nights conducting personal research on the Internet. It led him to the views of a handful of dissident doctors and researchers who had been challenging the conventional scientific wisdom about the origins of the AIDS virus for years.

Mbeki quickly began wondering aloud if South Africa's AIDS fighting program was on the right track. Staring down the barrel of drug costs that could bankrupt his treasury and plans for economic development, he provoked a debate about the proper strategies to pursue that is still reverberating globally.

Critics quickly elevated his stance into a heresy after he invited some of those dissidents to take part in a presidential advisory panel (which also included many mainstream researchers.) The thirty-member group was charged with investigating some critical issues, including the accuracy of AIDS tests, the safety of certain highly toxic viral drugs like AZT, which has been relatively effective in blocking transmission of the disease from mother to child, and the charged issue of what causes AIDS. Does HIV lead to AIDS, as most scientists insist, or are there other causes and contributing factors? It will make its report at the end of the year.

Mbeki never openly denied an HIV-Aids link, but his aggressively inquiring attitude appeared to many as if that's what he was doing. Such questioning was viewed as a distraction, evidence that he was in denial about an infection that the UN says is present in ten percent of the country's population, or some 4.2 million people, more than in any other comparable country.
For daring to challenge the consensus, Mbeki fell, in the words of a high-level

White House AIDS official I spoke with, "off the program." Soon he turned into a pariah and subject for ridicule in the world press, trashed by *60 Minutes* in the U.S. and criticized by one of South Africa's leading intellectuals, Dr. Mamphela Ramphele, for "irresponsibility bordering on criminality." Five thousand researchers and scientists worldwide issued a "Durban Declaration" to rebuke him, insisting that HIV causes AIDS, full stop. End of story. His defensive press secretary dismissed their statement as fit for the "dustbin." Local political pressure was then brought to bear on those behind the declaration to cancel a planned press conference that could turn embarrassing. Feelings polarized. Over coffee in my hotel, an HIV-positive ACT-UP militant from Brooklyn, New York, snarled, "Mbeki should be impeached and arrested."

Later he would join a small chorus of activists who booed and chanted at the president when he was introduced as part of a televised gala extravaganza that included a stage show, musical numbers, dance routines, scores of African drummers, and fireworks that rivaled what I had just seen in New York on July 4.

I have known and respected Thabo Mbeki for over thirty years. I have reported on him as an ambitious but pragmatic politician more comfortable in the mainstream than the margins. He never was a bomb thrower of any kind, and has been a centrist, not a leftist. Mbeki's whole career has been marked by consensus building, not making waves. I think he is sincere and brave to pursue his inquiry and stand by his views. At the same time, Mbeki is obviously on the defensive, and seemingly unable to understand why he is losing sympathizers like myself on this issue—I, who thought he was being picked on unfairly until I came here.

I had last seen him at his own inauguration in South Africa a year earlier. (I was one of his least visible foreign guests; Libya's Khadaffi was the best known.) At that time he spoke of his hopes for an African Renaissance, after being elected by a bigger majority than the one that had put Nelson Mandela into power five years earlier. The event was a celebration of a peaceful transition of power; a sign that a new, well-educated generation had taken over. Mbeki had been the darling of South Africa's business community for years, a champion of the type of neo-liberal economics that pleases cheerleaders for globalization. A close friend of the Clinton Administration, Mbeki was considered a man "we" could work with.

After laboring for years in Mandela's shadow, it was now his turn at bat.

But this AIDS controversy threatens to shred an image carefully woven over decades in exile and at the top levels of the ANC command. Unlike Mandela, the global icon whose charisma could often be mesmerizing, Mbeki is given to more studied scholarly pronouncements. Where Mandela combined moral appeals with legalistic precision, Mbeki is more the pipe-smoking intellectual, known for tough strategic thinking and hard-line backroom political horse-trading. More importantly, whereas Mandela, a tall man, was known for bringing people together, Mbeki, a far shorter one, now seems to be driving them apart.

Why? He has never been known as a leader led by emotions, ideologies, or irrationality. Mbeki's successes in the past were due to his unfailing ability to size up a situation, and neutralize potential enemies.

But on this issue, at least, he seems to have blown it—and for reasons that are still being hotly debated and speculated upon. At an event aimed at breaking "the silence," this president stirred a noisy debate, not about AIDS, but about his own ideas.

When Mbeki bounded to the stage, the crowd hushed, not sure of what to expect. Even ACT-UP quieted down. But those who wanted him to disavow his earlier concerns would soon be disappointed.

First, Mbeki welcomed the delegates and acknowledged the conference's importance. But then, when he appealed for tolerance for other points of view, he was talking, unmistakably, about his own. "The question which I and the government raised was akin to criminal and genocidal misconduct," Mbeki complained. He assured the delegates and those watching at home that South Africa is deeply concerned with HIV-AIDS and is committed to "a national action plan," a plan incidentally premised on the assumption that HIV is a cause of AIDS. He certainly was not in denial nor oblivious to the issue.

Mbeki acknowledged the health catastrophe facing Africa. But then took a turn that left sections of the audience stunned. Instead of focusing on AIDS, he delivered a lecture calling poverty Africa's biggest killer. "We cannot blame everything on a single virus," Mbeki said. "Poverty is the underlying cause of reduced life expectancy, handicap, disability, starvation, mental illness, suicide, family disintegration, and substance abuse."

Quoting the World Health Organization, he argued that disparities in wealth in the world were behind Africa's affliction, as that region of the world suffering the most with an estimated twenty-three-plus million people targeted for death. Mbeki refused to buy the idea that a single virus with a single cause could be responsible for the high number of deaths attributed to AIDS. Poverty, and the diseases and malnutrition that accompany it, is the world's biggest killer, he argued, and has rendered the continent so susceptible. The endemic poverty feeds the AIDS pandemic, Mbeki said, weakening individual immune systems on the one hand, and then making it impossible for countries such as his to afford expensive anti-viral drug therapies now used widely in the West.

He is not totally wrong on these points, nor is this a new issue for him. I remember covering Mbeki when he keynoted a conference on the grinding poverty in South Africa ten years ago at Duke University. He was there to endorse a well-documented study by Mamphela Rampele and others showing how deadly economic gaps in South Africa were the source of national misery, and apartheid's principal legacy. Yet today, poverty expert Dr. Rampele is on one side of the AIDS debate here, and Mbeki on the other.

He is not wrong in his desire to explore all options to fight AIDS, to insure affordable drugs and an approach that recognizes the social and economic nature of a crisis that cannot be solved just with the magic of medicine. Pioneering AIDS scholars like Jonathan Mann had made that point clearly in their seminal writings. The deprivation of human rights and the marginalization of people have helped fuel this global public health emergency. As Albina du Bosrouvray, a philanthropist behind the FXB foundation, once active in backing Mann and now supporting projects to help AIDS orphans, put it in an Op-Ed in a Durban newspaper: "An overdue discussion about the global dangers of the HIV-AIDS pandemic is slowly emerging."

Mbeki's speech—however valid many of its observations may be—went over like a lead balloon. "I was hoping and praying that he would find a way to gracefully back out of this madness," African-American AIDS activist Phil Watson told the *Mercury*, a local paper. "The house is on fire, and Mr. Mbeki is sitting around trying to decide whether a lighter or a match started it. He talks about a plan. He doesn't talk about action."

The next day, an eloquent response was heard from conference keynoter, South African judge Edwin Cameron, himself HIV-positive, who lashed out at the president for creating "an air of unbelief amongst scientists, confusion amongst those at risk of HIV, and consternation amongst AIDS workers." He blasted Mbeki's government for not doing enough to treat and support those suffering from AIDS. Five thousand babies a day, he charged, are born "unnecessarily" with HIV because of the government's refusal to provide drug interventions.

Mbeki's response to this furor was to play it down and reiterate that vigorous debate is good. "After fifteen years, we've still no solution. Nobody has come up with a cure, so I think it is important that everyone should be listened to," he said.

This flap reminded me of an earlier episode in South African history, also involving a speech by a South African president in Durban. It involved Mbeki's long-time enemy P.W. Botha, who had also come to this city on the Indian Ocean to deliver a highly anticipated speech, back in 1989, when he was expected to end apartheid with a "crossing of the Rubicon" address. Botha blew it then too, refusing to satisfy world opinion. He was later ousted by members of his own party.

Thabo Mbeki is alienating many of his own supporters by his peculiarly intellectualized approach. Hours before his speech, a march led by AIDS sufferers in the streets of Durban demanded access to treatment from the government and lower drug prices from the giant pharmaceutical companies. Mbeki was criticized openly in a fiery speech by Winnie Mandela, who is a fellow member of the ANC and a member of Parliament. People who spent decades marching against white governments were now marching against a black-led one they had elected.

This fight over AIDS issues mirrors other cleavages and discontents in South Africa. Whatever honeymoon the ANC may have enjoyed under Mandela is long gone. There is anger and resentment about unchanging realities, a slumping economy, and a government that says many of the right things but has serious problems delivering services.

There are intriguing and contradictory theories that purport to explain Mbeki's stance. He is an Africanist, some say, contemptuous of being told what to do by arrogant white westerners who have failed to stop the pandemic. He is just stubborn, say others, unwilling to concede his errors. Still others argue that Mbeki will bankrupt his country if he starts importing drugs that are so expensive to purchase and perhaps even impossible to administer, given the poor health infrastructure, and so he is right to look for alternatives.

There is even a rumor that he himself is HIV-positive but is in denial, unwilling to say so. Finally, there are suggestions that his stance is actually a brilliant tactic to force pharmaceutical prices to come down or even to insist that local companies, in which the ANC has an interest, get the lucrative business. There is no proof for any of these suppositions, but many are swirling around the conference.

Mbeki, bewildered by the anger and lack of tolerance shown by his critics, also seems unable to come up with a populist program for linking health and human rights and inspiring a people who are dying in droves. Paying lip service to the AIDS crisis won't save lives or help South Africans cope with an intensifying epidemic, or the AIDS orphans crisis which is just building steam.

Thabo: Come out of your bunker and dialogue with your critics the way you did so brilliantly years ago with the white power structure. The posturing and polemics about AIDS on all sides is not helpful to you, South Africa, or the world.

part five MEDIA MAKER

passions, pieces, and polemics • 1960–2000

CHARLES AND HOWARD
Tales of the Radio Wars from Then to Infinity
1996

The Story Behind This Story: In 1996, when shock jock Howard Stern, the self-styled "King of all Media" was moved into the morning slot at WBCN, the radio station I worked at for nearly a decade, I thought Boston *maga-zine might want a piece with my take on the end of an era in Boston radio. I found it disturbing that one of the most popular local disc jockeys, my for-mer colleague Charles Laquidara, was being pushed out of the station he virtually created. An old friend of mine had taken over editorial command at the slick city monthly. I knew him as a left-leaning journalist and was delighted when he responded positively to my pitch, commissioning my story. I wanted to track how monopoly media homogenizes programming, smearing big-name celebrities all over the radio dial and devaluing the local content that links stations to their communities.*

They seemed to like the idea, but then the bait and switch that so many freelance writers are familiar with came into play. I was asked to work with a staff writer, who never spoke to me. It could have been a gen-erational thing, or perhaps my writing was just not processed enough for such a glossy publication. But while I submitted a piece praising Charles, they ended up running a profile dissing him as over the hill and a burnout. Gone was my critique of corporate strategy in this corporate mag. Not only wasn't I consulted, but I wasn't even paid, and, only after bugging them persistently, settled, months later, for a small kill fee. Boston *did run a let-ter of mine dissecting the piece but, of course, edited out a reference to my experience with the magazine.*

Behind the scenes and unseen in this drama was the heavy hand of Mel Karmazin, Stern's patron, an ex–radio ad salesman who ran Infinity before selling it for $3.5 billion to CBS, which was itself soon acquired by Westinghouse. Karmazin, now that company's biggest shareholder, is also its new overlord, running what was once America's "Tiffany" network. One of his first programming decisions was to bring his protégé Stern's TV show to CBS on Saturday nights, where it has, at this writing, done poorly in the ratings, been skewered by the critics, and has been dropped by several CBS affiliates.

It was April Fool's Day and Howard Stern phoned it in. He couldn't be bothered to come to Boston personally to announce that he was now

WBCN's new morning man. We have the largest radio station monopoly in America to thank for this dark day in the history of Boston broadcasting, as Infinity Broadcasting, a name that spoke to a corporate ambition which the dictionary defines as "unbounded space, time, or quantity" imposed its nationally syndicated star on New England radio listeners.

According to a *Boston Globe* account, Stern's "ego filled every corner of the station's conference room" where an adoring press corps gathered to interview him via speaker phone while reveling in the crude and sexist remarks he made to all present including reporters who "seemed to play into his routine by volunteering to describe what they were wearing." We can thank this kowtowing, celebrity-obsessed press corps for further boosting this talented but demagogic blabbermouth into a popular national phenomenon.

As Stern moves in, the station's AM institution, its soul and defining spirit, Charles Laquidara, moves over to another Infinity property, WZLX, a classic rock station with studios in the Prudential skyscraper. The Pru, once home to 'BCN as well, is the place where I began dissecting news in the morning for Charles's show, "The Big Mattress," the only popular drive-time radio show to use a Yiddish word, *mishigas*, as a title for an interactive daily contest. That was 1971.

In the end, it was corporate *mishigas* that transformed the nationally admired station, once synonymous with the counterculture, insurgent news, and kick-ass rock and roll. It was that identity that rolled over the morning they kicked Charles out. When I read Charles's *public* response—praise for the radio gods of Infinity, I realized that he was just giving Caesar his due, damning with not so faint praise. After all, none of us are getting any younger, and fidelity to the corporate logo is the price you pay to collect that paycheck. Freedom of speech is not exactly rewarded these days in the bowels of corporate media. Privately, Charles was pissed and hurt.

Howardization is a product of media concentration in the radio industry with its cost-cutting, standardization, and lowering of quality and standards. Some years earlier, Infinity settled an obscenity complaint against Stern by "voluntarily" giving the FCC $1.7 million dollars in fines so their future buying binges would be unencumbered by regulatory delays. (Contrast that with how Infinity handled a phony FCC complaint years earlier over news bias! I will get to that in a moment.)

Howard's brash ballast buoyed Infinity's bottom line (how's that for a *Variety* headline?). Never mind its effect on American culture. Never mind his frequent racist and sexist commentary. There's big money to be made in dumbing down audience taste. It may be significant that the other American personality who dominated the media as no other, O.J. Simpson, had long been a board member of Infinity Broadcasting. When I asked an Infinity executive about that, he shrugged his shoulders and said, "you never know about people."

Like many in broadcasting, Charles had gone from being a person to becoming a personality; from being talented to becoming "a talent"; from producing great radio to being a great radio product. His consciousness over the years turned into a commodity in which personal principles and social values have little currency. A station once known for its collective spirit (and, in the early days, collective management) became one more affiliate of a national chain which parlayed telecommunications "reform" into the largest radio company in America. Like ballplayers and entertainers, the people who work there are now, at bottom, chattel in the marketplace. The local color that created a community of listeners has now metamorphosed into one more megaphone for Howard Stern's ego-maniacal self-promotional multimedia marketing hype machine reinforced with movies, books, TV shows, and pricey Pay Per View bacchanals.

At least Charles was not traded to another station for a player to be named.

This final act in the 'BCN drama has been building for years. WBCN has been through as many changes as the music culture itself—from free form, to progressive, to AOR, to punk, to alternative, and on and on, always searching for the sound that will get the most ears and sell the most ads. No institution can remain static if it hopes to survive, so 'BCN has mirrored all the cultural shifts of the last quarter of a century as well as promoted them.

Its political edge has long been gone. Activism receded after Watergate and the Vietnam War. Disco fractured the audience. Punk drove out the old rockers. MTV soon emerged, mimicking rock radio. (Led in part in its early days by ex-'BCN jock J. J. Jackson.) Over the years, some 'BCN jocks left to join the competition, which then challenged it in the marketplace with a similar sound or a slicker, more commercial format. 'CHR radio played all the hits all the time while classic rock and lite music formats clashed. Meanwhile, 'BCN jumped on the "alternative" music bandwagon where attitude replaced antagonism, and pose replaced radical politics. Being cool is all that matters. And getting rich. As 'BCN's on-air stars and behind-the-scenes managers began to get stock options and bigger salaries, their willingness to play by the company rulebook increased. They bought in. Many longtime listeners felt they sold out. It wasn't always that way. A look at 'BCN's past may refresh some memories. WBCN began as part of the Concert Network, a string of FM classical music stations that once blanketed the East Coast—WHCN in Hartford, WNCN in New York, and so forth—all founded by T. Mitchell Hastings, an engineer and radio pioneer whose claim to fame was inventing the car stereo and other technology indispensable to the spread of the FM phenomenon. Hastings was also more of a visionary than a businessman, in more ways that one. He once boasted of being in communication with the spirit world. His upper class–oriented classical music empire initially reached only a small elite of audiophiles who could afford the expensive new receivers. As a result, his network soon became financially moribund. It was shrinking until it caught the rock virus.

In 1968, T. Mitch was struck down by a brain tumor that required instant surgery. When he went into the hospital, his station was playing symphonies and barely paying its bills. When he came out, WBCN, under new management, had rolled over Beethoven and was rocking around the clock—and making money. Hendrix was in; Handel was out. The convalescing owner may have hated the music, but he liked the beat of the cash flow.

FM made stereo possible, and stereo broadcasting begot album-oriented radio. FM djs soon began to challenge and compete with the AM sound that they called "ugly radio." Soon Boston's famous screaming AM personality Arnie "Woo Woo" Ginsburg signed on for a stint as general manager. 'BCN soon shook him off as it shook up the audience, becoming a leader in shaping a new free-form formatless format, featuring hip on-air personalities with a laid-back style, playing longer sets of non-stop, commercial-free new music. Charles Laquidara, one-time schoolteacher and actor who tried out for a part in the *Boston Strangler*, emerged as the most distinctive of them.

WBCN called itself "the American Revolution," and it became one with jocks who fused countercultural attitudes and a large musical repertoire, experimenting with the art of the "mix" and the "set." They were known by the music they chose and the mood they created. Rock radio became a megaphone for "Sex, Drugs, and Rock and Roll," '60s-style. It was a generational thing, and it thundered with a political edge. While AM stations played Army recruiting ads, 'BCN offered information on draft resistance counseling. A Boston University student, Howard Stern, was among its listeners in the glory days.

Back then, only the national radio networks offered in-depth coverage of events outside the local broadcasting area. Locally, in most cases, radio news was seen as a loss-leader and not yet a profit center or important service. FM radio with its higher sound quality was more oriented towards music programming, and even less committed to news. "More Music, Less Talk" became a popular slogan then and a selling point. Years later in the Reagan era, when radio was deregulated and FCC news requirements dropped, many newscasts and news departments followed.

In the early days, WBCN committed itself to providing independently produced news that spoke to the concerns and passions of its youthful audience. It was news that didn't stop at the borders of Boston either. Listeners were interested in the war in Vietnam, so 'BCN reported it with some scope. Alternative news soon became a daily complement to alternative music. That commitment set the station apart and it stood out in an industry faithful to the institutional proposition that the audience doesn't need to know anything, and doesn't much care about anything anyway. (It's always been my experience that when managers say "people don't care," it's because *they* don't care.)

At 'BCN in those years rock radio was an adventure. Djs for the most part selected their own music and were willing to make a creative input to the news department. The spark plugs at the station, Charles and Norm Winer, were especially interested in informing and involving listeners. They were already providing information on activism, even encouraging protests. There was a hotline where callers could get concert info, hitch a ride in the days before car pooling, find a lost cat or dog, or request a song. The 'BCN "listener line" was always open and helped thousands deal with bad acid trips and career tips. 'BCN became the community switchboard that in turn reinforced a sense of youth community and listener loyalty.

It was often anarchistic, crazy, and wonderful, a place where anything could happen and when it did, Charles was usually in the middle of it: "There was the night someone put mescaline into my bowl of matzo ball soup. I had to come back to the studio to do a show and was totally crazed. They had to drag me out because I was just playing commercial after commercial, promos, IDs. I didn't know what song to play. There were only 5,000 records behind me, but I couldn't think of a song. The commercial I was reading dissolved right in the middle of my reading it."

On another occasion when the ratings results were disappointing,

Charles, through his invented radio alter-ego Duane Glasscock, told the audience to send "a bag of shit" to the Arbitron research bureau. He didn't say "ka-ka" or "feces" or "number two," he said "send a bag of shit." He also gave out Arbitron's address on the air every fifteen minutes. Duane, not Charles, was fired for that stunt.

The impact of this type of in-your-face programming on radio stations like WBCN was not lost on Washington.

In 1970, Vice President Agnew gave a speech criticizing certain unnamed radio stations for airing songs promoting "drug culture propaganda," code language for the still-growing youth counterculture. In March of 1971, as 'BCN prepared to celebrate the third anniversary of its rock format, the FCC warned broadcasters that there would be penalties, including a loss of license, for playing songs that would "promote or glorify the use of illegal drugs." This did have a chilling effect, although the only song specifically banned was John Lennon's "Working Class Hero" because it used the word "fucking." Andy Beubian, a departing dj, made sure to play it as the last selection of his last show. At 'BCN, our culture was adversarial towards any attempts at government censorship or management control. The staff was in charge, and mostly we got away with it.

Charles was political too, in his own way. After hearing my news reports about the use of Honeywell Corporation–manufactured anti-personnel weapons in Indochina, Charles added some unwanted content to an ad for Honeywell cameras being sold at a store called Underground Camera in Harvard Square. "Go out and buy yourself two or three Honeywell cameras and help support a corporation responsible for all those dead Cambodian babies." Underground Camera thought he accused *them* of killing Cambodian babies and sued for $200,000. The case actually went to court. I was even a witness at the proceeding that took place in the very Dedham Courtroom where Sacco and Vanzetti were tried. 'BCN used a "truth defense," proving that Honeywell—not the camera store—made the bombs. No big secret. We won.

Charles's principal appeal was not his politics but his wit, humor, musical range, and fast-paced programming. He virtually reinvented the radio morning show, complete with sidekicks, features, phone calls, and outrageousness. He was a magnet for an adoring army of student interns and production meisters who created satires, parodies, and distinctive audio collages that made his show feel like an event filled with surprises and spontaneity. I learned from him that how a message is delivered is almost more important than what it says, that style matters, and that being entertaining is not incompatible with being taken seriously.

At the same time, I began to realize that increasingly 'BCN, like most broadcasters, was aiming its product not at the community at large but at a smaller slice of the audience, certain key demographics prized by advertisers. Young men were the target group, and as a result the station's musical choices and banter were increasingly driven by sophomoric, adolescent humor, wild stunts, and on-air bravado. Macho talk and sexism was in; political concerns out.

And Charles could read the tea leaves. As he grew older, his shtick became slicker and sillier, reflecting and reinforcing a vacuous teen culture. When the station went on the air, TV watching was not as big a force in the lives of our listeners. As TV became a more dominant media, as fashion and sports culture became more pervasive, 'BCN echoed the shift. It now had MTV to compete with, and pressures from its corporate owners and their profit goals to meet. The station became more conservative even as it tried to keep its rebel, alternative spirit.

Charles probably felt he had no choice but to move downmarket to keep his ratings up. Being at 'BCN became more of a job than an adventure. And he became more of a very well-paid institution. He had moved to the suburbs years earlier, married and had children, and had little in common with many of his listeners. Soon he was commuting between his suburban spread and a ranch in Hawaii. It's a familiar story of going for the gold and the erosion of consciousness. Yet, I can't write him off or put him down. He's still on the air thirty years later, with fans who love him. He's an on-air artist behind that control board, ageless in a way, and an inspirational figure in the history of radio who probably won't get his due because he's wasn't on the air in a larger media market and media capital like New York or LA.

When I worked at WBCN, Charles Laquidara used to run a pre-produced musical insert to introduce the playing of a classic rock song or some golden oldie. It featured an announcer's voice, saying "One step forward—into the past." That's what had happened.

What came around has gone around. It was a long ride, but it's all over now baby blue. The 'BCN I knew is gone, and radio is the worse for it. I'm not just spouting nostalgia. I am expressing serious concerns about the dim future of independent and critical media in this age of media mega-mergers, with its many choices and few diverse voices. WBCN had been the model for insurgent broadcasting, and the demise of that model has now become the message. WBCN belongs to CBS now—a link in the Howard Stern radio network, an arm of the media beast. It had taken decades for 'BCN to cross the ratings Rubicon and abandon any pretense of serving higher values in an era marked by a gradual erosion of content and courage.

So say goodbye to a great radio experiment. Whenever I think of 'BCN, I recall one of New England's favorite sons and sometime 'BCN commentator, the late Abbie Hoffman, who remarked about the '60s: "We were young. We were foolish. We made mistakes. We took risks. But we were right."

And, at least, at WBCN, we were on the air.

Author's Note, 2001: After this article was written, Charles Laquidara retired from the classic rock station he had been exiled to after his long tenure at WBCN, and moved from Massachusetts to Maui—a far more desirable place of exile. His über-boss Mel Karmazin also moved (one notch up the corporate ladder) when the new CBS—a company which earlier swallowed Westinghouse, which had earlier swallowed the original CBS, which was itself swallowed by Viacom—named him its overlord. Gulp! As a result of all this consolidation, the Viacom/CBS/Infinity megalith now owns a total of seventy AM and FM stations. Along with fellow radio monopolist Clear Channel Communications, the two companies control nearly half the air space in the top fifty markets. All of this is a consequence of the Telecommunications "Reform" Act of 1996, which relaxed ownership rules; it was a bill sold to the U.S. public as a tool for promoting competition, though it actually facilitated concentration. Along the way, commercial radio has become more homogenized, formatted, and sanitized. And, at the same time, some of these same forces are now eating into the structures of non-commercial radio such as the once fiercely independent Pacifica network of listener-supported stations.

LETTER TO *NEWSWEEK* (UNPUBLISHED)

May 22, 1972

Dear Sir or Madam:

I can't say that WBCN-FM appreciated your reference to our news as "a lot of far-out weirdness and revolutionary craziness." Slick attempts at corporate journalism are prone to confusing a "soothing ideological massage" with occasionally irreverent but always truthful ideological demystification. I told your reporter that most straight media people would probably consider our alternative news weird and crazy. Funny thing. I had *Newsweek* in mind.

Danny Schechter
News Dissector

A HIDDEN HAND AT PBS?

1994

This article ran in International Documentary *magazine with the following unusual disclaimer:*

Editor's Note: This article, while not necessarily representative of the views of ID or of the International Documentary Association, raises important issues that we believe go beyond the interests of a single independent filmmaker. To generate discussion, we have circulated it to leaders and critics concerned with public television and asked them to respond. We invite our readers to write in as well and will publish as many responses as space allows.

> *"Just because you're not paranoid doesn't mean someone isn't following you."*
>
> —Anonymous

In 1990 our company, Globalvision, was producing the weekly news magazine *South Africa Now* when one programmer at KCET, the PBS station in Los Angeles, called to challenge us on one story. The report in question investigated allegations of a "third force" in South Africa, what Nelson Mandela had called the "hidden hand" behind the violence that had suddenly erupted in the form of massacres on commuter trains and a spate of political assassinations. We were told that KCET, L.A.'s public TV station, would be taking the show off the air because it considered the story "ANC propaganda"—in essence, advocacy masquerading as journalism.

The next day, the *Los Angeles Times* carried a report that David Horowitz, a leftist turned neo-conservative founder of the Committee on Media Integrity (acronym: COMI, pronounced "Commie"), "claimed credit" for the muzzling of *South Africa Now*. We later learned that he had been lobbying KCET to persuade the station to dump a wide range of PBS programming that violated his notion of political correctness. *South Africa Now* had, in effect, been offered up to appease him.

That disclosure prompted viewer protests in Los Angeles, several articles in the *Los Angeles Times*, and a debate within the station that led KCET to put the show back on the air, albeit with a disclaimer warning the unsuspecting that "this program reflects the views of its producers," a not-so-subtle attempt at further labelling our work politically. We called that decision a victory but knew that we had only won a small battle in a much more complicated war of images and legitimacy.

In the aftermath of this incident virtually every press article about *South Africa Now* resuscitated this controversy, quoting Horowitz to the effect that we were Marxist propagandists and the like, as if he had any credibility as a media critic, much less as an expert on South Africa. In the name of balanced journalism, we were continually put in the position of defending ourselves against charges that were never proven and were never true. There was no evidence, but there was an odor—and it stuck. Many people believe that where there's smoke, there's fire, or at least a flame.

Now fast forward four years to March 18, 1994. A South African judge charged with investigating the causes of violence in South Africa produced witnesses who for the first time conclusively implicated high-level South African police and security personnel in a well-orchestrated campaign of murder that claimed as many as 10,000 lives. Nelson Mandela was proven right: There was a "hidden hand!" The mystery of the "third force" was finally substantiated and solved! A furious President F. W. De Klerk, who insisted he was not implicated, suspended the accused amid another major scandal.

The *South Africa Now* story, which had been confirmed in bits and pieces over the years, had now met the ultimate test: truth. According to a *New York Times* report: "The evidence indicated that the police network orchestrated massacres of train commuters, trained Inkatha hit men, and took part in killings of ANC rivals."

The fact that our report, four years and 5,000 lives earlier, pointed in this direction did not make us such great journalists. The same suspicions and more fragmentary reports were appearing in many South African newspapers even as the American mass media largely ignored them. I have dwelled at length on this issue for only one reason: It was this story that was used as the reason, or perhaps the pretext, for dropping our series, which in turn damaged our credibility and reputations throughout public television. WGBH in Boston took KCET's signal and moved to drop the show too, wisely avoiding citing the same rationale but operating with the same spirit. Fortunately for us, in both cities, public pressure helped convince the stations to stay with the show, but the outcry was resented, and we were then blamed for orchestrating it, even though we had very little to do with it. It seemed like the last thing public stations wanted was to hear from the public!

That *South Africa Now* had been called into question on a story that was legitimate didn't seem to matter. The controversy took on momentum of its own as the consequences began to ripple through a system where the details of the subject seemed to matter less than impressions and prejudices. Many programmers became "uncomfortable" with the show. Our funding problems became more intense. Even after we won some major recognition, an Emmy and the George Polk award, the handwriting was on the wall. *South Africa Now*'s run was ending. Politically motivated critics—who wouldn't let the truth get in the way of a good smear campaign—prevailed, not because they were right, but because they *may* have been right. A Horowitz group publication later cited this campaign as their "defining moment."

Many leading PBS producers stood on the sidelines, wishing us well but not speaking out publicly—that is, until Horowitz and his new allies in Senator Bob Dole's office began turning their guns on them. The *Frontline* series was questioned. Bill Moyers was attacked. And then PBS itself stood accused of airing unbalanced programming. Suddenly a minor critic with a letterhead was able to get the Republican majority leader to threaten the refunding of PBS. Ironic? Perhaps, but to us it was just new evidence of the old dictum: "When they came for the Jews, I did nothing because I was not a Jew . . . and then they came for me!"

It is worth revisiting this controversy only for what it implies for the present. We have learned the hard way that inaccurate labels can lead to smears that leave a permanent stain; that administrative bureaucracies have no use for controversy; that political criteria are utilized constantly in PBS program evaluation, although it is very rare for public television programmers to admit openly that they are not carrying a show, or are consigning it to an unwatched time period, for political reasons.

When one reads about the 1950s Hollywood Red scare today, it seems so crude, so blatant, so pathetic to see how powerful corporations cowered before breast-beating political demagogues. While only a *relatively* small number of people may have been fired, the whole culture was diminished by the movies that were and were not made in a climate of fear and repression. Television was also "sanitized." A small-town grocer with a mimeograph machine and a press agent was able to turn a self-produced magazine called *Red Channels* into a widely utilized blacklist of TV writers and performers against which there was no appeal or even verifiable standard of proof. Accusation was conviction.

The chilling effect *then* is easy to see now. The chilling effect *today* is more subtle but just as real. Today's political litmus tests in news or entertainment are not as blatant. There are no loyalty oaths to swear to or congressional investigators to placate. Yet a fusion of conservative political ideology and conventional market-driven wisdom continues to guide media gatekeepers in decisions about what to commission, fund, buy, and broadcast. Only no one talks about the political effects of the process. It is largely invisible. In some circles, even being considered liberal is still outside the pale of respectability: it is a Red scare—but this time without the Reds.

There must be a reason why conservative pundits like neo-conservative columnist Fred Barnes, who has never made films, just received hundreds of thousands of dollars from the Corporation for Public Broadcasting, while a human rights series like *Rights & Wrongs*, with no less a PBS news star than Charlayne Hunter-Gault of the *MacNeil-Lehrer Newshour*, is repeatedly turned down. (I have nothing personally against Fred—the two of us were classmates at Harvard's Nieman Fellowship program for journalists.) But it is hard not to wonder if the fact that Nancy Reagan's former press secretary, Sheila Tate, is also CPB's chairman has anything to do with it. Or that Spiro T. Agnew's press secretary, Vic Gold, is also on the board? In politics, insiders have a way of staying in; outsiders are kept out.

That *South Africa Now* incident still hovers over us in an industry where perception is often more important than reality (the perception of imbalance, the perception of unfairness, the perception of perception, etcetera, etcetera). Today, PBS refuses to support our well-received human rights series, *Rights & Wrongs*, ostensibly on the grounds that "human rights is an insufficient organizing principle for a TV series." A credible weekly series on human rights, they say, is not "appropriate" at a time when human rights is *the* universal post–Cold War challenge. Is this a political judgement? You bet. Does it reflect an agenda? No question. Are those issues ever raised and debated within public television in these terms? Rarely, if ever.

PBS still has a mandate to air programming that promotes controversy and diversity. It has a new president and board. It remains the only channel—in the new multi-channel environment—that is at least committed in principle to serving the public interest. If a channel dedicated to serving the public is so closed to public input, how can we expect to have any impact on the so-called electronic superhighway of the future? Will independents and documentary-makers even have an on-ramp?

The PBS bureaucracy gets away with it because progressives—including many so-called Hollywood liberals—are not tuned into the issue. Many work in media but do not see it as a political arena for organization and lobbying. Right-wing extremists have mounted a permanent campaign to censor and suppress programming they dislike. They write letters, make phone calls, and use radio talk shows, direct mail, and newspaper ads. The far more numerous members of the liberal mainstream are disorganized, inattentive and ineffectual. They send in their PBS station pledge checks and complain that Rupert Murdoch will soon be running America. Self-fulfilling prophecies, anyone?

And as for *South Africa Now*? One of our anchors, Tandeka Gqubule, a South African print journalist who received her on-air training on the show, became the first black anchor for South African television's principal network. Nelson Mandela, on whose story we often focused, went from prison to the presidency and has now made human rights the cornerstone of his new foreign policy.

Rights & Wrongs went on the air in the new South Africa.

And while I was there recently, documenting the election for an insider film modeled on *The War Room*, many former viewers, mostly black South Africans but also fellow journalists, commented that I should be "proud" because "*South Africa Now* really contributed to the coming of democracy" in that country.

And that's a feeling that makes it all worthwhile—the sense that media work matters and can impact the real world.

This article originally appeared in International Documentary, *July/August 1994.*

SNATCHING DEFEAT FROM THE JAWS OF VICTORY
Making it to Hollywood and the Creative Artists Agency
1994

The screening was well organized. Joan Sekler, who cut her teeth as a foot soldier in the '60s, was on the case. If it can be organized, Joannie can organize it. Her time had come, and gone, and come again. If there was an Oscar for mobilizing the masses, she would win it hands down. No competition. The Laemle Sunset theater was full. Well, almost full. The crowd was multi-racial. Multi-everything. The post-screening reception was ready. Day-old croissants and donated South African wine available for viewer consumption.

It was showtime. My film *Countdown to Freedom* was having its first Hollywood screening. Its first screening anywhere—here at the Pan African Film Festival in a real movieplex, popcorn and all.

The film itself had only arrived a day earlier, shipped from London, where our video master tape had been transferred to film in an imperfect process which is always somewhat problematic. It is especially problematic when price is an issue, much less *the* issue. In this business, it is hard to hide cheap. That adage is unfortunately too true: you gets what you pays for.

And we did.

If God had wanted there to be one visual medium, would he or she have allowed film and video to inhabit separate worlds, much less the existing dazzling array of PAL, NTSC, HI-8, 3/4, HI-DEF, and VHS, with more techno-initials on the way? Why, Lord, why?

So the theater darkens. The audience is now in our hands. Months of work and years of sacrifice are about to be exposed to always fickle public taste. And this public could be particularly volatile in the sense that all political factions and militant tendencies are represented. There is at least one Masai warrior with a plate in his lip. Africa and Africa wannabes are here. I am sure that at least one guardian of some political orthodoxy will challenge a key fact or at least an interpretation. There are not many Jewish-American directors at African film festivals these days.

The projector cranks. The first light flickers—but then the projector jerks, the sound muddies, and, to my ears, the narrator, James Earl Jones, sounds like he is in a tin can somewhere *in* South Africa. What's happening? My blood pressure rises. Overwrought. Paralyzed. My celluloid world is collapsing just days after I'm told that the print has been checked and is fine. Finally, the projectionist himself comes down from his perch and shakes me into action. He invites me upstairs to his lair of whirring machines. He too is alarmed.

"Where is focus?" he asks. Something *is* wrong.

I can deal with the obvious. The sound *is* too low. We crank it. A little treble helps James Earl Jones. And when he taps the projector like some used car that needs a kick to get started—a living tap—the picture stabilizes and, whew, down below, the crowd is transfixed.

Another guy who works here tells me later this is the worst video-to-film transfer he's ever seen. Afterwards, a few others cheer me up by saying the technical stuff doesn't matter. But I know it does matter. It matters too much. We have spent a small fortune trying to get the technical crap right. Just not enough of a fortune.

Oh shit!

Fantasies of Academy Awards have just collided with reality. No way, José. The keepers of film kulture, those aesthete worshippers of the wonders of fine cinematography, and the we-marvel-over-great-lighting groupies will take one look at our print and consign it to some purgatory of movie apartheid—separate and unequal.

I can read the letter now. Nice try, kid.

In our film, Fidel Castro, who this audience cheers almost as much as Mandela, speaks of the death of apartheid and the birth of freedom.

I feel like it's my funeral now.

How to explain? Who the hell cares? This film was made on a budget more suited for a public access telethon. Whose fault was that? Like so many of our projects, it was cobbled together on will power with the video equivalent of scotch tape. It is like making a suit from those little pieces of cuff that a tailor gives you after a fitting.

I am feeling sorry for myself. Maybe it is my fate in this life. I don't seem to be able to marshal needed resources. Real budgets elude me. I start conjuring up Richard Farina's book from my days at Cornell, *Been Down So Long, It Looks Like Up To Me*.

Almost thirty years ago, I made my first political film. Again on no money, fueled then even more by innocence than by craft or skill. It was seen three times to my knowledge.

I vowed then that independent filmmaking was not a real career. It was the province of trust-fund kids and masochists seeking self-expression. It was a dead end that would leave me wandering like the lost Jew I fear I am becoming, in the desert of film festivals and rejection letters. You start chasing glory and end up in the real heartbreak hotel.

I got out of "the life" then—and I am feeling like getting out again. Throwing it in.

Am I snatching defeat from the jaws of victory? I never thought of myself as a loser, but I can't seem to engage them on their ground. I am just not stupid—or smart—enough to do stupid TV. I don't have the heart for it.

No one wants to read your press clips.

October 17, 1994.

P.S. CAA REDUX
1994/1999

Two days later, I caught another psychic wave. The surf was up in California.

This time we had a smaller VIP screening in the hub of Hollywood deal making, the Creative Artists Agency, the high concept ode-to-the-deal temple built by industry power broker Michael Ovitz, who has since defected to Disney.

We had visited the building earlier to check the quality of the projection, which this time was on that lowest of low formats: home video, VHS. Only we had a tape struck from our master in London, on PAL. The $2.99 dub looked better than the nine-thousand-dollar 16mm film transfer.

Rory and I were like two kids on a first visit to the candy store, marveling at how we slipped our film into these hallowed grounds. The two of us hung out for a while in the power lobby, hoping that this impressive setting would give us the aura of insiders, a status that has eluded us so far. We used their phones under a giant (read expensive) original painting by Roy Liechtenstein, read their trade papers, and pissed in their bathroom. (By mistake I used the ladies room and joked about it later with a kid pushing a mailroom cart in the hall. He snickered, and couldn't get over it. Fortunately, there had been no encounters with another gender. I was relieved on more than one level.)

Our day started well as well. The *Los Angeles Times* gave the film an enthusiastic review with adjectives to die for: "at once concise and compelling, this eloquent, proudly moving documentary," etc., etc. A day earlier, the *Hollywood Reporter* was also kind. We were now on the map—somewhere between Soweto and Beverly Hills.

As the nearly packed screening organized by the high-profile Hollywood Policy Center got underway, I began to sense another disaster in the making. Not again! Alfre Woodard started her eloquent remarks with an announcement. There had just been a tragedy below—an accident of unknown proportions in CAA's own parking garage.

Earlier in the day, when we brought our rental car into that labyrinth, I joked that the place looked like a Mercedes dealership. Like so many basement garages in LA, this one was manned by platoons of neatly attired Latino attendants. Parking may be a bigger industry than moviemaking here in this auto-addicted town. It certainly offers more jobs, but also represents a form of apartheid, U.S. style.

My fears were at the fore: I visualized the folks, now so calmly seated in these plush chairs, rushing out before the screening even began, racing down to the garage, to the vehicles they spend so much of their lives trapped in. How many cell phones and expensive sound systems were at risk? How much leather upholstery? I had visions of mangled steel that looked like that mashed mincemeat of a modern metal sculpture in the building's oversized entryway.

My mind raced ahead conceiving another possible scenario. Could this be a rebellion by the slaves of CAA, the masses forced to labor in the cellars, rising against the expensively dressed telephone headset–wearing yuppies upstairs? A revolution of valet parkers wreaking luddite-like vengeance against the machines that oppress them? Minions against mucky mucks. Hooray for Hollywood! But why now? Why at *my* screening?

Slow down, Danny. At the podium, a radiant Alfre Woodard is calm, citing just a few damaged cars by make and license number, to sounds of silent relief.

We later learn that there *was* a collision on level P-2. It was true. A parking attendant caught his foot between a rock and a hard place, the pedal and the brake. He careened into the wall, bouncing off into a head on head with a BMW. It was totalled. Ironically, one of the scenes in our movie takes place in a similar parking garage twelve thousand miles away.

I have said hello to the LA dream machine, and now I am saying goodbye. The audience loved the film—but will we find the deals to let others see it? Will we recoup? Will we find a distributor? Can this movie about the exploited be exploited?

Stay tuned.

UPDATE, 1999

Countdown to Freedom was sold to Cinemax/HBO and aired by MNET in South Africa on the first anniversary of the elections. It was not nominated for the Academy Award, but neither was the film that we saw as our principal competition, *Hoop Dreams*, which did get commercial distribution. The documentary selection process was widely denounced for overlooking *Hoop Dreams* and giving the Oscar to an insider, the woman who had run the documentary screening committee for many years. In July 1995, the Academy of Motion Picture Arts and Sciences sent me a letter calling my film one of the most outstanding of 1994, asking to show it under their auspices just before the 1996 Oscar ceremonies. The film was screened widely and generated considerable attention, including a positive write-up in the *New York Times* Sunday Arts and Leisure section. Like so many independent documentaries, it has yet to recoup its costs.

THE RIGHTS AND WRONGS OF MAKING HUMAN RIGHTS TELEVISION or WHY YOU MAY NEVER SEE TV'S MOST PROGRESSIVE NEWSMAGAZINE
1997

When we first came up with the idea for a TV magazine focused on human rights, a Hollywood syndicator thought it sounded "neat." The pilot was hosted by a former network anchorwoman, and segmented into solid features and analytical stories from all over the world, highlighting the real life passions and ongoing abuses of those crusading for freedom and dignity.

Much of the footage had never been seen on television before. Some was shot with home video cameras. In part, it was a global showcase of "Rodney King" type videos with dramatic footage.

We thought the show might be a hit. The video was "hot." There was emotion and storytelling. The production values were impressive for a low-budget effort. But the response from this well-known program distributor was telling. He liked the project but had to pass. "We only do reality television," was the actual excuse. We have it in writing.

Reality?

Years ago, George Orwell wrote presciently about the perversion of language. But even he might have had a problem with this dishonest use of terminology. The television newsmagazine arena seems to have a new entry each week, with every network competing for its share of the profitable "reality" market. With a tabloid sensibility increasingly driving story choices, network producers seem mesmerized more by what their promos will sound like than what their journalism will say. To add a Tina Turner twist: "What's reality got to do with it?"

In fact, as Ian I. Mitroff explains in his recent book *The Unreality Industry*, "With very few exceptions, most issues on television news are presented in a completely ahistoric context or no context whatsoever . . . the overall context is one of dazzling confusion. Little or no attempt is made to present a larger view in which the issues could be located in some coherent framework."

Amen! But this now-so-familiar critique seems irrelevant, if only because year in and year out it has had so little influence on changing mainstream programming. TV critics may blow the smoke but the industry is locked into a market-driven trajectory, with the mentality of salesmen programming networks whose real goal is programming viewers to consume more and question less.

Competition, Not Criticism

As network refugees and independent TV producers, the folks I work with at Globalvision have always felt that competition could probably be more effective in changing TV than criticism. We didn't like the way *they* did the news so we set out to do it another way. Sometimes you need a demonstration of other possibilities to prove that there are other possibilities.

News can be presented differently on television. Really. Although it's hard to find good models worth emulating. Most of the networks clone each other's look, homogenizing all differences away. "We have a TV screen that only has one scene," was the way an old friend of mine once put it in a song, and despite the plethora of channels, there is still very little choice when it comes to diversity of ideas, multicultural perspectives, or global content.

When you flip the dial—or, in today's parlance, "channel surf" with your remote control—you only see a very few formats, and so it is easy to believe that there are only a very few, and usually that boils down to only one legitimate and credible way of presenting information. We all know the news format: highly paid news stars "anchoring" broadcasts that look the same, sound the same, and feel the same. Reporters "voice-over" news "packages." The stories are short and self-contained, rarely linked to each other, rarely illuminating larger systemic problems.

That is why it is so important to try to offer a different approach, only it really can't be too different or no one will put it on the air. Our own series, *Rights & Wrongs: Human Rights Television*, is attempting to be just that by offering different content in a familiar newsmagazine format. Producing such a show is not as hard as getting it on the air at times people watch.

Rights & Wrongs is Globalvision's weekly newsmagazine, now on the air nationally. Yet it is still probably one of the best-kept secrets on television. It has no network backing or even official PBS sanction, although eighty-five public television stations air it weekly. [150 stations took the series before it went off the air in 1997.] You may have to scour the TV listings to find it. In contrast Europe's Super Channel, now available to fifty million homes in twenty-nine countries, plays it twice weekly in prime time. It will also soon be seen by viewers in Jamaica and South Africa.

A Well-Known Anchor—But Does it Matter?

The program's anchor is Charlayne Hunter-Gault, the most prominent female and African-American journalist in all of public television. A fifteen year veteran of the *MacNeil Lehrer Newshour*, you'd think her presence would be welcome on an innovative new series. If you do think that way, as we did, you'll end up realizing you are wrong.

Each week, *Rights & Wrongs* features a cover story that tackles some major human rights issue or theme and then follows it up with an interview or profile. We offer a news digest as well, only we call it a "rights reel," featuring footage that comes in from human rights monitors, independent journalists, and TV stations overseas. Much of it is shot on home video. Sometimes we also preview important documentaries that are not getting seen elsewhere. For example, we ran excerpts from *The Panama Deception*, the controversial exposé that won the Academy Award but not one network showing.

We close each show with a cultural feature, usually music videos with a human rights message. One week, it's a rhythmic cry from Haiti for an end to military rule; the next, a rap salute to women from Sweet Honey in the Rock. This is not the antiseptic stuff of MTV, but songs that speak out on the issues of the day.

What may be more unique is that *Rights & Wrongs* offers "video diaries," a form of first-person journalism, a kind of "inside-out" coverage that is so often missing in our personality-dominated news reporting. We think the most compelling stories come from the people most directly affected, often in their own voice . . . be they rape victims in Bosnia, or brave priests in Brazil. We don't mind if our correspondents have a "foreign accent" when they have something important to say. The other week, for example, we carried short films shot under fire in Sarajevo. The filmmakers are a multiethnic team called SAGA who are documenting the horror of a modern city under mortar fire while the world stands by cheering *Cheers*.

The Silencing of Sarajevo

Their work is extraordinary and powerful, the only authentic video coverage from the inside, the voice of those resisting aggression. Praised by the *New York Times*, it has been screened and hailed at film festivals from Cannes to San Francisco. An Annie Leibovitz photo spread on the heroes of Sarajevo in the current *Vanity Fair* includes a photograph of SAGA Director Ademir Kenovic.

But when Globalvision offered an hour special based on SAGA's material to television networks worldwide, not one responded positively. The rejections were overwhelming: "We've already covered Sarajevo,"

"Not for us," "Can't find a slot for it." Perhaps this group-think reflects some collective sense of denial about the horrors taking place in Bosnia. Perhaps it's just more evidence that the major media usually march in lockstep with the government on foreign policy. When Washington went to war in Iraq, TV news carried non-stop coverage. When Washington *didn't* resort to arms to save Sarajevo, media coverage remained lower key. And in almost every case, the networks rely on their roving correspondents, not better informed locals.

Perhaps there's something even more insidious at work here. I was struck by a recent story in London's *Independent*, reporting that newly unearthed documents show that the BBC—our Western paragon of broadcast journalism—had an actual policy of *not* covering the holocaust during World War II. (The reason: fear of awakening anti-Semitism in Britain!) They even had written guidelines prohibiting the use of "Jewish sources." One doubts such guidelines exist today, but the first war in the post-war period to be compared to a genocidal holocaust is hardly getting the kind of coverage commensurate with that categorization. To the Bosnians, however, the effect is not dissimilar. They feel their perspective is being ignored. "I used to think that if we had television during the Second World War, the world would never have permitted the extermination camps," a Bosnian filmmaker told me. "Now I no longer believe that."

There may be other factors at work. In the case of Bosnia, a majority of the victims are Muslims, who are part of a larger religious community that's been victimized by years of media scapegoating and stereotyping. They are victims who lack a powerful constituency or a slick public relations campaign to push for U.S. intervention. The lack of oil and other resources coveted by American industry has no doubt limited the enthusiasm for intervention.

So the Bosnians are seen but not heard—even as they insist that they are fighting a fascist aggression to preserve a multiethnic society in Sarajevo, and not to impose, as Serb nationalists claim, an Islamic fundamentalist state. This view really hasn't penetrated the news coverage, the principal frame of which is to picture the war as a confusing ethnic or religious conflict about land between Serbs, Croats, and Muslims. The human rights aspects of the war have been reported, but largely ignored.

TV's Year of Living Cautiously
Globalvision's brand of television is clearly out of step with what *Variety* recently called "TV's Year of Living Cautiously." There's more news pro-

gramming now than ever, but what do viewers absorb from this headline hit parade, from all that crime and slime on local news, and from the mush of hyped-up "storytelling" on the magazine shows?

Ironically, this steady stream of pabulum—the bread and circuses of an electronic age—is no longer even justified as journalism by those responsible for putting it on the air. When the priorities of some of our news managers are questioned, their response is to shrug and mutter a rationalization with the word "sweeps" in it. The drive for ratings has become its own unquestioned rationalization. There is just so much money to be made! Is it any wonder that Congress is up in arms once again about violence on TV, or that some entertainment programmers now say that the news is more violent than their trashy movies of the week?

The Question

Is this the best we as a society can do?

During the Gulf War, an opinion survey found that the more respondents relied on TV news, the less they knew about the causes of the conflict. Only four percent of Americans now even say they care about international affairs, even though their lives are increasingly being shaped by the dynamics of an interdependent global economy. Our ignorance of the world seems to be growing in direct proportion to our need to know more about it.

Our schools are losing this global education battle to television too. Kids are watching more, reading less. A *National Geographic* survey found that sixty percent of our high school students couldn't find Japan on a map. Twenty percent couldn't find the United States in relation to other countries! How can these young people compete in a global age? When it comes to understanding world affairs, we are an undeveloped country.

We are also still paying lip service to diversity. White males still dominate the "serious" talk shows, and the national debate follows all too narrow and predictable lines. Perhaps that's why popular singers like Bruce Springsteen are writing songs like "Fifty-seven Channels (Nothin' on)" while the telecommunications industry maps out ambitious multibillion dollar plans for five hundred channels to turn our homes into electronic shopping malls. More and more, viewers are being targeted as consumers, not citizens, as we enter the age of "information superhighways." Move over McLuhan. Marketing, not media, is the message.

At the same time, in this post–Cold War world, human rights has become *the* defining dividing line and challenge worldwide. Issues like Bosnia, China, and Haiti are now topping a Washington foreign policy agenda that for fifty years was obsessed with stopping "the Red menace." As ethnic conflict and wars *within* countries supplant ideological conflict and wars *between* countries, our television-driven democracy is being systematically *under-informed* about the real threats to the new global neighborhood.

Speak to the UN's Secretary General Boutros Boutros-Galli as *Rights & Wrongs* recently did and you get an earful of sober and well-documented complaints about how the leaders of the world are behaving irresponsibly in not funding urgent programs of humanitarian assistance, peacekeeping and preventive diplomacy that their own ambassadors have voted to support! By way of explanation, the UN chief says these same leaders complain constantly about the lack of public support for global solutions. Public opinion, they say, is lagging behind. But what shapes public opinion? Television.

Jimmy Carter had a similar complaint when he spoke with us, arguing that Americans have too limited an understanding of human rights. We tend to support principles when they are not really challenged, he says. Freedom of speech and religion are not that hard to get sanctimonious about. But social and economic rights are. The former president criticized the media and government for failing to recognize the importance of economic development in the third world, for refusing to focus on the need to reverse a growing polarization along North/South lines, between the haves and have-nots.

Media misinformation and manipulation can also promote ethnic conflict, hatred, and fear. When apartheid ruled South Africa, the government-dominated TV system branded all opponents as terrorists, hardening white attitudes and covering up the system's brutality. In the former Yugoslavia, the Belgrade regime used government-controlled television to promote ethnic chauvinism and war. The local media helped promote the conflict by muzzling opponents and blatantly distorting news. Today, international media perpetuate the conflict with confused and confusing coverage.

Isn't it obvious that television has an important role to play in spreading a respect for the values of human rights? Ironically, of all the channels, MTV has taken the lead in this arena with a "Free Your Mind" campaign to promote tolerance.

Pro-Social Television

We need more pro-social television in our own country whose population is becoming more mixed every day. There are now more Muslims in

America than Episcopalians. Human rights concerns are at the heart of securing justice for all in what is an increasingly multicultural society. The riots in our cities, from Miami to LA, our swelling prison population, and the persistence of growing inequalities, all speak to the perils of parochialism. It is an ostrichlike mentality that has turned so much of the prime-time TV schedule into a tool for titillation and diversion. Think of the attention the Amy Fisher case received and weep.

We could have kept *Rights & Wrongs* on the air for five years for what that gang bang of prime-time look-alike Amy Fisher TV melodramas cost. Our society is in trouble when the tortured lifestyles of its Joey Buttafuocos get more attention than the unspeakable torture being inflicted in the darkness in more than fifty countries. Shows like *Rights & Wrongs* can shine some light in—and perhaps even save lives—but so far we've found few funders with the guts to provide underwriting, and fewer networks with the gumption to put us on the air in accessible time periods.

Even the chiefs of PBS seem to put fear of controversy and criticism ahead of faith in content and conscience. Thankfully, many individual PBS stations have the option of selecting their own programming and will be airing the series through October. But after that, despite all the great reviews and viewer response, unless angels come flying and dollars come dropping, the only place to see *Rights & Wrongs* will be in the Museum of Broadcasting.

Cynics may say that the problem with programs such as ours is that no one will watch, that viewers just "don't care." Yet, episodic stories with a human rights dimension do very well on the highest-rated network shows. *60 Minutes*, which was almost cancelled before moving to its current Sunday night time slot, has won Emmys and audiences for its exposés of abuses in China's prisons and many similar stories. On its recent fifteenth anniversary salute to itself, ABC's *20/20* seemed proudest of its reports on famine victims in Africa and the plight of Romanian orphans. *Prime Time Live* has won critical acclaim and Nielson points for its few strong human rights related reports.

All of these successful TV newsmagazines have several things in common: they each took a while to develop a signature; they each took more than a year to build audience recognition and loyalty; and they each make great gobs of money airing reports from all around the world. In other words, when given the choice, Americans will watch the very kind of story that the pundits say they don't care about. Once again, the "conventional wisdom" is not so wise.

In government, a "need to know" criteria divides the informed from the truly informed. In our world, in this age, we all have a need to know. About the limits of power and the desire for justice. About the complexities and nuances of change in a turbulent world. About those grassroots heroes who are defining the values of democracy in countries where the freedoms we take for granted are not honored. We need less reporting about the machinations of the powerful in this new world disorder and more attention paid to human rights activists and innovative agenda setters.

The issues we face are increasingly complex. So are the solutions. Superficial sound bite journalism doesn't really inform us. We need contextual multicultural reporting as part of popular, regularly scheduled programming to outline problems and explore options for change.

We are not suggesting that one television program can reverse deeply rooted social trends or remake TV. We are also not unmindful of the limitations and constraints of doing a show on a shoestring. Most successful weekly TV series need adequate funding, constant promotion, and enough time on the air to fine-tune their story mix. Almost every successful series has needed many months, if not longer, to establish its on-air presence and generate viewer loyalty.

With all its problems, *Rights & Wrongs* is onto something important. We wanted it to become a model for a new type of global news programming on television, one that is built on a cooperative relationship with journalists and filmmakers worldwide.

We can't do everything, but we are doing something. It's worth a try. PBS, why aren't you listening? And if ABC's Roone Arledge wants to make an offer, we won't hang up. All we can do is keep trying.

Right or Wrong?

This article originally appeared in Toward Freedom, *Winter 1997.*

THE CONSPIRACY OF SILENCE
The Media and the Kennedy Assassination
1999

Speech for the Death of JFK Conference
May 15, 1999

I am Danny Schechter. Dan Rather is on vacation.
Will the camera crew from ABC in the back of the room please move over to make room for the crews from NBC and Fox? Excuse me, but can I ask the folks from C-SPAN not to block the CBS shots?
Oh—sorry—there are no crews.
I only wish we would have these problems. Even though the American people have expressed continuing skepticism about the official media-sanctioned explanations of what happened in Dallas thirty-six years ago next November, and have told pollsters year after year that they believe that some sort of conspiracy was responsible, serious news interest in the continuing debate and discussion has been conspicuous by its absence.

There are reasons why the JFK research community has not broken into the mainstream, why your conferences are not covered, why critics are marginalized. Largely, it is a function of the media's capitulation on coverage of the assassination and the cover-up—an institutional refusal to pursue the leads and flush out the truth. This has been compounded by the more recent merger of news biz and show biz, which has led to a decline of investigative reporting, and more sensationalism saturating the airwaves. There has been stereotyping, as well as a failure of nerve. But to be honest, part of media reluctance is based on the impression held by many skeptical and critical journalists that the conspiracy crowd is not credible because it accepts the views of kooks for whom one plus one equals five.

As one of those skeptical journalists, I know that my own interest in this subject was stoked and sustained by the emotional trauma of having been one of the millions of TV eyewitnesses who remember exactly where we were when those shots rang out, as if it were yesterday.

I had dropped out of college that fall to work with the civil rights movement. On that weekend before Thanksgiving, I had driven up to my alma mater, Cornell University, to see some old friends. It was a beautiful late autumn day, and I made good time reaching the student union in the heart of the campus, the building they call "the Straight." I pulled into the parking lot right around lunchtime. Bouncing up the stairs, I was unprepared for all the tears.

It had just happened.

I remember the sense of collective shock, and all those eyeballs glued to the sole public TV set on campus, as we watched Walter Cronkite pause, take off his glasses, swab dry his eyes, and report that the president was dead. I was impacted then—perhaps forever—by the horror of the events as well as by the power of media. Television brought all those images into our lives: the chaos in Dallas, the madness in the halls of the Dallas Police Department, Oswald's capture, Oswald's murder, the entire unexpected scenario of events. And in its aftermath, it was television that brought us together by reassuring us that our nation would go on. That sense of reassurance remained the media's mission over the years as it continually dismissed questions that could disturb a domestic tranquility it had helped reengineer.

The Kennedy assassination was the first great media event of the modern media era. Television news came of age with that event as well. Cronkite deviated from his role as objective anchorman to express emotion, and his tears deified him forever in the hearts of viewers who respected him as a human being, not some robotic reporter. It was also the story that thrust Dan Rather, another reporter from Texas famous locally for his hurricane reports, onto the national stage. Rather, of course, would succeed Cronkite when CBS unceremoniously dumped him years later. Nothing we saw that day would fully prepare us for the thirty-six year debate to come on the meaning of what we were watching.

In the years that followed, I observed the controversies that erupted, the criticisms of the Warren Report, the exposés of its many contradictions and improbabilities, the tales of the missing and dead witnesses and all that madness that turned "grassy knoll" from a strip of land into a global symbol, a part of our lexicon. Soon, European-style conspiracy analysis landed on the naïve shores of America, so much so that over the years suspicions about what really happened would become a national obsession.

The Kennedy assassination for many of us also represented the death of our belief in America the beneficent, the innocent. It marked the beginning of a disillusion with government that has driven my political life since then, through the credibility gaps of the Pentagon Papers, the CIA disclosures, Watergate, Iran-Contra, up until the present day with its Desert

Storms and NATO bombing campaigns for human rights. As secret documents surfaced, it became clear that parts of the government knowingly deceived the American people with lies and doublespeak.

At the same time, the Kennedy assassination, and the conspiracy mongering that soon surrounded it, also become a kind of side show—an almost sportlike political recreation with endless charges and counter-charges, disclosures, and intrigues. It spawned a library of books and monographs and a small army of people denigrated as buffs or buffoons. With the media only revisiting the issue episodically, a small army of citizen investigators stepped into the breech, churning out books, articles, and pamphlets that kept the allegation of conspiracy alive in the popular imagination. All of these self-appointed investigators began considering themselves a "research community."

Everyone had a theory. No one knew what really happened.

For years most serious mainstream news organizations devoted little time and fewer resources to investigating the unresolved questions. Instead, they downplayed it, debunking and denigrating independent researchers. "Big Journalism" somehow lacked the interest and the willingness to stay with the story.

In 1977, the screenwriter Nora Ephron explained why so many journalists "have kept as far away from it as possible . . . This is a story that begs for hundreds of investigators, subpoena power, forensics, experts, grants of immunity," she wrote. "A lot of people are dead. Some of the ones who are alive have changed their stories. The whole thing is a mess."

No one could or would untangle the mess either. The government failed with the Warren Commission and then failed again when the House Assassinations Committee took a second look in 1979. That investigation resulted in a finding of "a probable conspiracy" and called upon the Justice Department to pursue the matter. It didn't. More recently, the Assassination Records Review Board spent four years declassifying thousands of previously secret documents. Its work rated less press attention over all than Monica Lewinsky received in just one hour of saturation exploitation.

The press didn't seem to care. Collectively, it regurgitated its original view that Lee Oswald acted alone, concluding the case was closed. Oddly enough, despite all the big media guns and their one-note coverage, they were unsuccessful in pacifying public interest. By the time Oliver Stone rolled out his cameras, there was already a giant gap between the anti-conspiracy conclusions reached by the news media and the pro-conspiracy beliefs held by more than three-quarters of the people surveyed. The people didn't believe the government and they didn't believe the press. And they still don't!

This led to a kind of karmic standoff on the issue, that is until Stone's *JFK* hit the screen. Suddenly, with the power of a massive marketing campaign behind him, he offered a powerfully dramatized argument on an issue which up to that point had been presented, at best, sporadically and totally incoherently. In a country with a short attention span, his dramatization of a point of view took over two hours. Most importantly, his film included the still provocative but unproved thesis that Kennedy was killed when he decided to phase down the Vietnam War.

Big Journalism, no particular friend of coherence itself, went into action, unleashing its biggest debunking guns to blast away at Stone's movie as a "Hollywood happening," and a "conspiracy against reason." Oddly, critics loved the film, while most editorial writers and columnists hated it.

TV news coverage imbibed its hostile attitude towards Stone from the *New York Times* and *Washington Post*, the establishment press organs with whom they usually march in lockstep. Soon, TV news shows were denouncing Stone as if he had violated the "fairness and balance" doctrines that allegedly govern their news coverage—i.e. disclaimers, separation of invented footage and real footage, labeled dramatizations, showing "both sides" etc., as if their standards of so-called objectivity are routinely practiced.

Most of these attacks seemed to miss the fact that Stone is a dramatist, not a journalist; a moviemaker, not a TV news producer. Stone never claimed to be offering the whole truth; he always referred to *JFK*, perhaps disingenuously, as an exploration of one "theory." But the journalists bent on exposing his approach never reported his own doubts and modest claims. In setting up a *CBS Evening News* story on *JFK*, Dan Rather could barely conceal his own enmity when asking, "Is it an outright rewrite of history?" From his tone, there was no question that he thought it was.

Rather's attitude proved to rather accurately reflect the hostility that swept through TV newsrooms. ABC's *Nightline* was first off the TV block with a full-scale, one-sided blast at *JFK*. Fully half the program was devoted to exposing Stone's various "tricks" in the editing room. He was given only a short period of time to respond to this slickly edited ABC video assault on his thesis, peppered with sound bites from pro–Warren Commission "experts," all questioning his credibility.

Nightline returned to the subject a few weeks later after Stone's calls to open still-suppressed government files on the subject began to be taken seriously. Suddenly, his case appeared to deserve more respectful treatment, and he was given it.

Nightline was no stranger to the subject. Ted Koppel and Co. had spent an hour investigating the KGB's files on Lee Harvey Oswald in late November, a month before the movie opened. That show, which drew their largest audience of the season, never mentioned that our own CIA had many more files, nearly half a million documents on the subject, locked away. When our company Globalvision asked the CIA to give our cameras the same access to their Oswald files that the KGB gave ABC, we were turned down flatly.

We tried to interest CBS in airing our own film of the issues raised in *JFK*—a movie called *Beyond JFK*, directed by myself with two-time Academy award–winning documentary maker Barbara Kopple and HBO's Marc Levin. When we read that they would be airing a special on the subject, my partner Rory, who had worked for CBS, sent a copy of *Beyond JFK* over to Rather's producer at *48 Hours*. We never heard from them, but when we saw their show, a *48 Hours Special*, starring Dan Rather, we knew why.

48 Hours spoke with many of the same people we did, and featured so many similar segments that I suspected we had been ripped off. To my not inexperienced eyes, many of the elements and footage in their show look amazingly like the elements in ours. This is not to say that we don't offer a different interpretation. There is a vast content gap but . . .

Anyone who lines those two programs up against each other will see the similarities (and the differences.) At first I flirted with the suspicion that there may have been a bit of "creative borrowing," but you need hard evidence to make such a charge stick, and all I have is a gut instinct based on twenty years in the business.

As I thought about it further (Would they? Did they? Is this sour grapes or network envy on my part?) I was reminded of some Texas folk wisdom that Dan Rather himself used to spice his testimony in a trial that grew out of one of his *60 Minutes* stories: "If it looks like a duck, walks like a duck, and quacks like a duck—what is it?"

Quack.

Would they? You bet. Back then, CBS had already been caught copycatting. According to the *Village Voice* of June 25, 1991, the CBS newsmagazine was accused by HBO of attempting to rip them off after illegally obtaining a rough cut of a documentary on a rape crisis center, and then attempting to produce a similar show before it aired. In that case, a *48*

Hours producer actually apologized to HBO. I have been told of a similar incident involving another HBO project cloned by *48 Hours*. A former CBS producer suggested that cutbacks of research staffs and pressure for "hot stories" might be leading to "cutting corners" on West Fifty-Seventh Street.

As you would expect, CBS's approach was conventional: a centrist "on the one hand, on the other" approach with a predictable conclusion. We offer the view that there is more to conspiracy theories than meets the eye. They think that conspiracy theories clog the brain.

It was important, however, that for the first time on network TV, Dan Rather's *48 Hours* acknowledged that there are serious unanswered questions and doubts about the Warren Report's conclusions. The program even went so far as to concede that not all conspiracy theories are off base, a first for CBS. But staying on network course, they also recycled many of the conclusions of earlier CBS documentaries—that Oswald probably acted alone, that he killed Officer J.D. Tippet, that Jim Garrison was way off base etc. etc. *48 Hours* treated these controversial questions as articles of faith without offering any new evidence, as if assertion has the force of fact and truth. A score of books challenge their "reporting" on these points in detail.

I will leave those debates to others. What has not yet been dealt with is Rather's clever new twist in the debate, one that appears intended to end it. It is also a position calculated to portray the news business as above the fray.

To formulate it, Dan Rather uses an old debater's trick: When you don't want to deal with political analysis, trot out pop psychology. He did just that, taking refuge in a theory that dealt more with the motives of today's theorists than yesterday's assassins. This thesis is no doubt one of which Sigmund Freud would approve, perhaps in the spirit of Dan's own declaration that he is "going to keep coming on this one."

From the couch at CBS, here it is: Conspiracy theories must be explained by explaining their proponents away. Conspiracy buffs are best seen as people driven by personal psychological needs, rather than social or political agendas. Often paranoid, they are people who need to be "understood" in their groping, rather than heard on the particulars of their arguments, even when their books are on the best seller lists.

This is not surprising. It's called plausible denial. When CBS itself was under attack not long ago in two critical books, one by Dan's ex-boss, the other by a leading critic, Rather followed a calculated ostrichlike approach to not read them. "I liked the feeling of being able to say truthfully, I didn't read it," he boasted at a time when all of his colleagues were buzzing about their disclosures. He seems to have avoided the key conspiracy books too.

48 Hours' characterization of conspiracy theorists as "misguided" flows from the self-image that many mainstream newspeople cultivate about themselves as insiders, anchored in the "real world," pragmatists always, ideologues never. Hence Rather's charge that a belief in conspiracy involves an attempt to impose order and certainty on a world that lacks either. He asked us to accept that there are some matters which we will never know. In his program wrap-up, he dismisses conspiracy advocates as seekers after a coherent understanding of events that we journalists—pat, pat—know cannot exist. This put-down quite effectively marginalizes troublesome arguments instead of confronting them.

If we are looking for psychological motives here, why not turn the camera around? Rather himself has puzzled many an anchor-watcher with his own strange lapses of behavior over the years. What's it all about, Dan? What's the frequency, Kenneth? If the Kennedy assassination is a subject fit mostly for shrinks, what about the news business with its outsized egos, mega-salaries, and symbiotic relationships with those in power? The most insidious biases are the ones that are the hardest to detect or admit—like pervasive self-censorship, or conforming to institutional expectations and groupthink. If you want to see madness, look at the tapes of those Washington TV crews harassing grand jury witnesses in order to get a good shot or a stupid sound bite. If you like demented behavior, watch the Sunday morning TV shows with their banalities and bombast.

Dan, when is paranoia prophecy? You should know, as the man who gave Richard Nixon the Watergate willies, and who has time and again defended the sacred "Temple of News" at CBS against the infidels in the business office. Or, was his fire extinguished? Does co-optation just set in automatically when Richard Leibner negotiates a deal that reportedly brings in an estimated $13,409 a day? The camera blinked on that one.

Ironically, this psychobabble might not be all that inappropriate given the views expressed by *48 Hours'* most provocative guest, former CIA director Richard Helms. Interviewed to refute charges of CIA complicity, he was unable to explain why the CIA investigated itself in connection with the events in Dallas if the agency was, as Helms insisted, not at all involved. Even when ineptly confronted, he went somewhat ballistic on camera, sputtering that people who could believe that the CIA might have had a hand in the assassination are all "children." In effect, that is what *48 Hours* is also saying about those of us who suspect that Oliver Stone was on to questions worth pursuing.

Maybe I am being a bit unfair here to Dan Rather, implying that he was at one time more of an oppositional journalist than he thought appropriate. In *The Powers That Be,* David Halberstam reminds us of Rather's on-air sum-up on the night Richard Nixon stepped down. Listen to this:

> Rather: " . . . He did give, and I would agree with you Walter, what you said, he gave to this moment a touch of class—more than that—a touch of majesty—touching that nerve in most people that says to the brain: Revere the presidency and respect the president; the Republic and the country comes first . . ."

These are comments on a speech that virtually everyone who saw it or commented on it considered pathological, even psychotic.

What nerve does this touch, Dan? Perhaps the one that whispers: More than one brain is missing!

Freud's notion of a "split personality" might also be appropriate when you consider how Big Journalism reacted to Stone's movie. Initially, it confronted the arguments offered in *JFK* with one of the most hysterical media bashings in movie history. It took a Gary Trudeau cartoon on the *New York Times* Op-Ed page to dissect the absurd dimensions of the pounding Stone received from Big Journalists on all sides of the spectrum, from the cover of *Newsweek,* to every two bit Op-Ed pundit in the land. You had to laugh: Doonesbury's alter ego got their number by portraying Stone as JFK and the media as his assassins. This was one media firefight that could not hide behind a grassy knoll.

The media monitoring organization FAIR surveyed the coverage too, concluding that "the news outlets and journalists that attacked *JFK* the most vociferously were the ones with the longest records of error on the issue and defense of the lone assassin theory." It is almost as if journalists, who usually acknowledge that their own work is just history's "first draft," are insisting that if anyone has the right to distort history, it is they.

What seems obvious but is rarely acknowledged adequately is that all history—and by extension, all news—reflects someone's interpretation, a selection of some facts to the exclusion of others. Stone insists that "every historically based film in the history of the medium has utilized dramatic license and speculation, including documentaries."

For many newspaper columnists and TV commentators, the character assassination of Oliver Stone quickly became a higher priority than the questions he was raising about a president's assassination. Has anyone ever seen so much ink singing, or should we say, slinging the same song? Stone has confused facts with fiction; he has distorted history; Garrison was a fool; on and on? Only a handful of movie critics dissented from this self-righteous collective diatribe with its sound-alike regurgitation of identical posture and polemic.

When Stone's biopic on Richard Nixon was released four years later in 1995, the *New York Times* attacked it on the editorial page with an essay by Howell Raines, one of their top reporters. He criticizes Stone for believing the government is more competent than it is, and thus able to mount conspiracies. Once again, rather than rereading his own paper's clips on conspiracies—from the Pentagon Papers through Watergate—a top journalist dismissed the notion that people in power exercise their power to serve or conceal their own interests. After branding Stone naïve, he then offers up his own convoluted conspiracy theory, suggesting that Jim Garrison's case against the CIA was probably manipulated by the local New Orleans Mafia to shift attention away from them. His assumption, of course, is that the Mafia could do what the government can't: run a convoluted conspiracy.

The press claims to be committed to just the facts ma'am. Yet when confronted with the "fact" that no one agrees on the "facts," that every bit of "evidence" in this case has spawned counterevidence, that many documents may still be suppressed and hidden, honest media has had to take a second look and admit how little we know. As public opinion began to coalesce around the notion of opening the government's files, many of the journalists and public figures who had been so dismissive of Stone began to jump on the disclosure bandwagon, somewhat narrowing the gap between "news" and truth.

After all, what's a journalist to do when no one believes his or her spin on "the truth," when other interpretations of history start becoming acceptable, when the paradigm of official and "legitimate" reality begins to slip away? What to do? Do what Dan Rather does: lurch back and forth, embrace the theoretical plausibility of conspiracy while demolishing any practical possibility. And all the while, practice that polished politeness by treating Oliver Stone respectfully while producing a program that seeks to undermine his every premise. What a web we weave! Rather ended that *48 Hours* JFK special by proclaiming a pumped-up faith in facts and evidence over theories and beliefs, as if anyone really disagrees. But is this the case in most TV news coverage? Was it the practice during the coverage of the Gulf War when CBS and the other networks put jingoism ahead of journalism, when the Pentagon's "facts" were the only news all the time? Was it always "just the facts ma'am" over the years in CBS's embarrassing boosterism of the Warren Commission? And is it just facts that are driving today's coverage of Kosovo?

In our documentary, *Beyond JFK,* Walter Cronkite reveals that *CBS News* censored a comment by President Lyndon Johnson expressing his doubts about the lone assassin theory. The comment was deleted after our late president pressured CBS's late president with a fabricated concern about national security. For years Cronkite believed in the Warren Report. I was surprised then that he seemed to be changing his tune when I interviewed him in his office at CBS.

"Well I hold the view that he was a lone gunman, yes. I'm not sure as to whether it was part of a conspiracy or not any longer, however."

Tom Wicker of the *New York Times* was in Dallas when President Kennedy was shot and, like Dan Rather, came to national attention on the strength of his reports. At the time, he reported that the president was shot in the front. He later said he was mistaken. He was a sharp critic of Stone. Yet when I pressed him on the issue in his office at the *Times* just before he retired, Wicker confessed that he too had lost his certainty.

He told me: "For a long time I felt strongly that Lee Harvey Oswald was the lone assassin. I think there's evidence now that there certainly are doubts about that and I'm willing to concede those doubts. I don't know what happened."

Former PBS anchorman Robin MacNeil was there too, covering the event for NBC. He was the only journalist traveling with the president to get off the press bus after hearing shots in Dealey Plaza. Hardly a conspiracy "nut," MacNeil feels that Big Journalism may not be able to handle all the possibilities. "There is a predisposition still on the part of the mainstream media to believe it all works," he told me for *Beyond JFK,* "the system works. And it's only the crazies on the fringes that want to keep saying, no, it doesn't work, no it doesn't work, there's a conspiracy at work. And the two are converging all the time because the evidence has brought them together."

So, when pushed, Cronkite, MacNeil, and Wicker, leading lights of the journalistic establishment, all critics of Stone, admit to doubts, but those doubts rarely surface in major media coverage. Why? Most Big Journalists seem to make a fetish of facts, casting themselves in the pose of objectivity, often projecting deep-voiced expertise on the basis of the skimpiest of detailed knowledge. More often than not their interpretation of events and their "facts" are open to question. So is their point of view—an outlook that, above all, takes pride in denying its own existence.

CBS has been challenged over the years on its coverage of any number of issues—from Vietnam to Afghanistan— and it should be scrutinized for its honesty and integrity on the JFK assassination, the defining story of its news division, including this most recent *48 Hours* mishmash. After all, this is the issue on which Rather and CBS News built their reputations.

Big Journalism itself has to this day not explained the Kennedy assassination to anyone's satisfaction, including its own.

Yet at the same time, according to Robin MacNeil, "the country has become accustomed to, conditioned to, conspiracies at the very heart, in the very breast of its own government . . . Anybody would have to be a fool these days to dismiss conspiracies." Perhaps that explains the divergence between the views of the press and the people. The people believe conspiracies are occurring, while the press avoids reporting them.

WHAT IF?
1974

In 1974 I wrote a series of three articles for Papers, *a small magazine in Massachusetts, to try to imagine how the news could be presented differently; or at least how I wanted to see it back then. This was four years before I became a TV reporter.*

Dream I

One night, Walter Cronkite is preempted. Not by some network special or the like, but a daring and so far technologically unprecedented action by an as yet unknown revolutionary movement. Indulge my fantasy for a moment. The screen gets staticky. A "please stand by" announcement flashes. Then, a professional announcement: "Good Evening, the Free Video Commandos have preempted this program in order to bring you the real news, People's News."

I would like to think the viewer is transfixed. "People's News"? Where's CBS? The mind constructs a collage of street reactions. "Hey, wait a minute," a construction worker shouts, "they can't do that." A college student: "But Walter Cronkite was on the enemies list." An advertising executive: "This is ridiculous, they're only hurting their own cause." My instant sample is mixed. There is a sprinkling of "far out" and "hey can you dig that" from the long hairs. But for that minute in time, a national audience is captivated. Imagine: the revolution is not being televised, but, for once, there is something revolutionary on TV.

A camera meanwhile has zoomed down a ghetto street. It freezes on three people talking together on a tenement stoop. The locale doesn't look like a newsroom, but that's what it has been turned into. The three people identify themselves. First there's Fannie Lou Hamer, a middle-aged black woman, the former Mississippi sharecropper who came to national attention back in the days of the civil rights movement. Next to her, a younger man: Tom Hayden, a one-time student leader, an articulate radical intellectual known nationally as a Chicago Conspiracy defendant. And finally, Cesar Chavez, leader of the Farm Workers Union, a man of inspiration and quiet courage.

"We are your anchorpeople tonight," they explain, "invited to inform the American people about some basic problems that the news rarely touches on, or obscures when it does. Tonight, we hope to demonstrate that a real news alternative is possible and desirable. Stay with us as we take you to:

"The boardroom of Chase Manhattan, where Bank President David Rockefeller, now under the influence of sodium pentathol—that's truth serum, folks—will be interviewed on how the rich stay rich. The interview will be conducted by a Vietnamese peasant, an American autoworker, and a specialist on power structure research.

"And then, the Pentagon, where Pentagon Papers whistleblower Daniel Ellsberg debriefs the Joint Chiefs of Staff.

"From there, we'll go live to the publisher's office at the *New York Times*, where newspaper publishers from several major media empires, including William Randolph Hearst Jr., meet the surviving members of the Symbionese Liberation Army.

"And finally, we will all pray together in the prison chapel at Allentown, Pennsylvania, where former presidential assistant Charles Colson confesses to the deals he made with the Teamsters union to try to crush the Farmworkers union."

The anchorpeople continue: "In addition to exposing some of the plans of the people who rule America, we'll also be telling you about people struggling against them—activism which television news usually distorts or denigrates.

"Tonight, we'll be featuring reports on a black workers movement in Detroit; a feminist analysis on the state of the women's movement; a rap with a gay-media action group; and live via satellite Jane Fonda reporting from liberated zones in South Vietnam. Finally, we'll have some advice on how to beat high food prices with food co-ops. At the program's conclusion, viewers may call in questions and comments."

At that point, I blinked hard and awoke. The fantasy dissolved into the living memory of contemporary newscasting. My scenario seems unlikely, even to me. And that's perhaps because it is. Even a temporary interruption of the nightly news routine could not fundamentally transform it. Given the structures of American society, a basic change in the system itself is what's needed. Until then, our images of what newscasting is—and what it could be—are shaped by what the networks are currently doing.

Not accidentally they're all doing it the same way. You can prove that point to yourself easily enough. Just exercise your highly vaunted "right" to a freedom of choice. Flip the dial! Compare the range of stories and their treatment. Listen to the language that's used, the style of presentation. Oh, CBS's Walter Cronkite may be more liberal than ABC's Harry Reasoner, and NBC's John Chancellor's dour puss might turn you off or on. But basically they're birds of one ideological feather: members of the same species, sharing more in values and worldview than their competitive positions suggest. In form and content, they're interchangeable and perform a similar function.

Dream II

(Last month, Danny Schechter had a dream of what newscasting could be like if we weren't so locked in to the standard format now being used by all three major television networks. This month he goes a bit further in explaining his concepts.)

Television news is packaged. In form, it aims primarily at reinforcing its own credibility. TV journalists are groomed to become personalities and paid on the same scale as entertainers. Their journalistic skills are evaluated in equal measure with their visual appearance, manner, and professional style. Few people have friends or neighbors who look or sound like most broadcast people. More and more television stations are hiring consultant firms to make the news even slicker than it is. Advertisers pay handsomely to sponsor newscasts because they want some of the credibility to rub off on their products. The news programming seeks also to legitimize the media itself.

The form is well-suited to the content it transmits. That content is neither as comprehensive nor as objective as it pretends to be. Edward Epstein's study of television news (*News from Nowhere*, Random House, 1973) documents how the internal structures and capabilities of the networks define what is presented on the national news. He shows the pressures which limit and distort the picture Americans receive of what's going on in the world. Epstein concludes with a plea for more alternative sources of news.

As for objectivity, one doesn't have to agree with the critique commonly identified with Spiro T. Agnew (remember him?) that most news programming has a bias or slant to it. A totally bias-free approach is impossible, even as Agnew's attacks were aimed merely at substituting his own slant for theirs. Officially, the networks still cling to the chimera of objectivity. "Our reporters do not cover stories from their points of view," *TV Guide* quotes the President of CBS News as saying. "They are presenting them from nobody's point of view." It's a position, incidentally, which usually leans towards supporting established power and authority.

The debate over objectivity and bias often obscures the actual impact that news programming has on the consciousness of those who consume it. The tendency towards "up to the minute" reporting plays an important role in mystifying those at whom it is aimed. According to Herbert Schiller, a professor of communications, the process is quite intentional. He notes in his book, *The Mind Managers*:

> . . . The insistence on immediacy tends to inflate and subsequently deflate the importance of all subject matter. Consequently, the ability to discriminate between different degrees of significance is impaired. The rapid-fire announcement of a plane crash, an NLF offensive in Vietnam, a local embezzlement, a strike, and a heat wave, defies assessment and judgement. This being so, the mental sorting-out process that would ordinarily assist in creating meaning is abandoned. The mind becomes a sieve through which dozens of announcements, a few important but most insignificant, are poured almost hourly. Information, rather than helping to focus awareness and create meaning, results instead in a subliminal recognition of inability to deal with the waves of events that keep breaking against one's consciousness, which in self-defense must continuously raise its threshold of sensitivity.

Our minds become victims of media overload. We have more information than ever before and less ability to evaluate and understand it.

This process is not unintentional. There's a whole industry of media specialists who study and perfect television's ability to influence people. It's a mistake to believe that the calculation that underlies a sales campaign is not present when information is the product. Middle-of-the-road sociologists Paul Lazarsfeld and Robert K. Merton noted this phenomenon, explaining that the media's power comes "not only from what is said, but more significantly from what is not said. For the media not only continues to reaffirm the status quo but, in the same measure, they fail to raise essential questions about the structure of society."

The Dream is Over

TV is used as an instrument of mental and political pacification. Former '60s activist and political sociologist Todd Gitlin explains:

>   Whether deceptively labeled as *entertainment, news
>   culture, education, or public affairs,* TV programs aim
>   to narrow and flatten consciousness—to tailor every-
>   man's worldview to the consumer mentality, to pla-
>   cate political discontent, to manage what cannot be
>   placated, to render social pathologies personal, to
>   level class consciousness.

The aim of manipulating and packaging consciousness is to insure
the passivity of the people at large. Politics becomes a spectator rather
than a participant sport. The emphasis is on the people in power, the men
at the top. The whole approach has a counterinsurgent intent.

Not all of these intentions are realized. There would be very little
hope for change if the people on top had absolute control. Sometimes, the
media managers have to cope with the unanticipated impact of their
efforts. Conflicts within the media, and the media's impact itself, produce
contradictions between the managers and the managed. The medium
becomes an instrument for change whether it wants to or not. The reporting of the Vietnam War, although never really sympathetic to the
Vietnamese revolution or clear about the war's causes, certainly mobilized
people against government policy. It produced the *credibility gap*. The
same goes for Watergate reporting, which has undermined respect for
political institutions. Media attention gave various action-oriented movements a national audience. The civil rights, anti-war, feminist, gay, and
other social movements all cultivated that media attention. Consequently,
their concerns rose to the level of public issues. In some cases the media
themselves produced issues and groomed national *leaders* or spokespeople. All this had its costs, of course.

For the movement, a media focus often becomes a substitute for real
organizing work. Some of its leaders may temporarily capture public attention, but the process often transforms serious people into celebrities. Political
goals get obscured; outrageous statements or sensational actions get the publicity. A group such as the Symbionese Liberation Army might be able
momentarily to force some newspapers to carry its communiques, but it has
no control over the more extensive coverage of its own liquidation. The
media will be more responsive to forces for change only when it is more democratically controlled. "There's no such thing as unmanipulated writing,
filming or broadcasting," contends German writer Hans Magnus
Enzenberger. "The question, therefore, is not whether the media are manip-

ulated, but who manipulates them. A revolutionary plan should require the manipulators to disappear; ironically, it must make everyone a manipulator."

Making everyone a manipulator seems a rather utopian aspiration, and will require a radical transformation in the society at large. In the meantime, there are many ways of thinking and talking about reforms and alternatives. Nicholas Johnson, the maverick former FCC commissioner, wrote books filled with proposals to innovate and regulate. Most of the proposals were defeated. The broadcasting industry had no use for restrictions and many were quite prepared to go along with White House proposals to tighten (and righten) up politically in exchange for relaxed licensing regulations. With its ever slicker commercials, gun-happy cops-and-robbers shows, banal entertainment, and anti-educational children's programming, television remains the wasteland that former FCC commissioner Newton Minow once called it.

There's always the impulse, as Todd Gitlin notes, to chant, "Smash the TV sets, smash them all!" But destroying the technology is not, he recognizes, a plausible or even desirable solution. Instead, people concerned with changing society need a strategy for dealing with the media and their impact. The objective must go beyond simple reformism. "A revolutionary movement," he writes,

> . . . must aim to transform mass media by liberating communications technology for popular use. Nationalization of the technology by itself does not solve the problem of access—who is to have it, and under what conditions? The producer-consumer relation must be changed to a relationship among communicators. This requires a transformation of production (for subsistence, joyful human relationships) which would drown out the clamor of partial compensations.

This is heady stuff, I realize, and may be a long way off. In the meantime, I recommend talking back to your radio and television set by every means possible. Letters, calls and criticisms help the people on the other end of those microphones realize the extent of dissatisfaction. Inside the studios, there is some space to innovate and subvert. Thanks to various access rules, there is literally time to be seized.

So while you're flipping those dials, folks, think of what might be. Indulge your own fantasies. The media you transform might be your own.

part six MEDIA CRITIC

passions, pieces, and polemics • 1960–2000

DISSECTING THE TUBE
The Gulf War and the Death of TV News
1991

I've been dissecting news for a long time. Professionally that is. Back in Boston in the '70s when rock radio was in its infancy and WBCN was redefining the FM sound, I was known on air as the "News Dissector," the anchorman who specialized in reading between the lines. The name was given to me by a goofy dj because it rhymed with my last name. The label stuck because listeners realized it was descriptive of my "method."

That method of news analysis was something I learned on the job, once I understood that real and revealing information is not always where it is supposed to be, like on the front page or in the lead paragraph of a news story. It is certainly not to be found in any rip-and-read radio newscast or on any TV news "show" that calls itself "Eyewitness" or "Action."

Often, the real tip is buried in the back of the paper, in the business pages, where real power hides in the P&L stats; or in the obits, where the AIDS crisis takes no vacations; or in the wedding announcements, where the upper classes parade their wealth and power. Finding the buried facts and the defining details usually involves poring over lots of sources simultaneously, a form of comparative shopping in this information age. My nosing for news led me to appreciate why so many people read the paper backwards, sometimes starting and finishing with the sports page. Scores don't lie.

But sometimes television news does—and figuring out why and how is not always as easy as it looks. The coverage of the Gulf War has upset me more than any story I ever saw. It was probably the biggest, most expensive, and most sustained undertaking in the history of the television news divisions. It preempted the whole tube for weeks on end. It was a marathon, a news-athon. It hooked us into a state of addictive anxiety where we stayed tuned in to saturation updates without end. It rallied the country behind the war while promoting the illusion that what we were watching in our living rooms was what was happening in the deserts of Arabia.

The coverage was so one-sided and so well-managed that the Bush Administration would sweep the "GULFIES" if such an award were ever created to honor the media work in this conflict. Michael Deaver, President Reagan's PR honcho, was ecstatic about its impact, contending, "If you were to hire a public relations firm to do the media relations for an international event, it couldn't be done any better than this is being done." Hodding Carter, President Jimmy Carter's former chief flack, seconded the emotion: "If I were the government, I'd be paying the press for the coverage it's getting."

Yet the press—and this was a television story above all else—did not have to be paid. Pete Williams, the man who "handled" the media for the Pentagon, put his finger on this greatest accomplishment before hostilities erupted. "The reporting," he boasted to his superiors, "has been largely a recitation of what Administration people have said, or an extension of it."

But let's scratch deeper. Was this a case of meanies in the military manipulating the messengers of the media? No way. Listen to Michael Massing in the *Columbia Journalism Review:* "Access was not really the issue. Yes the pools, the escorts, the clearance procedures were all terribly burdensome, but greater openness would not necessarily have produced better coverage." For him, what we lacked were not freer reporters in the field, but more digging into the real reasons for the war; fewer "Scud Studs," as NBC's Arthur Kent was called, and more I. F. Stones to burrow in the bowels of official Washington to get at the story behind the story. (Kent himself was later fired by NBC, sued the network, won, and then wrote a book denouncing the manipulation of news.)

The critics of the war coverage now include many of the people upon whom we relied for our information. CNN's Bernard Shaw told a university conference that the American people "never got the whole story." Veteran *New York Times* war reporter Malcolm Browne was so disgusted with the news management that he said that the reporting on this war spelled an end to war reporting as we have known it. *Newsday* quoted one correspondent as saying: "The line between me and a government contractor is pretty thin."

This skepticism found more adherents because of the way the war ended—with what the UN called "apocalyptic" damage in Iraq, a country that suffered as many as 150,000 military fatalities, many inflicted as their troops fled Kuwait only to be massacred in what an Air Force pilot called a "turkey shoot"; with Saddam's massacres of the Kurds and the Shia Muslims; with nearly five million people displaced across the region; with a new wave of human rights abuses in Kuwait, and Saddam Hussein still in power in Baghdad. The television news coverage of the war never showed us the scale of the suffering or prepared us for the cycle of upheavals, reprisals, and arms sales to follow.

It often substituted images for information as well. We only learned later that the power of the Iraqi army has been deliberately misrepresented; that only a minority of the munitions used were so called "smart weapons;" that we may have been as responsible for the oil spills in the Gulf as Hussein; that the Patriots caused more damage than the Scuds; that there may have been no basis for the chemical weapons scare; that the cost of the war could end up being ten times the official estimate, once you factor in veterans benefits and war debt, and on and on. My point here is not to set the record straight, only to suggest that it never was.

The packaging of this coverage, with its cast of military experts, nose-cone footage, and absence of critical analysis, is the product of a television system that is itself rarely covered. While there have been some TV programs devoted to polite debates about the efficacy of press pools, there has been virtually no digging into why or how the networks became such willing partners in this orgy of patriotic chest-beating.

To dissect all this means delving into a medium that is less fact-filled than picture-driven. Packaging and marketing is far more dominant in the mode of production. To decode the product, you have to understand its manufacturing process, and recognize that TV news has its own political and economic signature. You can't understand what's on the tube without delving into the business behind the box.

To get at how TV news gets at us, you have to put the news itself into the kind of context into which it rarely puts the issues it is covering. And unfortunately the people who can do that best—the professionals who sit in at the morning meetings and decide the story lineups, who sit in the appropriately named "control rooms" to decide what images to send our way, and the correspondents and producers who know what part of their scripts get approved and what parts don't—may be too close to the electronic trees in this particular forest. Its hard to achieve the distance required to attempt that when you are part of the news system, when you are wearing those "golden handcuffs" that come with so many seductive privileges like high status and higher salaries.

When you are on the inside, you tend to think like an insider. Sometimes you take criticisms of your employer personally, as if any attack is directed at you. Unlike critics who throw broadsides from afar, you know how much time TV stories take to produce and how much competitive and deadline pressure there is. It's hard to be reflective when you are caught up in the day-to-day, especially during those periods of crisis, like around-the-clock Gulf coverage, when the adrenaline rush is contagious. You are often too busy counting the overtime to think about the impact your work is having.

As an insider, you soon discover that corporate cultures exist within news organizations the way they do in other organizations—with unwritten rules steering you towards being part of the team. At *ABC News*, a daily list is circulated detailing where everyone in the organization can be reached. It's labeled "the Troops." It should be no surprise that dissent and democracy are no more encouraged inside the "News Army" than inside "Today's Army." In both places there are clear limits placed on your "being all that you can be."

TV news organizations are structured into hierarchies and governed by codes of conduct and routines of coverage that tend towards a sameness of approach, even a homogenization of what programmers call "product." That's why when you flip the dials, you quickly notice how similar the shows all are, how their formats, structure and tone tend to look alike and sound alike. Without a doubt, different programs are "positioned" in different ways. Some reporters are better than others, and there are still many examples of reflective and distinguished work. But the differences are increasingly subtle when they are apparent at all. Ask any visitor to this country. When they cruise the channels, it all looks alike: American television.

It hasn't always been this way. For years, the big three networks had worked hard to project distinctive identities, although they were not always evident to the viewing public, which knew them on the basis of their stars, their shows, and their anchormen.

I once heard an executive describe the different network news organizations this way: CBS was referred to as "the Church"; NBC "the Morgue"; and ABC the "Asylum." Here's why: William Paley's CBS built itself on image and moral purpose—from the understated simplicity of its eye-like logo to its mystique as the network of Murrow and Cronkite. NBC was its staid alter ego, with newsrooms known for the lowest decibel level and the most waspy decorum. ABC was considered the most aggressive and experimental, the new kids on the block known for being younger, more personality-driven, the network of Howard Cosell and Geraldo Rivera.

Today all these differences are blurred, with Dan Rather's former producer producing Ted Koppel, with former NBC executives on ABC's payroll, and on and on. Their graphics may feature different colors and designs but their stories, their approach, and their "feel" are pretty much the same. Even CNN, which came to life in the '80s, has essentially copied existing formats, putting pictures to "all-news radio." Its ability to "go live" has been its signature, but the content of CNN is the content of mainstream TV news—only there's more of it.

Why the sameness? Why do the networks ape and imitate each other rather than compete by offering different visions and values? Shouldn't our free market promote competition, or are there monopolies of control and ideas?

One new book offers a provocative way of looking behind all of this. It is the effort of two media scholars who may yet be "discovered" like the late Marshall McLuhan, a once obscure Canadian scholar who became famous coining the phrase "Global Village." David Altheide and Robert Snow's new tome features their buzz words in its title: *Media Worlds in a Post-Journalism Era.*

The TV media, they say, has its own imperatives—what they call "media logic," turning this news world ultimately into a world of its own—with its own language, grammar, ideology, and interests. What is and isn't covered often has as much to do with how a program is seeking to position itself, the perceived or real demographics of its audience, as the inherent importance of any one story.

Media mechanics—the compression of all information into prefabricated formats—has already brought us the death of journalism as it was traditionally practiced. "The journalism enterprise," they contend, "especially TV news, is essentially reporting on itself; it addresses events that are cast in its own formats and frames of relevance," rather than attempting to understand the events in their own terms, and then trying to communicate the complexities and ambiguities of "real world conditions."

Fast forward to 1991 and soon you're one of four billion eyeballs around the world glued to CNN, watching a smart weapon get dropped like a suppository into the waiting rectum of some Iraqi weapons installation. Wham, bam, thank you ma'am. Soon you had what Gary Indiana calls TV war: "the Home Shopping Channel by other means;" made-for-TV Pentagon home videos, ultimately designed more for selling weapons systems to envious allies than for bringing information to news hungry Americans.

The Gulf War was the kind of story TV news organizations live for. It was a chance to show their stuff, prove their mettle, and make their reputations. Almost all of the super reporters of the Murrow era established their bona fides during World War II. Another generation of journalists catapulted to the top of their profession thanks to Vietnam. The Gulf War seemed to offer another such opportunity. For TV news organizations struggling to justify their outsized budgets to owners with bottom line orientations, the war promised more resources and higher ratings. What more is there?

Well, for starters, there is understanding. At the height of Desert Storm, a University of Massachusetts survey research team probed ordinary Americans for the basis of their jingoism and concluded that: a) most people actually knew very little about the issues on which they had strong opinions; b) they tended to echo government policy justifications believing they were their own independent viewpoints; and c) the more TV news they watched, the less they actually knew.

That's because news and truth were frequently worlds apart. Before Congress authorized the war, when the question was whether sanctions could work, there was a semblance of debate and evenhandedness. The behind-the-scenes story of the politics and economics that created Saddam's power—including the role of the United States—was rarely told. In fact, a poll showed that seventy-three percent of the American people say they didn't know the U.S. was arming Saddam during the ten-year Iran-Iraq war. No wonder then that the events that led to the war, and their context, were barely explained. Hussein was demonized early on, and anti-war sentiment was no match for the yellow ribbons and the appeals that made for patriotism.

Given the determination of the president to make his stand in the sand in this climate, giving peace a chance never had a chance. (Literally and metaphorically: a documentary about the making of the Sean Lennon-Lenny Kravitz version of "Give Peace a Chance" was never broadcast.) Once supporting the troops was framed as supporting the war, dissent was branded as treason. CNN's Peter Arnett became a target of right-wing criticism for his coverage from Baghdad despite the network's constant efforts to point out that Arnett's reports were often being censored. Friends at CNN tell me that the network was very sensitive to the well-orchestrated anti-Arnett campaign and were careful to insure that his reporting was surrounded by disclaimers and quickly followed by interviews with experts who treated Arnett as an advocate, not a journalist.

A new book by CNN's general-in-residence, Major General Perry Smith (retired), *How CNN Fought the War,* recounts his battle to keep the Pentagon position the dominant one while operating inside CNN's Atlanta newsroom, a place that insiders often call the "bunker." Smith explains how he waged his own war to "balance" Arnett's "misleading" coverage. "Throughout this entire period of time," he writes, "I kept trying to figure out Peter Arnett. Was he biased in favor of the Iraqi government? Was he an anti-war advocate . . . Was he fundamentally anti-American?"

This TV general finally decided that Arnett was not an ideological bad guy after all. His ultimate diagnosis: "The more I watched the Arnett coverage, the more I talked to people who knew him well, the more I came to believe that he was a 'feeler.' In other words, Arnett is someone who empathizes with the people around him." Feeling and empathy are apparently considered a high crime and misdemeanor in some circles. From General Smith's point of view, the fact that the UN later spoke of the bombing damage in Iraq as "apocalyptic" is not relevant to the accuracy of Arnett's reporting. The important fact was that Arnett's message and his "feelings" were out of line with the official line.

There is another factor that brought the networks into line with government policy—a factor which has not been commented on much elsewhere because it raises that distasteful notion of "self-interest." It turns out that January 1991 was not the best time for the networks to take on a popular president and his popular war. And the reasons were economic.

Just as the smart bombs started flying, a lot of smart network money was engaged in a massive lobbying effort to change the FCC's Financial Syndication rules. Those rules, enacted at a time when the public airwaves were thought fit for regulation in the public interest, limited the networks' rights to own and market their own programming, ostensibly to limit their power to monopolize the marketplace. This meant that pro gram suppliers, not the networks, would forever make the big money when the Cosby show and others went into syndication. Needless to say, this arrangement pleased the producers, not the programmers. As television became more competitive, thanks to cable and VCRs, network profits began to plunge. Hence the high stakes campaign to change the rules to more amply reward the broadcasters.

The Federal Communications Commission had the power to revise the rules, and it was dominated by a group of Reagan-Bush FCC appointees. One of the commissioners, James Quello, a former station manager of Detroit's ABC affiliate, was the network point man on the issue. Just before the war started he made a very public point of criticizing aggressive questioning at Pentagon press briefings as unpatriotic in a speech to the Indiana Broadcasters Association. What kind of signal do you think that sent to network higher-ups? What "Network Big," to use a *Variety*ism, would want to antagonize the very administration it was then asking for a big financial dispensation?

By the war's end, when I spoke to Quello, he had moderated his critique, saying that he now felt the networks did a good job. Incidentally, he voted for changing the FCC rule—but the networks did not get all the changes they sought; they only won a limited but lucrative compromise giving them the right to sell their shows overseas.

I don't have hard evidence yet of just how this FCC sideshow affected the war coverage in the main ring of the media circus. But a friend at one of the top television shows—a producer who insists that his anonymity be protected—told me a relevant story. He had suggested that more debates be built into his network's coverage; his executive producer agreed and invited him to draft a proposal. He did, but he never received a response. It was explained that a prominent network "fixer" was in the White House regularly in that period lobbying on the FCC rule change, and that there was no way the administration could be confronted when the networks had such an important economic agenda under consideration in Washington. There is no way to confirm this story, but other journalists I've told it to say it "sounds right."

It was in this same period that Michael Gartner, president of NBC's news division, personally intervened to kill a story about civilian damage in Iraq. The story had been shot and produced by the network's long-time stringer Jon Alpert, one of the few independent journalists to regularly report for a network news program. Alpert was fired after fifteen years. The circumstances were these: Thanks to an invitation from former Attorney General Ramsey Clark, Alpert wrangled a visa into Iraq at a time when NBC News could not get its own principal correspondent in. Tom Brokaw's *Nightly News* program agreed to run his report, although the network news managers resented his getting in when their guy couldn't. The traditional newsies never liked Alpert's unconventional, non–button down style. Alpert told me that the president of NBC told him that he was considered a "loose cannon" and didn't want one of his people associating with the "Ramsey Clarks of the world."

Gartner says he never saw Alpert's piece so he was not censoring that specific story, and that the network belt-tightening meant that freelancers were no longer needed. But, among journalists who examined the case, there is no question that it was the content of Alpert's report, with its striking images of civilians in hospitals and people weeping over their dead, that doomed the report. It may or may not be relevant that Gartner was hired by General Electric when it bought the network. GE is the country's second largest defense contractor. One of its divisions was mak-ing the weapons that the other division was reporting about.

Slowly, as hard information leaked out from under the blanket of state censorship and news management, media organizations began to admit they had been had. Months after the war ended, the organization representing the bureau chiefs of fifteen news organizations that had earlier agreed to work within the Pentagon's restrictive system wrote to Defense Secretary Dick Cheney to protest the pool system that the networks helped create. This after-the-fact disclaimer was pathetic, especially in light of what occurred in France, where all the leading news anchors had threatened to strike rather than become passive conduits of official briefings and packaged press releases. What's most worrying about all of this is that it can happen again. The government has learned, in Norman Mailer's phrase, to "feed the media." And the television media has not learned very much at all.

This article originally appeared in Spin *magazine, 1991.*

HELICOPTER JOURNALISM AND ITS LIMITS
Why Reporters Who Only Look Down Tend to Cover Up
1994

The helicopter provides a useful metaphor for assessing the state of con-temporary American journalism and for understanding how the majority culture covers the minority.

Ninety-five million Americans were mesmerized as the TV news hel-icopters tracked O. J. Simpson's bizarre Bronco ride on the freeways of Los Angeles last summer. A scene that seemed inspired by a look-alike chopper shot in the movie *Speed* was fascinating enough to disrupt prime-time programming and the NBA basketball championship. The prospect of a black celebrity blowing his brains out, live and in color before the cameras was too tantalizing for our TV programmers to turn down. We would later learn that Simpson had told his pursuers at the beginning of the chase that he was heading home—but we never found that out until the chase scene was shamelessly milked.

This was not the first time, of course, that aircraft were pressed into service as the prime means of reporting news in L.A. Who can forget those helicopters circling over South Central Los Angeles in the after-math of the verdict in the trial of the policemen who beat Rodney King, video cameras zooming in vicariously on the excitement and danger of a community upheaval and rip-off spree in progress, with fires and plumes of smoke providing the kind of eerie special effects usually produced in nearby Hollywood.

To be sure, not all of the coverage came from the comfortable van-tage point of an airborne helicopter. Some gutsy reporters were down in the streets taking notes while trying to safeguard their equipment and persons, knowing all too well that rage and frustration can spill over to the press, often perceived in inner-city neighborhoods as a proxy for the pow-ers that be. The "facts" of the L.A. riot were ultimately reported, but their larger meaning may have been obscured. While America fixated on the chaos below, it was broadcast safely from above.

The top-down angle of vision sums up the dominant "outside-in" media approach to racial stories in America. When there are no distur-bances—only what some call "silent" riots—coverage is more episodic and usually linked to retrospective and ritualized coverage of commemo-rations such as Martin Luther King, Jr.'s birthday or Black History Month. Occasionally the media focuses on minority communities and their issues in the aftermath of the latest police brutality incident. As chronic problems resurface or boil over into destructive rebellion, media institutions dust off clips from the morgue or rerun archival footage to remind us that the news is not all that new. If this occasional use of archival material really drew historical parallels, or focused attention on long-standing structural racism, it would be welcome. But most of the time, footage is replayed for its action quality or to illustrate superficial points of comparison.

Substantive analysis is rare, especially if it points to how government policies or police behavior contributed to the problem in the first place. When was the last time you saw a report on ghetto violence that explained how red-lining by banks, inferior education, benign neglect by city government, decaying housing stock and infrastructure, or white business flight contributed to racial tension? Such reports air occasionally as post-mortems in the aftermath of events. But by that time the images and first-day story have usually defined how we understand "what happened."

The larger challenge to journalists becomes apparent as the truth of the 1968 Kerner Commission's report on civil disorders is recycled from one generation to another, with its honest—and all too rare—admission that we live in two countries, one white and one black, that racism has an institutional character, and that white indifference is as much of a problem as white prejudice.

The Kerner report did more than document a growing gap between white and "Negro" Americans. It took aim at the news media in a "finding" that was buried in 1968 and is all but forgotten now, concluding that the media totally distorted the causes and significance of the racial uprisings that tore urban American apart. "We have found a significant imbalance between what actually happened in our cities and what the newspapers, radio, and television coverage of the riots told us happened," it concluded.

Twenty-five years later, these words have an ongoing relevance, serving as an indictment of corporate journalism's self-image, mission, and performance. How far have we come from criticisms of a press that "repeatedly, if unconsciously, reflects the biases, the paternalism, the indifference of white America?" The Kerner Commission's final words bear repeating: "This may be understandable but it is not excusable in an institution that has the mission to inform and educate the whole of our society."

Reporting about race is a small industry in America. It has produced superficial and distorted reportage, as well as some of our greatest literature, spiced with insights and wisdom. My own experience as a journalist has been enhanced by immersion in the civil rights movement of the

1960s and coverage of the international human rights movement today.

These days, I think about the coverage of race in America in a global context, believing that when we look outside this country and find other angles of vision and methods of analysis worthy of applying, we can see our own society a bit more clearly.

Outside the United States, the coverage of race does not just focus on one "c" word, like color, but explores others, such as context, class, community, commerce, and consciousness. Race may be a key factor in all kinds of conflicts, but it is neither static nor the only one. There is confusion in America's public discourse about the vocabulary of race: We often use the term "race" when we mean racism, a concept that implies a relationship between an oppressor and the oppressed.

In other countries, especially in Western Europe, there are newspapers and public service broadcasters who tend to examine the causes of social problems as well as their effects, with journalists less likely to conceal their political leanings in a blather of self-congratulatory pretensions about "objectivity." I subscribe to the Manchester *Guardian Weekly*, which offers reporting from the *Guardian, Le Monde,* and the *Washington Post,* precisely for such reasons: it allows me to contrast coverage as well. The spectrum of discussion in such liberal European media seems much broader and less likely to delineate political differences the way we do along narrow Republican-Democratic lines.

Television abroad, unlike American TV, is not totally dominated by commercial values. In France, England, and Germany there are annually hundreds of hours of TV documentary programs that tackle social and political issues. The BBC, Channel Four, and other outlets are able to remain competitive with commercial broadcasting. The infotainment sensibility and tabloid "reality" programming have not yet prevailed.

As the major American media corporations and media barons such as Rupert Murdoch gobble up more media institutions globally—or launch their own—some of the differences between what we see in the United States and what they see overseas are disappearing. The so-called American influence, driven by corporate interests, continues to insinuate itself into the fabric of an emerging global popular culture. First Hollywood and now made-in-the-USA movies are driving out other fare simply because local cultures have neither the resources nor the distribution channels to allow them to keep up or compete.

The annual TV market in Cannes is a good place to measure what's selling—and who is selling out. A Warner Brothers marketing executive speaks of "moving tonnage of product" in one corner; in another, the American networks are gobbling up production entities and positioning themselves for global expansion. For example, the European owner of the Superchannel—the pan-European satellite that linked East, Central and Western Europe with a mix of programming that included shows about the environment and our own human rights series—was forced by a European bank to sell the station to NBC, owned by General Electric. The new owners rechristened it the NBC Superchannel and recast it in their own image as an outlet for NBC shows and CNBC financial chatter. Roger Ailes, President Reagan's image-maker and now a top NBC executive, played a key role in the program refit.

One of NBC's first decisions was to withhold broadcast of a *Rights & Wrongs* show that reported criticism of G.E.'s labor practices in Mexico (it was later broadcast after this small act of censorship was exposed in *Variety*), and then to drop the series altogether on the grounds that it lacked "European content." A week later we received a grant from the European Community because of our European content.

We are all witnesses to the disappearance of serious journalism in the United States, as tabloid styles increasingly set the news agenda. Our media devote little attention to putting news in context. Judged by the way the mainstream press in the U.S. shuns the past and marginalizes memory, we might conclude that history doesn't count in grasping the present. Yet journalists, especially those who report on sensitive issues of race—often buried, as they are, in mine fields of nuance—can only make these issues intelligible if they locate a historical context and larger meaning.

And sometimes we need familiarity with the past to help us recognize that race is a significant factor in a story where it seems on the surface not to be. Otherwise we contribute to a fog of collective amnesia. For example, the legacy of slavery in America has to be acknowledged in reporting on race relations. At the same time, this must be done without regurgitating all those cliches about the "pathology of the black family," which so often result in a "blame the victim" news frame.

In the international media, but rarely here, economic issues are treated as integral to an understanding of politics. In the coverage of politics, journalists attempt to trace and explain the relationships between who owns what and how power and opportunity are distributed in the society.

Ownership and interests are usually linked. This goes for the news business, too: The concentration of the American media in fewer and fewer hands has had an impact on what does and does not get covered.

The distribution of economic power has maintained a class-stratified society in which our beliefs and worldviews are shaped by class experiences and socialization. That's why labelling people racially and monolithically ("the Blacks," "the Latinos," or "the Whites") is so misleading.

In the case of the Los Angeles upheaval, for example, the circling helicopters brought us images that could not explain who was rioting or why. The fact that there were as many Latinos and other minorities arrested as blacks meant that it was far more than just a black reaction to the Rodney King verdict. A new independent film, *The Fire This Time*, explores the roots of the disturbances, examining the parallels with the 1965 Watts rebellion and the city's failure to act in its aftermath. Shot from the ground, not from the air, the film focuses less on the people in the streets than on the neglect by those in the suites—the city's power structure. Perhaps because it looks around, rather than down, *The Fire This Time* is having problems getting on the air in Los Angeles.

Once again, an international parallel might help us see our society more clearly. There has been extensive coverage of South African apartheid in the American media but rarely in a way that helps us understand what our two countries have in common. Typically, apartheid in South Africa is presented as another version of the overt racial segregation that long divided Americans, as if the African National Congress's (ANC) liberation struggle was just a replay of our civil rights movement. What we are rarely told is that apartheid's founders based their system in part on the U.S. policy of forcing Native Americans onto reservations. The ruling white minority used apartheid not only as a rationalization for dumping so-called surplus populations but as a tool to manage and exploit black labor. Propped up by American-based multinational corporations who flocked to South Africa in pursuit of the profits such exploitative policies promised, the pass system was a way of controlling and subjugating the workforce and enabling giant mining enterprises to flourish. The American press reported South African police atrocities, but the structure of the apartheid system, and its creation of a vast gulf between wealth and poverty, was rarely explained.

Furthermore, while people of color in South Africa certainly have been oppressed on a racial basis, deep divisions also have existed along rural-urban lines and according to loyalties of ethnicity, tribe, and politics. This destructive factionalism contributed to the decision by the African National Congress to make non-racialism a basic tenet of its philosophy.

Yet as far as much of the American press was concerned, Mandela contin-ued to be identified as South Africa's "black nationalist leader," simplify-ing his movement's ideas and political culture and subordinating them to his pigmentation. A conflict over values and power was presented to American audiences for years with one formulaic racial description— "black-on-black violence"—an explanation that explained nothing, mak-ing it virtually impossible to assess, for example, the real significance of the struggle between the ANC and the Zulu-nationalist Inkatha Freedom Party led by Gatsha Buthelezi.

The American press habitually resorts to this black-on-black refrain in covering politics in Africa, yet never uses similar terminology to cover Europe. We do not read about "white-on-white" violence as an explana-tion of neo-fascism or the war in the former Yugoslavia. The Western media use another variety of false labelling in the case of the war in Bosnia, characterizing the warring parties along equally artificial ethnic lines—*the* Serbs, *the* Croats, and *the* Muslims. Such monolithic categories subvert any clear understanding of the war's political dynamics because they deny ideological differences and confuse authoritarian ruling elites with the people they ostensibly represent. For example, the people of Sarajevo of all ethnic backgrounds who are fighting to defend their mul-ticultural city against an ultra-right-wing nationalist onslaught can't understand why so much of the coverage treats the aggressor and the vic-tim with parity. That Western diplomats have proposed a plan to carve up the country along ethnic lines—á la apartheid—is rarely commented upon. And despite all the references to "ethnic cleansing," the war is rarely depicted as an expression of racism.

The South African experience has relevance here as well. "Ethnic cleansing" is but another form of forced relocation in which a people is dispossessed because of who they are. It is unmistakably a racist concept, since it targets people on the basis of their ethnic-racial difference. The Bosnian writer Kemal Kurspahic refers to the so-called peace plans that have sought to partition Bosnia along ethnic lines as "classical apartheid," a solution to which the West once again, in another part of the world, has acceded. Other Bosnians have made parallels with the genocide of Jews during World War II. A Muslim cleric, Musta Spahic, has referred to Bosnia's Muslims as the "new Jews of Europe." Marek Edelman, the Jewish hero of the Warsaw Ghetto resistance, has also stressed the paral-lels, indicting Europe for "behaving the way it did toward the resistance in the ghetto."

Listen to Rabia Ali and Lawrence Lifshults put forth the Bosnian perspective in their book, *Why Bosnia*, and ask yourself how many times this perspective has informed the news coverage you have watched:

> The reality, as the Bosnians saw it, was that the West was complicit in engineering their defeat and the destruction of their society. Their emphatic denials to the contrary notwithstanding, the Western powers had made their position unmistakably transparent: they would not permit Bosnia[ns] to defend their country themselves or to allow others to join in their defense and they would compel them to accept defeat, and accede to the internationally legitimized carve-up of their country.

And yet if the majority of the Bosnians were not Muslim, would the West have looked away as long as it did? If Haiti were not black, would its refugees be returned to the high seas? Jesse Jackson once asked if the media response would have been different in South Africa "if twenty-six million blacks were holding down four million whites under the gun."

These international references are relevant to a discussion on the reporting of race in America because the United States is bound by the same international protocols and covenants on the protection of human rights as other nations. Our media could, if it chose, legitimately examine domestic racial issues in the broader context of international human rights. Over the years, American civil rights leaders began to appreciate this connection and internationalize their own perspective, broadening their civil rights emphasis into a human rights focus. W. E. B. Dubois, an early NAACP leader, became a pan-Africanist and intellectual of global stature. Malcolm X and Martin Luther King, Jr. followed in DuBois's footsteps. Malcolm X went from the black Muslims to black nationalism to black internationalism, demanding in his last years that the United States be judged by the standards set out in the United Nations Declaration of Human Rights. He saw black oppression in America as a crisis of human rights and traveled worldwide preaching the gospel.

Martin Luther King, Jr. is usually remembered for his "I Have a Dream" speech in 1963. But later in his life he too developed an international outlook, attacking the war in Vietnam while arguing that "a true revolution in values will soon look uneasily on the glaring contrast between poverty and wealth . . . the Western arrogance of feeling that it has everything to teach others and nothing to learn from them is not just."

In December 1993, Human Rights Watch and the American Civil Liberties Union published a comprehensive and detailed report on human rights abuses in America. They studied how the United States government applies human rights law, and whether our country is in compliance with the International Covenant on Civil and Political Rights of the UN Declaration that Washington signed in 1992. The 128-page report catalogued serious and widespread violations in the areas of race and sex discrimination, prisoners' rights, police brutality, the death penalty, immigration rights, language rights, religious liberty, and freedom of expression.

Most Human Rights Watch reports get lots of coverage and are cited by broadcasters throughout the United States. Their findings about other countries routinely make news. This one didn't. "It got almost no pick up," an official of the organization told me. "We were surprised because it is such a powerful story."

Powerful maybe, but also willfully ignored. Why?

The challenge for those reporting on race is to cover the many struggles to right wrongs. It can be done: *Freedom on My Mind*, the audience award–winner at the 1994 Sundance Film Festival, is a case in point. It offers an intimate insider view of the civil rights movement that transformed Mississippi and challenged America in 1964.

The film gets at truths deeper than most journalistic accounts because it encourages you to feel that movement's texture and passions through the eyes of those who made it history. It humanizes rather than distances, while offering a real contextualized chronology. It tells stories based on the lives of ordinary people at the grassroots level, not just the better-known leaders, with compassion and a bottom-up, not top-down perspective. It also points toward the kind of reportage we see so rarely now on television but could, if the television networks had a different agenda.

Helicopter coverage could never have told that story, or many others. Perhaps that's why the helicopter pilot who brought the great O. J. freeway spectacle to world attention is now being wooed with movie deals and an offer of a "reality" series of his own. Let's face it: the choppers just chop it up. It's time for journalism to parachute back to earth and start reporting from the ground up, not the top down.

This article originally appeared in Tikkun, *September/October 1994.*

UNCOVERING THE PRESS
The Revolution in Portugal
1975

"If you can't understand the situation in Portugal," an English journalist told a BBC audience recently, "it's probably because you've been reading the newspapers too regularly."

An extremely complex political event, the Portuguese revolution has been reduced by Western press coverage to a contest for power at the top, a jockeying for position by personalities and forces who are for or against communism. While editorial writers and U.S. government officials sound a chorus of support for Portugal's "moderates," the coverage on the scene is a throwback to the pre-détente '50s.

Time's "Red Threat"

Time magazine's recent "Red Threat in Portugal" cover, with its hammer and sickle and grotesque caricatures of the "troika" then governing the country, was a portrait of unconcealed bias. "A revolution that began by freeing Portugal from a dictatorship of the far right is rapidly evolving into a dictatorship of the far left," it stated categorically. "In Portugal the dream that the April revolution would lead to a democratic and pluralistic society is fast fading, and the nation's eight million people have only a slim hope of seeing a centrist or moderately socialist civilian government."

Now, less than a month later, Portugal has a moderate and centrist government, and the Communist Party has suffered a clear setback. Although last week *Time* carried no news from Lisbon, the *New York Times* pronounced the event a "new start for Portugal," while the *Wall Street Journal* confidently asserted that "Portugal seems to be teaching us that the worst doesn't always happen."

The *Journal*'s worst fears are not necessarily shared by the people of Portugal, depending, of course, on which class of people one talks with. The specter of counterrevolution is a genuine concern for a wide range of people I spoke with, whose lives have been transformed by the revolutionary process launched in April 1974.

Simplistic Categories

Anti-communist protests in the North received splashy, front-page coverage, with rarely a mention of their organized, rightist character. The Western press made little attempt to explain or analyze the economic grievances of the northern peasants, or the role the reactionary Catholic Church has played in inspiring the rioting.

If the press considers the "Reds" the main danger to Portugal, it has projected the Socialist Party as the country's savior. A wire-service reporter admitted to me that the crowd estimates for socialist rallies were consistently exaggerated.

Political conflicts are reduced to simplistic categories. The communists are all "hardliners"; their leader, Alvaro Cunhal, is the "party boss." Their political program is stigmatized as "East European-style communism," although they deny it.

The Socialists, Popular Democrats, and Center Democrats are grouped together as the "democratic forces" who, despite their differences, are presented as representatives of the majority will. The press views the results of the April 1975 constituent assembly elections as the only legitimate measure of public opinion. However, the high percentage of illiteracy among the electorate, the use of fear tactics by the far right, and the popular Armed Forces Movement's support for socialism—erroneously taken by many voters as an endorsement of the Socialist Party—are never mentioned as having influenced the election.

Boiled-Down News

A prominent American correspondent feels that Americans need simplification to understand the situation. "We have to write for the milkman in Idaho," he explained. "We have to boil it down."

But the effects of distorted and oversimplified reporting are serious. Largely because of fear generated by Western press coverage, Portugal's economically vital tourist industry was practically destroyed this summer. Further, a hostile public opinion, officials note, can create an environment conducive to overt Western intervention.

No major newspaper has even reported, much less investigated, the charges by former CIA agent Philip Agee detailing covert CIA maneuvers in Portugal.

I asked an officer in the Armed Forces Movement for his assessment of U.S. press coverage. "I have met many of your journalists, including some of your more prominent columnists, but I find it very difficult to talk with them," he responded, on the condition that I not use his name. "They come with preconceived notions, and get very upset if you disagree with their definitions of democracy or socialism."

U.S. correspondents have little understanding of Portuguese history, he told me, and even less sensitivity to the needs of the Portuguese people. "They speak as if there are no classes in our society, as if history is all the work of a few men. They have no tolerance for explanations which do not fit into their formulas."

Portugal was always a backwater for most of the Western press. International newspapers based their correspondents in Madrid and kept stringers in Lisbon. The repression of the old regime and the resistance against it received scanty coverage. Not surprisingly, the events of April 25 caught most of the journalistic establishment off-guard.

Having now defined the "story" as a quarrel for power within the ruling circles, reporters usually cultivate sources who share their outlook. It is rare for a reporter to seek out or quote the opinions or analysis of the radical left, or, for that matter, independent observers. In the end, Portugal becomes, like so many news stories, a never-ending series of the reporters' own notions of communist treachery, of violent protests, of economic chaos.

Washington Post/Newsweek correspondent Miguel Acoca, for example, found a maid at the Tivoli Hotel, the closest thing to an American press club in Lisbon, who "caught the mood best."

"Several weeks ago, when a Ukrainian folklore troop from the Soviet Union stayed at the Tivoli," Acoca wrote recently, "she did the dancers' laundry. 'Mother of God,' she exclaimed, 'their underwear was coarse stuff. It wasn't as good as mine. So tell me, what do we need communism for?'"

Paper to the Printers

"We want to create a paper that will be in the hands of the working classes, free from all compromises and from all partisan solidarities," declared the workers at *Republica*, a privately owned newspaper with a strong independent tradition. When they took over the paper last spring after a long struggle with an owner linked to the Socialist Party, the event shook Portugal. The American press referred to it as a clear-cut case of communist suppression of the free press.

Carlos Albino, current coordinator of the workers editorial commission at *Republica*, told me two weeks ago that the conflict had its roots in the workers' resistance to the owners' efforts to convert the paper into an organ of the Socialist Party. Albino stated categorically that the workers were opposed to control by both the Communist and Socialist Parties.

The *Times* of London did report that the *Republica* conflict "is essentially a clash between the owners and journalists of the newspaper, who happen to be Socialists, and the printing workers employed by it—some, but by no means all, of whom are Communists." The American press did not report this.

In fact, many of the *Republica* journalists aligned themselves with the workers against the owners during the conflict. Throughout, the Socialist Party continued to publish its own weekly organ.

This article originally appeared in Seven Days, *October 6, 1975.*

BOSNIA: A FAILURE OF JOURNALISM
1994

Two recent editorial cartoons defined the problem. The first shows an army of news satellite trucks and minicams staked out at the Lorena Bobbitt trial. A passerby asks one of the TV crew members, "Why don't you people give this kind of coverage to the tragedy in Bosnia?" He responds, "Did someone there get his penis cut off too?"

A second cartoon shows a movie theater with *Schindler's List* on the marquee. A couple are leaving, shaking their heads, wondering how "such a thing" could have happened. In the foreground, you can see the headline on a newspaper in a sales box: 150,000 DEAD IN BOSNIA; WORLD DOES NOTHING.

When a recent edition of *Nightline* looked closely at the parallels between the Nazi Holocaust and genocide in Bosnia, two of the three "expert" guests admitted that they didn't really understand the dynamics of the war in the former Yugoslavia, and didn't think most Americans did either. Paradoxically, *TV Guide* reported that week that Bosnia was one of television's most-covered foreign news stories.

Despite all the coverage and the courage of those who bring it to us, Bosnia represents a frightening failure of journalism—a failure of analysis, interpretation, and explanation. However shocking the images of carnage, the lack of editorial clarity about the causes and meaning of the war left us unable to perceive a connection to our own lives.

To be sure, some intellectual opinion journals and a few leading newspapers have done an excellent job of setting out the issues. But for the most part, the mass media have not. When the history of this conflict is written, future generations may wonder why so many did so little for so long.

Death in Sarajevo hits the headlines only when the atrocity is on an unspeakable mass scale, like the February 5 attack on the central market that tore sixty people into body parts and left another two hundred wounded. It happened on a slow news weekend, but was followed by newspaper accounts falsely putting the event in the context of "warring factions." Lower visibility murders had been going on almost every day. Like some daily horror-scope, the roster of the departed is duly noted and forgotten. Four by shelling, five by machine gun fire, three by starvation, one by freezing . . .

A stunning picture of a woman in a pool of blood grabs us for one media second. For another, the story of a little girl's diary evokes comparisons to Anne Frank. The muffled sound of mortars becomes part of the soundtrack of daily life.

The people of Bosnia are not just dying, they are being silenced. We rarely hear their analysis. To the Bosnians, this conflict is not just about land or nationalism or even survival. It is also about defending the principle that people from different ethnic groups can live together—a principle Americans would relate to if it were ever presented clearly to them. But it isn't, and that is partly because Western journalists and news organizations have framed and reported the issues superficially, almost invariably in terms of ethnic war, without acknowledging or, perhaps, even understanding that they are doing so.

The war's policy issues have been debated, by and large. But the performance of the media, especially of television, has not. In a picture-driven medium, what you see is what you get. Here, the corollary also applies: You don't get what you don't see. For starters, we never really saw how the war came to be.

From its very inception, this was a television war in a way that Vietnam was not. In Central Europe, television is not just an appliance but an instrument of power. That's why the Romanian "revolution" started with an armed battle for control of a TV station and why Boris Yeltsin fired on the Russian parliament after its dissidents stormed a TV network.

The right-wing nationalist regimes in Belgrade and Zagreb recognized the power of the tube as a political tool. First, they purged independent journalists. Then, they used their respective state-owned electronic media to mobilize and consolidate political support through crude ethnic-ideological appeals. TV propaganda pitted people living together against each other. The news was manipulated to promote distrust, grievances and hatreds. Serbian state television initially targeted its own domestic opposition, then Croatia, and later Bosnia. Croatian television fired back. Sometimes the two stations presented the same atrocity pictures as evidence of each other's barbarism.

The American people rarely saw reporting on this media war or how it turned into a shooting war. American television was not paying much attention. We were never clearly told who was the aggressor or why. We didn't understand the neo-fascist character of the dominant ideologies in Serbia and Croatia or how undemocratic regimes there were encouraging extremists and militias staffed by thugs. Instead, events were made to seem crazy, as if all parties were equally to blame in a region with a predisposition toward chaos. "Well, you know the Balkans."

When the international press started paying attention, the environment had already been infected with disinformation and misinformation about who and what was responsible. Not many outlets made it clear that the war was not ordained by a higher being but began as a conscious act of policy by the regime in Belgrade.

Of course, most of us knew Sarajevo because of the 1984 Olympics, but that was all we knew. Suddenly, distant memories of sports camaraderie, of skiers in flight and skaters on the ice, turned into scenes of bloodletting. Only then did the international media move in *en masse*, providing dramatic images of ethnic cleansing and civilian massacres. There was no shortage of bang-bang footage of the kind for which TV is known.

Then leading newspapers assigned award-winning journalists to pound away on the issues day after day. And they did an impressive job, often relying on their local colleagues. Soon, we all saw Europe's new concentration camps on TV and were shocked by stories about desperate refugees fleeing armed onslaughts and mass rapes. Many journalists paid with their lives; more correspondents died covering three years of war in the former Yugoslavia than during a decade of fighting in Vietnam.

But while the initial coverage was intense, it was sometimes wildly inaccurate. Many mistakes flowed from omission rather than commission, from relying on information that it may have been impossible to check.

The Bosnians have been dehumanized in much of the coverage, rendered nameless and faceless, seen only as "victims," as objects—not subjects—of media attention. What are we told of their culture, their history, or the character of their resistance? Who speaks for them? Can we name three of their leaders, or poets, or journalists, even now after three years of intense coverage? Which of their representatives gets on the air regularly enough to be known or remembered?

The Bosnians have become the classic "other." Spoken in terms of religious preference rather than national identity. Their country may have been recognized by the United Nations, but the media recognize Bosnians only as followers of the Prophet Mohammed. What Edward Said calls "orientalism" is usually reserved for the Middle East, but today it is being practiced in the center of Europe.

There is a more generic problem too: The American television network brand of "sound-bite journalism" is especially superficial when it comes to reporting on people with foreign-sounding names and thick accents. The Bosnians might as well be from another planet. Unfortunately, they are also neophytes when it comes to waging a propaganda war. Had they invested early on in a high-powered PR firm and a slick advertising campaign they would have had a better shot at winning friends and influencing the spin on coverage. (They did hire the American PR firm Ruder and Finn to help them promote their views. The campaign was only partially successful.)

The "Bosnia story" has been filtered through a media system with a short attention span, where images supplant ideas, where "foreign news" itself has become an endangered species as bureaus and resources are cut back. As a result, TV news becomes a numbing blur of charge and countercharge. At a certain point, the sheer madness of it all becomes too much to bear. We become desensitized. There is no way to digest it at all because so little context is offered to advance comprehension.

Is it a surprise, then, that many tune it out as too obtuse and complicated for mere mortals to understand? Rather than empower us with information that might lead to action, the coverage deadens the brain and paralyzes the emotions.

It is one major reason why Americans don't seem to care.

This article originally appeared in The Progressive, *April 1994.*

SELLING CHINA
How Mike Wallace Became China's Favorite Journalist
2000

The east side of Manhattan is an armed camp as streets are closed and security units prepare for the arrival of 150 heads of state attending the UN's Millennial Summit. So far, China has been receiving the most media attention, fostered by a multimillion dollar PR offensive and the presence of two top leaders.

Li Peng, the chairman of China's National People's Assembly, left New York in a rage after being served with legal papers filed by Tiananmen Square survivors under a U.S. law allowing lawsuits against foreign human rights offenders. Other protesters supporting Tibet and the outlawed Falun Gong spiritual practice are planning protests against Communist Party Chairman Jiang Zemin.

In advance of his trip, China, with advice from American PR agencies, mapped out a plan to win over the American public. An exclusive interview was offered to *60 Minutes* which promoted it in advance—and then plugged it on air—as if it were their own booking and a rare unique exchange of views. They neglected to note that CNN's former Beijing correspondent Andrea Koppel (daughter of Ted), did a similar personality-driven half hour Q&A with the Chinese leader not that long ago. CBS hyped its "exclusive" thus: "The discussion between Wallace and Jiang ranges in tone from slightly tense to lighthearted and humorous. Wallace asks all the difficult questions." For his part Jiang made clear that the interview was intended as a propaganda exercise to "win understanding" from the U.S. public. He grinned personably, sang a song, repeated aphorisms, but was never confronted by the kind of tough cross-examination for which Wallace is well known. CBS was using Jiang to score a celebrity-style media coup; Jiang was using CBS to score a political one.

My eyebrows go up when news organizations pat themselves on the back for asking "difficult questions." "Difficult" for whom, Mike or Jiang? Did I miss something? Isn't asking difficult questions what journalists are supposed to do? Would news programs in an earlier era boast of "lighthearted and humorous" exchanges with a repressive dictator? Yes, Wallace asked some serious questions and tried to follow up with lots of dramatic fingerpointing and cliches about democracy, but if it was a prizefight I would judge it a TKO for Jiang.

This *60 Minutes* snow job had curious fallout. It turns out that

President Bill Clinton was watching. When he met Jiang at the UN later in the week, he complimented him on his ability to turn Wallace into a "purring kitten. It was great," he said, "I was so jealous." Both leaders had a good laugh together. A month later, Jiang was in Hong Kong where he was grilled by local reporters about his government's support for a political leader there. He turned on the journalists, lambasting them for their attitude and naïveté. Why, he asked, can't they be more like Mike Wallace? "I go laugh and joke with him."

Jiang's big TV score was just the beginning. China hired a high-priced PR firm best known for hyping China-booster Rupert to publicize the opening of a $7 million cultural expo at New York's Javits Center which will then travel nationwide. (From the press release: "The exhibition will offer an unprecedented look at the beauty and diversity of China. The event is being presented free to the people of New York as a gift from the People's Republic of China.") This gesture is all part of upgrading China's image before the U.S. Senate takes up the China Permanent Normal Trade Relations question this fall. PNTR's passage would permit China to avoid an annual review of its human rights record.

As for China's big budget expo, I was struck that two U.S. media moguls are honorary sponsors: Time Warner's Gerald Levin and Viacom's Sumner Redstone. Both do business in China, and both have toadied up to the Chinese government before. On September 28, 1999, in the midst of China's fierce crackdown on Falun Gong, Sumner Redstone, who was about to merge his giant Viacomese nation with CBS, was in Shanghai for a conference hosted by Time Warner–owned *Fortune* magazine and keynoted by President Jiang.

To the delight of the Beijing regime, Redstone called for American press restraint in the coverage of China. The media, he said, should report the truth but avoid being "unnecessarily offensive" to foreign governments. "As they expand their global reach, media companies must be aware of the politics and attitudes of the governments where we operate . . . Journalistic integrity must prevail in the final analysis. But that doesn't mean that journalistic integrity should be exercised in a way that is unnecessarily offensive to the countries in which you operate." Right, Sumner, let's keep it lighthearted and humorous. (Redstone's company now owns *60 Minutes*!)

What kind of signal do you think this sends? And talk about one-way appeasement. At the conference itself, the Chinese brazenly censored a *Time* magazine special on China, published by Mr. Levin's Time Warner.

As one news report explained, "The edition, whose masthead was emblazoned with the headline 'China's Amazing Half-Century,'" fell foul of Chinese censors by including articles by exiled dissidents Wei Jingsheng, Wang Dan, and the Tibetan Dalai Lama. Obviously, Time Warner was not perturbed enough to stay away from openly endorsing the Chinese government's New York expo.

Apparently, human rights do not register too highly on the media's corporate agenda, any more than they do on the UN's. At Beijing's request, that body also excluded the Dalai Lama from a meeting of world religious leaders. An "official" Chinese delegation was permitted to take part. It promptly hewed to the government line by further denouncing Falun Gong as an "evil cult," just as Jiang did later on *60 Minutes*. (Wallace had turned down a chance to interview Falun Gong's Li Hongzhi a year ago. The problem, I was told, was that he "only spoke Chinese"—as did Jiang!)

There have been some hard-hitting press reports about Falun Gong's resistance campaign lately in the *Wall Street Journal*, *Los Angeles Times*, and *Washington Post*, but the public still has very little idea of the extent of China's human rights violations. In little more than a year, twenty-four Falun Gong practitioners have died under mysterious circumstances and 50,000 have been arrested. Pervasive torture and incarceration of people without due process in labor camps and mental hospitals continues.

Falun Gong's perspective (real interviews, not sound bites) was mostly missing from the news stories, not only after Chinese practitioners were silenced, but also for institutional reasons that have to do with the structure of overseas news coverage. Few news organizations solicit comments in the United States for China-based stories. So if voices are silenced in China, they are rarely heard at all, since what human rights groups or Falun Gong followers do overseas is not usually considered part of a China correspondent's beat. This, though Falun Gong practitioners are accessible on the Internet.

As the world's leaders gather in New York, and as protesters challenge the Chinese government and speak out on other issues, pay attention to whose voices are reported—and whether already compromised media companies give them the attention they deserve.

This article originally appeared online at www.mediachannel.org.

WATCH LOCAL, SEE GLOBAL
1990

In April 1990, over half a billion people in sixty-three countries watched Nelson Mandela speak to a packed stadium of rock fans at a London concert in his honor. The only part of the world not watching was the biggest television market of them all—the United States.

Once again, American television was out of step with the world, isolationist and isolated in an increasingly globalized electronic community. Not one network here, including MTV or PBS, would touch what programmers apparently considered an event that was either too political, not adequately commercial, or both. It was the American viewers who lost out this time, but in the long run it will be the folks who run our TV networks who will lose out if they bury their heads in the sands of outmoded thinking and status quo behavior.

American myopia is not new, but strong economic pressures are now reshaping the nature of broadcasting and are likely to force the United States to jump on the emerging global television bandwagon.

Three powerful forces are at work.

First, the three major networks are facing a growing erosion of their viewing audience. Their power and popularity are shrinking, partly because of proliferating competition, partly because they are exhausted—when they are not insulting—as a creative and inspirational force.

Second, the spread of cable and satellite technology and the penetration of VCRs gives viewers more choice. The widespread use of remote controls has turned TV viewing into expeditions in "zapping" as viewers dart through the dials looking for something compelling, and usually find little of substance to engage their interest.

Third, production expenses are increasing even as viewership declines, forcing producers to seek less expensive programming methods. "Under the circumstances," writes Les Brown, one of our most respected writers about television, "there seems little choice for the U.S. networks but to deal abroad, cultivating the kinds of relationships with foreign suppliers they've had with Hollywood studios."

Already the big U.S. communications companies are buying up European production facilities and taking a stake in cable and newly privatized channels. (Japanese companies are also gobbling up U.S. firms.) As Europe approaches economic union in 1992, a vast new market is on the horizon. There are billions in pent-up advertiser demand, with hundreds of hours of new programming needed. Americans want into this market, and Europeans, whose own TV program–making skills have matured significantly, want out. They are asking for access to the American market at the same time that U.S. companies seek to flood Europe with their latest product.

What this could mean is a new era in television—a chance for viewers everywhere to literally tune in the world and be exposed to a diversity of voices, entertainment, and points of view. There's a danger, of course, that in this process cultures could be homogenized into one mushy TV soup by media moguls who see the world as *The Deal of Fortune*. But there's also the opportunity for television to realize Marshall McLuhan's global village aspiration and become a force for the exchange of ideas, fashions, cultural events, and practical problem-solving across all borders and boundaries.

So far the American market has been resistant to diversity, for all of its talk of faith in free markets and fair trade reciprocity. U.S. programmers would much prefer to monopolize the terms of the international television interchange. American-made TV shows, from pro wrestling to religious pros like Jimmy Swaggart, are already shown worldwide. In contrast, foreign-made programming has a hard time penetrating our living rooms. Last year, only seven percent of all prime-time programming came from overseas—and that figure includes all the British imports on PBS.

This situation is not only unfair in the abstract; it deprives U.S. viewers of a window on the world. Our own parochialism is fed and reinforced by one-note news shows that march in lockstep with government and corporate agendas and by the freeze-out of entertainment, sports, and information from abroad. Our ability to relate to and empathize with other peoples will increase to the extent that we get a feel for their points of view, passions, heroes, humor, and cultural idiosyncrasies. An occasional overseas ambassador or president on *Nightline* is not enough.

In the age of satellites, the technology exists to crack our cultural isolation and promote a cross-fertilization of ideas. Global programming is now technically feasible and economically viable. "World television" is poised to penetrate an insularity fed by the kind of educational underdevelopment that led to sixty percent of our high school kids not being able to find Japan on a globe and twenty percent unable to locate the United States.

Tuning in to the world need not be sold as something that's good for you, as some kind of elitist antidote to illiteracy. It can be marketed in the same way we market all TV shows: as worth watching, informative, or just plain fun. Already, broadcasters who are willing to take risks and introduce a more global perspective are getting a good response. Ted Turner has built CNN on the strength of its overseas reach, and he is now making money as a global broadcaster. The Discovery Channel is also doing well with programming with international themes.

As we approach the turn of the century, as TV thrusts itself on the cutting edge of change from Romania to South Africa to Tiananmen Square, it is no longer a question of *whether* we will see what the world sees, but when. Soon we'll be watching local—and seeing global!

This article originally appeared in the Utne Reader, *July/August 1990.*

DON'T MESS WITH PUBLIC ACCESS
1993

Public access television makes news only when outrageous ideas threaten to disturb the domestic media tranquility. In July, "Race or Reason," a neo-Nazi show on Queens public access, was yanked off the air after protests. And in September, a Manhattan cable show planned to treat viewers to the "Chef de Cocaine," a crazed crack aficionado offering up his distinctive "home cooking" lessons.

Why do only these kinds of shows provoke debate, or even comment, about public access? The scenario is usually predictable. Some reporter or Mrs. Grundy sees the offending show late at night. An exposé appears and public outrage mobilizes. The cable companies deny responsibility, complaining that they are forced to carry such electronic swill. They have even asked the Supreme Court to free them from the requirement to offer any public access.

The original concept of setting channels aside for public programming was forced down the throats of cable companies when they sought the right to wire our communities. It was argued then that their promises of diversity would never be realized unless the public was guaranteed the right to participate. The companies were supposed to help out with equipment, training, and advice.

The spirit of public access has been honored more in theory than in practice. Producers have been given few resources to work with. Production values are laughable, programming concepts amateurish, promotion nonexistent.

And yet public access has brought new voices into our living rooms, sometimes as a novelty, sometimes with real passion and information. Public access has never cloned the slickly packaged eye candy on the commercial spectrum. It remains idiosyncratic, plays to small audiences, and is usually ignored. After all, the cable companies have better uses for their escalating subscriber fees than to plow it into programming by and for the public. If they did that, they wouldn't have the billions needed for new acquisitions.

Besides, cable companies would have you think all public access is just "junk" programming. But ask yourself: Is it really any junkier than so much else that's on cable? The proliferation of channels has not ushered in a new dawn of diversity. The electronic Goliaths now positioning themselves to monopolize this growing media marketplace have no public interest agenda. Their vision of interactivity includes little more than personalized buying services, home banking, Hollywood movies on demand, and video games. So far, the brave new world of the "information superhighway" sees viewers as consumers, not citizens.

That is why it is so important to safeguard and defend public access. The irony is that the very worst of current TV programming—those tacky home video shows—may hold the key to the very best in the future. Thanks to home video cameras, if you don't like the news, you can report your own. What Charlayne Hunter-Gault calls the "Rodney King Weapon" has become enormously powerful—and empowering.

And there are public access programs worth watching. Manhattan Neighborhood Network offers a fascinating smorgasbord of community and entertainment programming. Some of it is excellent, but it is rarely reviewed or even listed in the TV guides—probably because more people would watch if it were.

Recently, there were 2,000 entries in a Hometown Video Festival. The winner, Paper Tiger, a local video group, was honored for a show called "Video Dial Tone: Mailing our Free Speech," about the danger of telephone companies controlling your TV set. FAIR, the media reform group, has been presenting shows on media trends. Labor unions, like Local 1180 of the Communications Workers of America, are taking their cause to the public via public access. CrossWalks, a city-operated network, is providing multichannel access to community-based groups in all the boroughs.

Global issues can be covered too. The Deep Dish Network, a consortium of public access producers based in New York, created an award-winning series on the Gulf War, offering perspectives not seen on networks, which seemed to allow the Pentagon to program their coverage.

A growing segment of the public wants to be involved with new media. The boom in online computer networks and even radio talk shows demonstrates the demand and the need—which the media giants are unlikely to satisfy. Let's hope that the congressional watchdogs who are questioning the anti-trust implications of these new monopolies-in-the-making will speak out to preserve public access. In commercial television, everything is slick, but little matters. Its edges may be rough, but public access should matter to us. Not only for what it is, but for what it can become.

This article originally appeared in New York Newsday, *November 3, 1993.*

(LOW) POWER TO THE PEOPLE
1999

Franz GourGue had been a ham radio operator in Haiti; Sara Zia Ebrahimi, an activist at Gainesville Florida's Civic Media Center; and Pete TriDish, as he's now known, a student in Philadelphia. None of them knew each other, but their lives converged when they discovered the joys and dangers of becoming micro-radio broadcasters, a currently illegal but increasingly popular "new media" in the oldest sense.

I met the three radio rebels at an energized and sizable weekend seminar of micro-radio enthusiasts held at a reconditioned firehouse near New York's Chinatown, home of New York's Downtown Community Television Center. They had come to share experiences and teach others how to get on the air with a few hundred dollars in rather primitive equipment as community broadcasters. Powered by no more than forty watts, these stations reach an average two to five miles in range. No one is sure how many exist. Some say 1,000; FCC regulators report shutting down 360 in the last eighteen months. Some are clandestine and fancy themselves pirates; others, like Radio Free Allston in Boston, operated openly in an ice-cream parlor until Feds pulled the plug.

However small in reach, these micro-radio stations are now in the crosshairs of a far bigger battleground in the broadcasting industry. For years, the federal communications laws were interpreted to permit only licensed stations. This quite naturally limited their number and the number any one company could own. Once telecommunications laws changed, large companies were able to monopolize the marketplace. According to former FCC commissioner Reed Hundt, four media companies have bought ten percent of the country's 10,231 radio stations since the passage of the Telecommunications Act of 1996. Media observers like Dan Kennedy of the *Boston Phoenix* noted the consequences. "The corporatization of radio matters because it is destroying a uniquely intimate medium, replacing real community voices, people with a sense of place and purpose, with the same soundalike shows. In city after city, town after town . . . it's highly profitable. And it sucks."

Micro-radio broadcasters say they are the antidote. It now looks like the FCC may be convinced by the soundness of their arguments. FCC Chairman William Kennard, concerned that minority ownership of broadcast outlets has recently fallen from a whopping three percent to a mere one-and-a-half percent, now sees micro-radio as one remedy. "We can create a whole new class of voices who can use the airwaves for their communities," he says. The Commission is now receiving comments on its proposal to license smaller stations, including low power outlets. Micro-radio activists have flooded the commission with supportive letters, even as they privately fear that the regulations accompanying any new rules might limit more countercultural and subversive initiatives. For example, one proposal would deny licenses to stations currently operating in defiance of the law.

The FCC is supposed to make public all the comments in April, but its rulemaking could drag on for years. That is, if it is not killed earlier by a powerful politically connected broadcast lobby that has already declared war on the plan, charging it will gum up its digital strategies. Says Eddie Fritts, president of the National Association of Broadcasters (and college roommate of Senate Majority Leader Trent Lott) "This proposal will likely cause devastating interference . . . to broadcasters."

Ironically, that is precisely what the insurgent micro-radio movement wants: to interfere in plans that concentrate control over radio in so few hands. Their seminar was plastered with posters like "Let 10,000 antennas radiate" and "FCC: Enemy of the People." Activists wore T-shirts with slogans saying, "If it wasn't for commercial radio, we wouldn't know what to buy."

This movement is quite diverse, organized by a coalition of college-age radicals and community-based businessmen, with help from the Promeatheus Radio project. At least forty percent of those attending the workshop in New York were minorities.

Franz from Haiti, for example, runs Radio Nago in Brooklyn (89.3), offering a blend of Haitian music, culture, and conversation that can't be found on the commercial dial. It also features immigration lawyers—a service popular with listeners. Twenty-one-year-old Sara Zia from Florida took to the airwaves because she couldn't find her kind of music in a town of college students where public radio, she says, "plays only classical music 24/7." When her shows were silenced by FCC action, she moved north with hopes of launching a women's station. It was then she met PeteTriDish (many of these radioactive-ists use names de media guerres, like dj Tom Paine) who launched Philly's Radio Mutiny after Temple University radio censored commentaries by Mumia Abu Jamal. "Everything I do links getting the right to broadcast to challenging the monopolies of the media order," he told me.

The stations see themselves as part of a movement. They even download and air news reports from each other via a website. They have been waging a hit-and-run guerrilla media war with FCC enforcers who use sophisticated tracking equipment to locate them. On New York's Lower East Side, a station calling itself "Steal This Radio," a la Abbie Hoffman, was ejected from a squat after investigators persuaded the electric company to disconnect the tenement. Now, they're based in a community center but can't transmit until a nursery school that shares the space sends the kids home. Their programming includes hip-hop records "by kids in the projects." The station was founded by a squatter who named himself after a member of the whaling crew in Melville's *Moby Dick*.

Will micro-radio make a difference in our tightly controlled broadcast spectrum? The short answer is that it already is—pressuring the FCC to reconsider its stance, and illustrating, even by the pathetic reach of its puny radio signals, how much still has to be done to open up the communication system to many more voices and real media choices.

Reprinted with permission from the May 24, 1999 issue of The Nation.

HOW TO CHANGE THE MEDIA
1996

In this era of Mickey Mouse and Westinghouse, when six or seven giant monopolies are poised to dominate the mediascape, what are those of us concerned with this two-ton Goliath to do? How do progressives fight back?

On the face of it, we are not doing a very good job. Forces to the left, if not on the left, including that alphabet soup of liberal advocacy groups, have been silent and ineffective as the right wing–dominated Congress rolled back an array of welfare-state legislation.

A *New York Times* page one story, "In Centers of Power, Fewer Voices on Left," reported that liberal advocates admit that they are not skilled in framing issues, using technology, or transmitting electronic media. In short, they acknowledge not being sophisticated enough to compete with a far smaller but better funded opposition. (Needless to say, the *Times* has not been particularly aggressive in reporting the extent of popular resistance to Republican-initiated cutbacks. Right-wing pundits still get more ink and airtime than their counterparts on the other side of the spectrum.)

As a media professional with a unique vantage point, having worked in alternative and mainstream media, print, radio, and television, I am always struck by how the right properly pinpoints media at the top of its strategic plan, while the left thinks about media strategy as an afterthought, when it considers it at all. If you examine just how Newt Gingrich did it, you'll realize that his whole "go-pac" blitzkrieg started as a communications strategy.

If we want to promote democracy and challenge vested interests, we have to focus on understanding and explaining how the media fits into all this—as both a hegemonic force of domination, and an indispensable tool for outreach and organization.

We cannot even talk about changing America without confronting and remaking media power.

There is no denying that media is a central force in American life, and potentially an instrument for social change. We live in a media culture where the issues we discuss are framed by media coverage and echoed through a TV-dominated popular culture. When an issue is not on television, for most Americans it doesn't exist.

The fact also stands that most Americans like TV. They watch it for hours. It transports them out of their day-to-day lives. The stupider it is, the more popular it can become. We have to understand why—and make sure that our criticisms of the media industry do not become viewed as attacks on the people who watch—knowing as we do that viewers choose between the choices they see, between narrow choices they have been conditioned by constant repetition to accept.

Most media alternatives are not presented in a compelling way. They are neither professionally promoted, nor professionally marketed. Many are also not that accessible. It is far too simplistic to blame the viewers, or, for that matter, to deduce that because a mass audience watches TV religiously, that they like what they are seeing. We can't become as self-righteous or as arrogant as the TV industry itself. A recent *New York Times* poll found that over half of TV viewers could not name one program that they considered really memorable. Not one.

The "fact" of television's popularity does not explain another fact: that popular criticism of television is growing exponentially even as most people know that there are few channels to express their concerns and fewer still that seem to have any impact. We have all heard the homily about having the wisdom to know what we can and cannot change. TV seems to be a distant and immutable force.

Yet, there are other contradictions at the heart of the industry itself that may be opening up new arenas for challenge and change.

Media businesses may be dynamic, but they are also inherently unstable, because market forces and new technologies are forever shaking their dominance and changing their modes of coverage. Just look at what's happened in the last quarter of the century in almost every sphere of communication from telephones to satellites, from TV to cable, and now in the "new media" arena: the world of computers. Increasingly, futurists are banking on the new technology, evolving visions of the seemingly unlimited potential of cyberspace, and by clear implication admitting that the "old media" has had it, is already history.

Ironically, just as big media merges to become more concentrated and centralized, a new decentralized media built around the Internet is devolving power. Technologies with awesome powers for communication are potentially in the hands of ordinary people.

One of America's most commercially successful writers, Michael Crichton, best known for *Jurassic Park*, has identified a new soon-to-be-extinct species. "I want to focus on another dinosaur," he writes, "one that may be on the road to extinction. I am referring to the American media. And I use the term extinction literally. To my mind, it is likely that what we now understand as the mass media will be gone within the next ten years. Vanished without a trace." Crichton quips, "A generation ago, Paddy Chayefsky's *Network* looked like an outrageous farce. Today . . . *Network* looks like a documentary."

If the economic forces within the media industry generate acute contradictions, political pressures are also at work, as the impact of mass media becomes more and more of a political issue. Opinion polls continue to register mounting dissatisfaction with the products of our commercial popular culture, as well as with much of the news media. More and more people are now complaining, writing letters, feeling distressed and even outraged. Public protest is building, steaming up from below.

The politicians who play to this sentiment, in effect running against Hollywood and the news media, have tapped into a growing popular vein, however demagogic and hypocritical their stance. We need to speak out on these issues too.

The first step is to build awareness. Happily, even seasoned professionals are now speaking out, coming to terms with their own roles and responsibilities. Writer Carl Bernstein, who rode high as one of the reporters credited with unmasking the Watergate scandal for the *Washington Post,* is among them.

"We are being dominated by a global journalistic culture that has little to do with the truth or reality or context" he was quoted as saying in *Editor and Publisher,* a trade paper aimed at the newspaper industry. "The result of the misuse and abuse of free expression in Western democracies actually disempowers people by making them more cynical about public life."

Even former network executives are admitting that there is a deep institutional problem at work here. Here's Reuven Frank, former head of *NBC News*:

> It is daily becoming more obvious that the biggest
> threat to a free press and the circulation of ideas is the
> steady absorption of newspapers, television networks,
> and other vehicles of information into enormous corpo-
> rations that know how to turn knowledge into profit,
> but are not equally committed to inquiry or debate or
> to the First Amendment.

This was a network honcho talking, not Noam Chomsky!

This situation breeds cynicism which leads to passivity and people dropping out of the political process all together. It reflects itself in low voter turnouts, in public indifference, and ignorance. Already a Harvard study has equated more TV watching with a drop in civic participation. For young people, "what's cool" is often more significant than what's important.

We need to move beyond criticism to consciousness-raising and creative action. Enough critique. Enough pointing out what is increasingly obvious. The shallowness, superficiality, and vapidity of so much of our media has to be redefined as a political challenge, as an issue around which to mobilize. Media priorities have to be confronted, and they have to become a priority of a more urgent kind on any progressive agenda for change. In the '60s, corporations like Dow Chemical became targets of protest and symbols of corporate greed and irresponsibility. In the '90s, many media companies deserve similar contempt. The same people who would be outraged if toxic waste were dumped on their doorstep have to be encouraged to express similar rage at no-less-toxic junk TV shows being dumped into their living rooms and brains.

The right to information has to be presented as a human rights issue. Article 19 of the Universal Declaration of Human Rights speaks of it as such, linking the right to speak out with the right to take in. "Everyone has a right to freedom of opinion and expression," it reads. "This right includes freedom to hold opinions without interference and to seek, receive, and impart information and ideas through any media, regardless of frontiers." In America, the Carnegie Commission that gave public television its mandate spoke of a "freedom to view."

Democracy itself can only thrive when and if an electorate is informed. The Institute for Alternative Journalism expresses concerns for which it hopes to find support among the public at large: "We believe that democracy is enhanced, and public debate broadened, as more voices are heard and points of view made available," they write. "In today's political and media environment we are especially concerned about increasing media concentration, and about the success of conservative and far-right ideas and personalities in framing the issues relevant to us all." They and many others, including a newly organized cultural environment movement, are sparking a needed political debate about the relationship between media and democracy.

Some Europeans have also put forth a "People's Communication Charter," "mindful that communication can be used as a tool to support the powerful and to victimize the powerless" and "affirming that the development of just and democratic societies requires just and democratic communications structures." This document deserves to be more widely known because it spells out a vision of what media can and should be. Without a collective sense of what we want, we will never be able to create momentum on the issue.

It is my hope that our visions can speak to growing public anxieties and complaints and someday find organizational form and focus in a broad-based media reform movement.

So far, too much of this momentum for media change has been generated by right-wing political forces, which for years waged a relentless campaign against what they described in one word as the *"liberalmediaelite."* Only once it had become obvious that the right itself was more deeply embedded in high places and low in almost all opinion media, and in fact in a position to guide its trajectory, did honest conservatives like John Podhoretz, a political-strategist-turned-TV-critic-turned-editor of Rupert Murdoch's conservative weekly magazine, admit that the term itself was a politically motivated concoction that was widely used but never really believed. Only fooling, guys.

Yet when right-wing monitoring groups like Accuracy in Media (AIM) inspire left-wing counterparts like Fairness in Accuracy in Reporting (FAIR), the mainstream media tend to pit them off against each other with claims that attacks from the right and left only prove that they are doing their job. They take refuge in the middle, refusing to audit their own behavior by any measures other than ratings and the bottom line. Clearly, a new force is needed to break a log jam that celebrates the status quo.

How can that be done? And who can do it?

Towards a Strategy for Change

There are a growing number of media professionals who are open to participating. Not everyone on the "inside" is happy. Many, perhaps most, are demoralized. I have been involved in two industry initiatives that show the potential of reaching out to insiders.

"The New York Media Forum," an irregular effort by a small group of journalists from a variety of institutions—two networks, the *New York Times*, and others—organized panel discussions at which colleagues could hear debates and discussions of media coverage issues. We drew several hundred people to these events from a wide range of media posts: newspapers, the magazines, radio, and TV. There have been few organizations that have managed to bring such a broad range of media workers together. It was clear that in many media organizations there is a hunger for intellectual stimulation of a kind that is conspicuous by its absence. Before the underfunded organizing group ran out steam, the ad-hoc group held many successful events that created opportunities for networking, informed journalists about issues in a non-threatening way, and actually led to enhanced coverage of important issues.

The second industry initiative was an effort by "concerned media employees" to rally behind striking writers at *CBS News* in the late '80s. Several hundred media employees responded, for the first time, across craft and network lines—engineers and producers, correspondents and editors—all protesting CBS's treatment of its employees. Unfortunately, their union, the Writer's Guild, like many unions, practices a parochial trade union politics, not realizing that their only hope for long-range security rests on mobilizing a coalition inside *and* outside the industry. They did not show up. Ralph Nader was there, speaking to us about the irresponsible practices of the industry and appealing to our commitment to the public interest as well as to our job interests. A rally and petition effort was successful, but there was no follow-up, and the initiative floundered.

If media change is to be successful, we need to reach and motivate media workers at every level in the system. And they can be reached. Their alienation is great, even though their consciousness still tends to buy in to the conventional wisdom rather than to opt-out or challenge it. Like viewers, they have been conditioned by years of exposure to the rituals and culture of news gathering.

A program for change needs to have at least five components. To start, it needs to build awareness of media power and irresponsibility throughout our communities. Educators, journalists, and organizers have to start talking about this issue and popularizing it. It has to be placed squarely on the agenda of all unions and issue-oriented organizations. A coalition of support for a charter for media accountability is badly needed. Critics cannot hope to be effective without a constituency and a program for change.

Here are some of the steps that are needed:

1. More Monitoring
Everyone can monitor media performance. Groups like FAIR have developed manuals and lists of criteria. If teachers and their students, labor unions and their mem-

bers, begin tracking what's on TV and radio, and how the news is being reported, they will be better able to detect and challenge bias. Media literacy has to become part of the school curriculum and of everyday life.

2. Demand Media Accountability

Once armed with more information—especially information that is collected by people themselves—citizen groups will be in a better position to demand responsiveness and accountability from media corporations. When media executives are forced to meet with their consumers, they will be forced to be more responsive. Most are sure to resist so-called "pressure politics," but they will not be able to ignore it.

3. New Legislation and Enhanced Regulation

Deregulation has given media companies a free hand to pollute the airwaves. Tougher antimonopoly laws and enhanced regulation in the public interest by a revamped FCC are in order.

4. Transform Public Television

It is time to put the public back into public television, with more locally elected community boards and a return to public television's original mandate to provide alternative voices and more program choices. Pressure will be needed to democratize and properly finance PBS. PBS should be funded through a tax on commercial television stations and their advertisers. There needs to be at least one channel that serves the public interest in the broadest possible way. The financing of Channel 4 in London might be a model worth examining and emulating.

5. Support Alternative Programming

Creating channels in and of themselves will not make for changes in the system unless new programming reflecting a non-corporate view is available. Congress recognized discrimination against America's independent filmmakers when it created the Independent Television Service (ITVS). That agency and other media centers on the local level need to be adequately funded with their programming guaranteed some form of distribution. The human rights series that I help produce at Globalvision, *Rights & Wrongs*, has only survived because of ITVS backing. 145 companies turned down our bid for funding on the grounds that an association with human rights could be bad for business overseas.

In this context, it is essential that independent journalists and producers find better ways of cooperating with each other and realize that they cannot be really successful unless the media system opens wider. It is discouraging to see so much competition and one-upmanship among people who are fighting for a fraction of the pitiful funding base that exists. Just compare the U.S. to Canada and you will see that state support for independent journalism and filmmaking is significantly higher north of the border. That's what happens when a society values culture and is willing to support it.

It is not my role to produce a blueprint, but unless someone does, to put media issues on the agenda, my own complaints will seem trivial when compared with what's to come. A media system targeted at more consumerism is in conflict with a media spirit committed to promoting citizenship. The choices are becoming clearer even if the solutions are not. A state system of censorship and government control is certainly not desirable, but citizen attempts to rein in a media system that is out of control are worth encouraging. Business rarely operates in the public interest unless it is required to do so. The movement for social responsibility in business has so far not reached the media industry. Only public awareness and pressure will move the mountain of media inertia.

A new media reform movement is needed.

May the Media and Democracy Congress be a first step.

This article originally appeared in Media and Democracy Congress Book, *1996.*

A CALL FROM MY DAUGHTER
1997

My daughter Sarah is on the phone from college in Santa Cruz, California. She's reading Erik Barnouw's excellent history of American broadcasting, puzzling over an unexpected fact.

"You always told me that Edward R. Murrow was one of your heroes," she says, "so how come he joined the U.S. Information Agency and tried to stop his own exposé about migrant workers from being seen in England?" Oddly, that very night Ed Murrow was in my living room as a sound bite in an endless parade of clips, in a collage put together by the TV Academy to glorify the industry and extol its Emmy Award. Once again, after all these years, there's Murrow on TV blasting Joe McCarthy, but, of course, nothing about CBS years later easing Ed out the door.

"The instrument can teach, it can illuminate, yes, it can even inspire," he would write in the sunset of his career. "But it can do so only to the extent that humans are determined to use it to those ends." By then, however heralded, he had outlived his usefulness. What he did was no longer valued. His partner Fred Friendly quit when CBS refused to interrupt *I Love Lucy* reruns to show important Senate hearings on the Vietnam War. CBS dumped their spiritual successor too, newscaster Walter Cronkite. He was forced out by an executive I later met, Van Gordon Sauter, who Cronkite says treated him like a "leper."

"I felt like I had been driven from the temple where for nineteen years, along with other believers, I had worshipped the great god News on a daily basis."

So how come?

Well Sarah, it's like this: like Icarus, you can be among the chosen and still lose your wings when you fly too close to the sun. When an institution decides you are "trending down," or believes it can make more money using that other guy or gal, you're gone. Also, some folks do get co-opted or just plain give up, burn up, or burn out. Or they go for the gold. Remember, at the end of the day, *they* own the candy store. When I grew up, I read the muckraking accounts of how the big industrial magnates crushed the workers and shamed America. Your generation will be reading about today's media moguls.

Murrow mattered because he did at times illuminate and inspire, and there are still moments like that on the tube—for us it was when we watched men walk on the moon, for you and your friends, probably, it was when Ellen came out. For us it was when JFK was gunned down or the cops were televised breaking heads in Chicago; for your generation it may have been when Murphy Brown took on the Vice President or when Seinfeld first said "yadda yadda" or when you became addicted to watching *Beverly Hills 90210*. Reality was what focused us; fiction seems to be what grabs you and your friends. Why is that?

The problem is this: Not that much in the media seems to matter at all. If that isn't troubling enough, few even expect that it should matter. That's what gets to me. How do we convey to the public that it is being cheated, that there is another way of seeing, that there are concrete alternatives and real options? How do we inspire a public when oligopolies rule and ordinary people are, in effect, electronically disenfranchised?

These are the kind of "big" questions that have tormented me, because there are so few really good answers. Having come of age in the '60s, fired by that "everything is possible" attitude, I still believe that people can make change happen. If wars can be ended or presidents driven from office, the media networks can be reintroduced to the values of democracy.

And yes, Sarah, I know I am not in the '60s anymore. I know that the conditions and consciousness are different—in no small part because of the mass media. So the strategy of this fight is as hard to define as it is to wage. I cherish freedom of the press. I am part of a small media company which has survived but not thrived. I vacillate between wanting in and preferring to be out. Sure, I would like to be "commercially viable." And why not? I spent years in commercial media. I want to reach people. I have shown I can do it. Yet that commercial world may no longer be an option. I may have crossed that Rubicon. In public television, some bureaucrats today call the tension between audience and mission "tired." But for me it is still crucial, because in the end it gets down not only to what the public gets exposed to, but what you want to do with your life, and what values you want to serve.

Late in his career, Ed Murrow was writing about what future generations will find when they pore through the real archive of what so many Americans have become addicted to watching over all these years. It's not the glitzy exhibits on display in the front of the Museum of Broadcasting, but the tons of trash and stuff buried in the basements and the closets. The public, he said, "will find there recorded in black and white, or color, evidence of decadence, escapism, and insulation from the realities of the world in which we live."

You are that "future generation." It's your job, metaphorically speaking, to help us change the channels. Here's the baton. Your turn is coming. It will not be an easy or quick fight, and cannot be won before the next commercial break. The status quo will have you believe it's the only quo. Fighting to democratize the media, or taking on the vast power of the well-financed global media machine, will be a protracted battle because we are up against cherished myths, embedded ideologies, subtle techniques, and masterful moguls. There will be name-calling, evasive tactics, and resistance.

The fight for more freedom *in* the press will be falsely characterized as an attack on freedom *of* the press. Perhaps we can take strength from the words of a lead character in Ken Kesey's *One Flew Over the Cuckoos Nest*: "The thing he was fighting, you couldn't whip it for good. All you could do was keep on whipping it till you couldn't come out anymore, and somebody else has to take your place."

And someone will, Sarah, someone will.

ALSO FROM AKASHIC BOOKS

Falun Gong's Challenge to China: Spiritual Practice or "Evil Cult"?
A report and reader by Danny Schechter
254 pages, hardcover / ISBN: 1-888451-13-0
Price: $24.00
The only book-length investigative report on this severe human rights crisis that is affecting the lives of millions.
". . . a persuasive analysis of this strange and still unfolding story . . ." —*New York Times*

We Owe You Nothing: Punk Planet, The Collected Interviews
334 pages, paperback (6" x 9") / ISBN: 1-888451-14-9
Price: $16.95
"This collection of interviews reflects one of *Punk Planet's* most important qualities: Sinker's willingness to look beyond the small world of punk bands and labels and deal with larger issues. With interview subjects ranging from punk icons Thurston Moore and Ian MacKaye to Noam Chomsky and representatives of the Central Ohio Abortion Access Fund, as well as many other artists, musicians, and activists, this book is not solely for the tattooed, pierced teenage set. All of the interviews are probing and well thought out, the questions going deeper than most magazines would ever dare; and each has a succinct, informative introduction for readers who are unfamiliar with the subject. Required reading for all music fans." —*Library Journal*

Adios Muchachos by Daniel Chavarría
245 pages, paperback / ISBN: 1-888451-16-5
Price: $13.95
"Daniel Chavarría has long been recognized as one of Latin America's finest writers. Now he again proves why with *Adios Muchachos*, a comic mystery peopled by a delightfully mad band of miscreants, all of them led by a woman you will not soon forget: Alicia, the loveliest bicycle whore in all Havana."
—Edgar Award-winning author William Heffernan

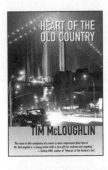

Heart of the Old Country
by Tim McLoughlin

216 pages, trade paperback / ISBN: 1-888451-15-7
Price: $14.95

"Heart of the Old Country is a wise and tender first novel, though its youthful narrator would surely not like to hear that said. His boisterous, irreverent, often hilarious tough-guy pose is his armor, for he comes from the heart of old Brooklyn, where compassion and emotion are considered fatal weaknesses. Yet underneath it all, he shows a love for humanity so deep it might equal Dostoevksy's. Tim McLoughlin is a master storyteller in the tradition of such great New York City writers as Hubert Selby Jr. and Richard Price. I can't wait for his second book!"*
—Kaylie Jones, author of *A Soldier's Daughter Never Cries*

The Big Mango by Norman Kelley

270 pages, paperback / ISBN: 1-888451-10-8
Price: $14.95

She's Back! Nina Halligan, Private Investigator.
"Want a scathing social and political satire? Look no further than Kelley's second effort featuring 'bad girl' African-American PI and part-time intellectual Nina Halligan—it's X-rated, but a romp of a read . . . Nina's acid takes on recognizable public figures and institutions both amuse and offend . . . Kelley spares no one, blacks and whites alike, and this provocative novel is sure to attract attention . . ." —*Publisher's Weekly*

***

These books are available at local bookstores. They can also be purchased with a credit card online through www.akashicbooks.com. To order by mail, send a check or money order to:

Akashic Books, PO Box 1456, New York, NY 10009
www.akashicbooks.com, Akashic7@aol.com

(Prices include shipping. Outside the U.S., add $3 to each book ordered.)

Franklin Pierce College Library

00132203

Danny Schechter grew up in the Bronx and graduated from DeWitt Clinton High School. After graduating with honors from Cornell University in 1964, he was a civil rights worker and community anti-poverty organizer. In 1966 he was an assistant to the mayor of Detroit on a Ford Foundation grant. Between 1966 and 1968 he studied at the London School of Economics, gaining a Master's degree in political sociology in 1968. From 1970 to 1977 he was the news director, principal newscaster, and "News

Dissector" at WBCN-FM in Boston, where he won two Major Armstrong Awards. He was a Nieman Fellow in Journalism at Harvard in 1977–78. His television career began in 1978 at Boston's WGBH, and included stints as a producer at CNN as well as eight years as a producer for ABC's *20/20*. Since 1987 he has been executive producer of Globalvision, a New York–based television and film production company which he co-founded, and since 1999 he has also served as executive editor of MEDIAchannel.org. Mr. Schechter has one daughter, Sarah Debs Schechter (see resemblance above, circa 1977), and lives in a New York City loft with his eight-thousand-album record collection and an Apple computer that is nearly out of memory.

At Globalvision he produced 156 editions of the award-winning series *South Africa Now*, co-produced *Rights & Wrongs: Human Rights Television* with Charlayne Hunter-Gault, and created *The World of Elie Wiesel*. He has also produced and directed many other TV specials and films. His writing on politics, current events, and media issues has appeared in leading newspapers and magazines including the *Boston Globe, Newsday, Detroit Free Press, Village Voice,* and *Columbia Journalism Review.* His first book, *The More You Watch, The Less You Know: News Wars, [sub]Merged Hopes, and Media Adventures* was published by Seven Stories Press in October 1997 and reissued as a paperback in January 1999. In 2000, Akashic Books published Schechter's groundbreaking report and reader, *Falun Gong's Challenge to China;* later in the year, he produced a corresponding film by the same name. *News Dissector: Passions, Pieces, and Polemics* is drawn from forty years of writing on politics, current events, and the media.